THE U.S.A

CUSTOMS AND INSTITUTIONS

A Survey of American Culture and Traditions

An Advanced Reader for ESL and EFL Students

THIRD EDITION

Ethel Tiersky and Martin Tiersky

PRENTICE HALL REGENTS
Englewood Cliffs, New Jersey 07632

Library of Congress Cataloging-in-Publication Data

Tiersky, Ethel, 1937-
The U.S.A : customs and institutions : a survey of American culture and traditions : an advanced reader for ESL and EFL students / Ethel Tiersky and Martin Tiersky. — 3rd ed.
p. cm.
ISBN 0-13-946385-2 :
1. Readers—United States. 2. English language—Textbooks for foreign speakers. 3. United States—Civilization. I. Tiersky, Martin, 1935- . II. Title. III. Title: USA.
PE1127.H5T5 1990 89-48289
428.6'4—dc20 CIP

Editorial/production supervision and interior design: **Shirley Hinkamp**
Cover design: **Ray Lungren Graphics, Ltd.**
Manufacturing buyer: **Ray Keating**

Illustrations: **Rodney Quiriconi**

ACKNOWLEDGMENTS
"Columbus" by Joaquin Miller from the *Complete Poetical Works of Joaquin Miller*, (New York: Arno Press, 1972) distributed by Ayer Publishers, Salem, N.H.

Printed in the United States of America

10 9 8 7 6 5 4 3 2

ISBN 0-13-946385-2

Prentice-Hall International (UK) Limited, *London*
Prentice-Hall of Australia Pty. Limited, *Sydney*
Prentice-Hall Canada Inc., *Toronto*
Prentice-Hall Hispanoamericana, S.A., *Mexico*
Prentice-Hall of India Private Limited, *New Delhi*
Prentice-Hall of Japan, Inc., *Tokyo*
Simon & Schuster Asia Pte. Ltd., *Singapore*
Editora Prentice-Hall do Brasil, Ltda., *Rio de Janeiro*

DEDICATION

To our loving parents, three of whom went through the transition from immigrant to citizen;

to our wonderful children—Howard, Arthur, and Marcia—who have kept us in touch with the customs and language of younger Americans, and who helped immeasurably with the editing and proofreading of this book;

to our editors at Prentice Hall/Regents for their assistance, confidence, and trust;

to the many ESL students at Harry S. Truman College in Chicago who classroom-tested this manuscript and whose questions helped us discover what immigrants want to know;

and, especially, to ESL and EFL teachers everywhere who juggle instruction in language, culture, and history to help their students gain a rich understanding of the American experience.

CONTENTS

PREFACE

TO THE STUDENT:

This third edition of *The U.S.A.: Customs and Institutions* has two main goals. One is to introduce you to the lifestyles, attitudes, customs, and traditions which are characteristic of Americans. The second is to increase your knowledge of the most widespread American custom of all—the custom of speaking English.

Let's begin with a brief description of the book's content. As its title promises, *Customs and Institutions* deals with customs—how Americans celebrate their holidays, what they like to eat, which forms of entertainment they prefer, what sports they play and watch, and how they behave toward one another. It also deals with the nation's most important institutions: its schools, churches, and governmental structures.

In addition to describing life in the United States, *Customs and Institutions* also attempts to analyze it. Why is the divorce rate so high? Why do so many American mothers work? Why is there racial tension in the U.S.A.? Why do so many adults attend school? These are questions that every student of American society wonders about, so we have tried to answer them.

We want to tell our readers not only about how Americans behave but also about what they believe. American philosophies of education and government; American attitudes toward religion, marriage, and family life; the American outlook on life in general; and the American dream—all are given as much attention as space allows.

A word about what this book is *not*: It is neither a defense of American culture nor an attack on it. Though the text does mention obvious strengths and weaknesses, its primary intent is to describe and analyze rather than evaluate.

Now let's turn to the second goal: to improve your comprehension of English. If you're ready to read this book, then you are already well on your way toward mastering the world's most popular and useful second language. But it's not quite correct to speak of mastering English. In truth, no one ever does, not even those who speak it as a native language. Learning English is a lifelong process. That's why this third edition of *Customs and Institutions* has a totally revised set of exercises designed to help you read with greater understanding, discuss your reactions to the ideas presented, learn a specific set of vocabulary words and idioms, and note some important characteristics of written English.

Why, you may ask, is there no end to the study of English? First, of the 2,700 or so languages in use today, English has the largest vocabulary—perhaps as many as one million words, including all of the scientific and technical ones. New technology keeps adding additional words to the language, as did the nuclear age and the computer age. Of course, a person can communicate fairly well with just a few thousand words, but the more you know, the better you will understand what you hear and read.

Second, English is a highly idiomatic language with thousands of two- and three-word phrases that have meanings quite different from the meanings of the same words used individually. (For example, *give up* does not mean either *give* or *up*.) This text, written in informal American English, introduces and provides exercises to practice idioms and expressions that often confuse the non-native speaker.

If your past instruction in English has been in British English, don't worry. The switch to American English will present no major problems. In terms of sentence structure, these two main versions of English are basically the same. The differences between the two Englishes are greater in pronunciation, colloquial usage, and slang than in the written language. British English has more irregular verbs than American English does (*learnt* versus *learned*, for example). There are some minor spelling differences (such as *colour* versus *color*) and some differences in vocabulary. (The British *lift* is the American *elevator*.) Still, you will find that British and American English are very much one language.

As you improve your English, you will learn more about the world's most widely used international language. Today, at least 750 million (and perhaps as many as one billion) people speak English. About 350 million speak it as their native language. (Only the speakers of the combined varieties of Chinese surpass that figure.) The rest know English as a second or foreign language. In terms of international communication, no language is more useful. English is the language of more than half the world's technical and scientific journals. It is the language of international business, sports, and travel. In short, English has become the global language of our shrinking world.

Whether you are living in the United States now, just visiting the country, working or studying with Americans who live in your country, or perhaps meeting Americans for the first time in the pages of this book, welcome to the U.S.A.!

TO THE TEACHER:

If you are familiar with the first two editions of *The U.S.A.: Customs and Institutions,* you will find this third edition quite similar in terms of the topics covered and quite different in many other ways. The second edition was published in 1975. So much has changed in the U.S.A. since then that, in the process of updating, we have almost completely rewritten the text. There is one totally new chapter on etiquette. Many of the other chapters have been reorganized. The words are new, the facts updated, but the book continues to create a general portrait of the U.S.A., both its virtues and its shortcomings. It provides answers to many of the questions that foreigners and immigrants ask about this nation, and it will help them understand and relate to Americans better.

What's been changed? You will find this third edition a more effective teaching tool because of several revisions:

1. The book now begins with a multiple-choice quiz designed to stimulate student interest in the text and indicate the wide range of information contained in it.
2. The vocabulary and sentence structure have been simplified somewhat (though not drastically) to make the information more accessible to intermediate and advanced ESL or EFL students.
3. There are now headings in all of the chapters so that students can follow the flow of ideas more easily and teachers can divide chapter assignments into smaller segments more easily, if they wish.
4. The paragraphs are numbered for easier reference.
5. Perhaps the most important change is in the design of the exercises. The exercises have been totally revised so that they now develop a wide range of language skills. Comprehension Questions (I) ask students to explain what they've read and also to react to the content by making cultural comparisons and stating their opinions. Vocabulary Practice (II) lists 20 vocabulary words to master after each reading. These words are in boldface type the first time they appear in the chapter so that students can study them in context. Students then select some of these vocabulary words (using them in a new but similar context) when they fill in the blanks to complete the sentences in the exercise. Word Study (III) teaches word parts, homonyms, common noun and verb endings, and more. Idiom Study (IV) provides practice with the phrasal verbs, other idioms, and common sayings used in

the chapter. In Reading Skills (V), many different styles of exercises provide practice in recognizing main ideas, finding significant supporting facts, making inferences, identifying facts versus opinions, determining word meaning from context, recognizing pronoun references, and more.

Accompanying this edition of *Customs and Institutions*, there is (for the first time) an *Instructor's Manual* containing teaching tips, exercise answers, and a test for each chapter.

This third edition will help non-native speakers of English better understand both the life and the language of the U.S.A. We hope you enjoy using it as much as we enjoyed researching and writing about this exciting country.

Ethel Tiersky
Associate professor
Communications Dept. (English & ESL)
Harry S. Truman College
Chicago, Illinois

Martin Tiersky
Attorney-at-law
Chicago, Illinois

THE U.S.A.—A QUICK QUIZ

(Answers to the following questions can be found in the chapters of this text. They are also listed at the end of this test.)

1. What famous landmark symbolizes the U.S.A. as a country that welcomes foreigners? a) the Statue of Liberty b) the Golden Gate Bridge c) the Empire State Building d) the World Trade Center.
2. A famous figure that symbolizes the United States government is a) a cowboy b) a thin, bearded man called Uncle Sam c) George Washington d) a fat, bearded man called Santa Claus.
3. The United States government spends about ______________ a year. a) $35,000,000 (35 million) b) $5,000,000,000 (five billion) c) $400,000,000,000 (400 billion) d) $1,000,000,000,000 (one trillion).
4. If an American woman tells you that it is her birthday, the polite response is a) Merry birthday! b) How nice! How old are you? c) My condolences. d) Happy birthday!
5. The animal that symbolizes the U.S.A. is the a) bear b) donkey c) elephant d) eagle.
6. The national motto, which has been printed on all U.S. currency since 1955, is a) "In God We Trust" b) "America, the Beautiful" c) "Stars and Stripes Forever" d) "With Liberty and Justice for All."
7. The U.S.A., the oldest democracy in the world, came into existence in the year a) 1492 b) 1685 c) 1776 d) 1812.
8. The American flag has a) 50 stars and 13 stripes b) 13 stars and 13 stripes c) blue stars and red and white stripes d) white stars and red and blue stripes.
9. In terms of the amount of land it possesses, the U.S.A. is the ______________ largest nation in the world. a) second b) third c) fourth d) eighth.
10. The largest state in population is a) California b) New York c) Illinois d) Texas.
11. The President of the United States lives in Washington, D.C. in a building called the a) Capitol b) Sears Tower c) White House d) National Mansion.

12. The tallest building in the world is 1,454 feet high. It is the a) Empire State Building in New York City b) Sears Tower in Chicago c) World Trade Center in New York City d) Capitol Building in Washington, D.C.
13. What percent of those Americans eligible to vote actually voted in the 1988 presidential election? a) 90% b) 75% c) 60% d) 50%.
14. Americans are considered adults when they reach the age of 18. Then they can legally do all of the following actions, except for one. Generally, Americans must be age 21 to a) vote b) buy alcoholic beverages c) get married d) enlist in the military service.
15. The average American woman gets married at about age a) 18 b) 20 c) 23 d) 26.
16. About what percent of married American women work? a) 15% b) 30% c) 55% d) 75%.
17. What is the average family income in the U.S.A.? a) $15,000 b) $30,000 c) $45,000 d) $60,000.
18. What percent of today's American adults are college graduates? a) 10% b) 20% c) 30% d) 40%.
19. A baby born in the U.S.A. today can expect to live to about age a) 55 b) 65 c) 75 d) 85.
20. The number of people employed by the Executive Branch of the federal government is about a) 35,000 b) 100,000 c) 500,000 d) 3,000,000.
21. American children believe that on Christmas Eve a) a witch rides through the sky on a broomstick b) Santa Claus rides through the sky in a sled c) Pilgrims ride through the sky on turkeys d) people should play jokes on one another.
22. What percent of American households have at least one TV set? a) 66% b) 82% c) 91% d) 98%.
23. The three American cities with the largest populations are a) New York, Los Angeles, and Chicago b) New York, Boston, and San Francisco c) Los Angeles, New York, and Philadelphia d) Los Angeles, Detroit, and Chicago.
24. About how many words are there in the English language? a) 200,000 b) 400,000 c) 1,000,000 d) 2,000,000.
25. What sport is known as the national pastime? a) baseball b) football c) hockey d) basketball.

Answers to Book Quiz

1. a	6. a	11. c	16. c	21. b
2. b	7. c	12. b	17. b	22. d
3. d	8. a	13. d	18. b	23. a
4. d	9. c	14. b	19. c	24. c
5. d	10. a	15. c	20. d	25. a

1

THE AMERICAN CHARACTER

1. "What a country!" says the Russian immigrant and popular comedian, Yakov Smirnoff. This exclamation expresses his surprise, delight, confusion, or disapproval as he learns something new about the U.S.A. Most newcomers to the United States probably share his mixed emotions. It's a wonderful country, they realize, but it's not heaven.

2. Most newcomers arrive in one of the large **urban** areas. Some find the crowds, high-rise buildings, and noisy traffic overwhelming; however, they usually adjust to the urban **environment** rather quickly. It is the American people—their customs and their language—that remain a long-term mystery.

3. This book attempts to uncover some of the mystery, beginning with the attitudes that most Americans share. What do Americans love, hate, want, and believe in? Any statement about the American outlook must take into consideration the nation's great size and geographic **diversity,** and the fact that it is (as John F. Kennedy said) "a nation of **immigrants.**" Generalizations about third-generation, white, urban, middle-class Americans may not accurately describe new immigrants, blacks, rural residents, or the poor.

A LAND OF DIVERSITY

4. In area, the United States is the fourth largest nation in the world. (Only the Soviet Union, Canada, and China have more territory.) Its 50 states cover about 3,600,000 square miles (5,800,000 square kilometers). Forty-eight of its states form one territorial block of land. The other two are Alaska, located northwest of the nation's mainland, and Hawaii, a group of islands in the south Pacific Ocean. They became states in 1959. In addition to these 50 states, the United States government has some control over 12 island territories in the Caribbean Sea and the Pacific Ocean. These include Guam, the Virgin Islands, and Puerto Rico. Residents of these territories are American citizens.

5. "No one should have to see America for the first time," said one visitor, **overwhelmed** by America's size and the great variety of its climate and **geography.** A homesick immigrant from anywhere can probably find a place in the U.S.A. that is similar to his or her native land. The United States has tall mountains and flat cornfields, deserts and tropical regions, prairies and forests, rugged coastlines and gentle, rolling hills. The climate, too, covers all extremes. Throughout the United States, summer weather is warmer than winter weather; but temperatures vary, from southern Florida, where visitors come to swim and sunbathe in December, to northern Alaska, where, in winter, the temperature may drop to –75° Fahrenheit.

6. The United States is also the fourth largest nation in population after China, India, and the Soviet Union. In 1988, there were about 240 million people living in the U.S.A. Although about 95% of the people now living in the U.S.A. were born there, the United States has one of the most varied populations in terms of national ancestry. Racially, the U.S.A. is about 83% white, 12% black, and 5% Asian. About 8% of the population is Hispanic, making the Spanish-speaking people the second largest ethnic **minority** in the country. Newcomers are often surprised by the variety of skin colors they see, but Americans take it for granted. These differences are more than skin deep. It may take a few **generations** before the values and customs of the "old country" are altered by an American outlook. Some are never revised.

7. Traveling around the U.S.A., one also becomes aware of regional differences, not only in geography, but also in the ways that Americans speak and act. Most Americans can tell what part of the country another American comes from just by listening to the speaker's accent. (The Midwestern accent is closest to what is heard on national TV.) Styles of cooking vary from place to place, influenced by the different immigrant groups that have settled in that area and by the edible plants that grow there. Recreation varies from place to place, determined in part by climate and geography.

8. In addition, American personalities may differ somewhat from one region to another. For example, New Englanders are often described as stern and self-reliant, Southerners as gracious and leisurely, and Westerners as casual and friendly. People from southern California are considered especially eager to try new fads. Midwesterners are considered more **conservative** than Californians and less worldly than New Yorkers.

9. However, many regional differences have been erased by modern transportation, communication, and mass production. From the East Coast to the West Coast, travelers see the same kinds of shopping centers, supermarkets, motels, homes, and apartment buildings. Franchise businesses have created stores and restaurants that look alike wherever they are. National advertising has created national tastes in consumer goods. National news media determine what Americans know about world events and also influence attitudes and styles. Thus, it is safe to make some generalizations about this diverse nation, but it must be done with caution.

THE MEANING OF DEMOCRACY

10. The courage to try something new has been an American characteristic since colonial times, when the nation's founders started one of the greatest experiments of all times—the creation of American **democracy.** The citizens of the United States, through their elected **representatives,** establish the nation's laws and determine its foreign policy. Those who disapprove of these laws and policies may openly express their disapproval and try to elect new representatives.

11. American democracy is based on **majority** rule, but it also protects minority rights. There are certain freedoms which the United States promises to all its citizens. Members of minority groups cannot be denied these rights by a vote of the majority. The basic rights of every citizen, outlined in the first 10 amendments to the Constitution, are known as the *Bill of Rights.* These include freedom of speech, freedom of religion, and freedom from unreasonable search and arrest.

12. In the United States, democracy is not only a form of government, it is a way of life. The idea that those who must live by the rules should help make them is basic to nearly all American institutions and organizations. American children are introduced to the democratic concepts of majority rule and representative government at a very early age. Many families hold weekly meetings to determine household rules and activities. Most schools have student councils with elected representatives so that students can voice their opinions about school regulations and activities. Social, civic, labor, and charitable groups elect their officers and make decisions by voting. In publicly owned businesses, stockholders elect the directors who control the company. Local and state governments are also based upon democratic principles.

13. "All men are created equal," says the Declaration of Independence. This statement does not mean that all human beings are equal in ability or ambition. It means, instead, that all people should be treated equally before the law and given equal privileges and opportunities.

14. The American belief in equality of opportunity is illustrated by the Horatio Alger myth. Horatio Alger was a 19th-**century** American novelist who wrote stories about poor boys who became successful. His books told about the little newsboy or shoeshine boy who grew up to become rich and respected. These popular rags-to-riches stories exemplified the American dream—the belief that any individual, no matter how poor, can achieve success through honesty and hard work.

15. For many immigrant Americans, this dream became reality. Most of them, particularly those who came to the United States during the 19th century, were peasants or laborers in their native lands. Within a generation or two, nearly all these immigrant families rose on the social and economic scales. Financial success was often the result of taking a risk, of quitting a salaried position and starting a new business. Becoming an **entrepreneur** is still an open, though sometimes difficult, road to prosperity. Social mobility—movement from one social class to another—has always been characteristic of the United States, and it is closely tied to financial status.

"TRY IT—YOU'LL LIKE IT"

16. The great American novelist and humorist Mark Twain pointed out the difference between the more conservative European and the more experimental American temperament. He described the Englishman as a "person who does things because they have been done before" and the American as "a person who does things because they haven't been done before." Americans love to try something new mostly because of a belief that newer may be better.

17. As a nation of immigrants, the United States has had a continual influx of people with a pioneering spirit, with the courage to make major changes. In the mid-19th century, this spirit led American settlers to make the long, difficult, and dangerous journey westward in search of gold or free land. The desire to start a new life in a new place is still noticeable throughout the nation. About 40 million Americans change residences every year. The average American moves about 14 times in his or her lifetime. Most of these moves are local ones, occurring when families get bigger or smaller, richer or poorer. Some moves are due to job changes. Others are the result of a spirit of adventure or the desire for a change of climate. Moving away is less lonely today because it is so easy to travel or phone a few thousand miles to keep in touch with relatives and old friends. Out of sight is no longer out of mind.

18. The pioneering spirit of Americans is evident in many other aspects of their lives. Mid-life career changes are quite common and reflect American adaptability as job opportunities change. Americans of all ages are quite willing to return to school to learn something new if that will lead to a better job. Americans also change marriage partners more often than most other people in the world.

19. Americans love science and technology because these fields of study bring the excitement of new discoveries. The United States has embraced the new age of communication with great enthusiasm. From preschoolers to senior citizens, Americans are learning to use computers—at school, at work, and at home. Robots, lasers, and other creations of modern technology fascinate them. Americans subsidize all kinds of space exploration, ranging from outside the earth to inside the atom, in order to uncover the secrets of the universe. Most Americans are looking forward with great excitement to the beginning of a new century and the scientific wonders it will bring.

20. This love of change is closely tied to faith in improvement. Americans have always been **optimistic** people, believing in the perfectibility of people, the basic goodness of their country, and the ability of American ingenuity to improve the quality of human life. But in the past 30 years, people have come to realize that if life can become better, it can also become worse. The dangers of air and water pollution, nuclear power, and overpopulation have become clear. Americans now realize that it is not only possible for living conditions to **deteriorate;** it is even possible for the inventions of modern science and industry to destroy life on earth totally.

JOINING AND PROTESTING

21. In movies and in literature, Americans love a story about a person who, all alone, fights a social evil and wins. But in the real world, Americans are more likely to organize a group when they want to bring about social change.

22. These groups can be divided into three types, based upon their goals. First, groups have been organized to **protest** some government action and demand a change of policy. For example, the groups that protested American involvement in the Vietnam War during the 1960s were quite influential in persuading the government to leave Vietnam. Groups have also protested the government's large stockpile of nuclear weapons and pleaded for nuclear disarmament.

23. Second, many groups protest social evils, such as drunk driving, pollution, and the sale and use of handguns and illegal drugs. These groups urge the government to pass more laws restricting dangerous behavior and to punish more severely those who disobey the laws. Some of these groups accomplish a great deal. For example, those fighting pollution have created recycling centers for glass, metal, and paper, and have encouraged local governmental agencies to check automobiles and factories to be sure that they are not excessively polluting the air.

24. The third type of group is the one that campaigns for the rights of minorities. In recent years, women, blacks, American Indians, and Hispanics have all given their versions of American history and destroyed any illusions that this nation really offered justice and equality for all. Homosexuals have campaigned actively not to be discriminated against, especially on the job. Handicapped people have fought for the installation of ramps and other devices so that they have access to public buildings and public transportation. Senior citizens have organized to promote their interests. And women (who have been discriminated against although they are in the majority) continue their organized efforts to obtain equal opportunity in the working world and to defend their right to obtain legal abortions.

25. In general, these various groups have two main goals. The first is to educate the public. The second is to influence governmental bodies to pass legislation that will benefit their causes. These groups reflect the American belief that the efforts of ordinary citizens can improve conditions, especially if people unite in a common cause.

HURRY, HURRY, HURRY

26. Almost every American wears a watch, and, in nearly every room in an American home, there's a clock. "Be on time." "Don't waste time." "Time is money." "Time waits for no one." All of these familiar sayings reflect the American obsession with promptness and **efficiency.** Students and employees displease their teachers and bosses when they arrive late. This desire to get the most out of every minute often affects behavior, making Americans impatient when they have to wait. The pressure to make every moment count sometimes makes it difficult for Americans to relax and do nothing.

27. The desire to save time and handle work efficiently also leads Americans to buy many kinds of machines. These range from household appliances to equipment for the office, such as calculators, photocopy machines, and computers. One popular machine is the video cassette recorder (VCR), which gives Americans a new kind of control over time. Baseball fans don't have to miss the Sunday afternoon game on TV because of a family birthday party. They simply videotape it. Then, for them, the Sunday afternoon game occurs on Sunday evening.

ARE AMERICANS MATERIALISTIC?

28. Americans have one of the highest standards of living in the world. Because they spend so much money for goods and services, Americans are often accused of being materialistic, of valuing above all else money and the things it can buy. Of course, advertising encourages people to keep buying things far beyond what they need. Sometimes purchases are made in order to "keep up with the Joneses," to show friends that one can afford a bigger house or a fancier car. Expensive possessions are symbols of the owner's financial success. In the mid-19th century, the American author Henry David Thoreau advised his readers, "Simplify your needs!" But 20th-century Americans have moved in the opposite direction. Now, just as Thoreau predicted, many find that their possessions own them. They must work hard to make enough money to pay for and maintain the house, car, TV, stereo, computer, and many other things they consider necessities.

29. In defense of the materialistic American, one expert on American culture points out, "...however eager we are to make money, we are just as eager to give it away. Any...disaster finds Americans writing checks to relieve distress....Generosity and **materialism** run side by side."

STRAIGHT TALK

30. Most people agree that the direct, assertive American personality is a virtue, but it sometimes surprises foreigners. In many cultures, respect for older people or those in positions of authority keeps others from expressing their true feelings. But in the U.S.A., children often argue with their parents, students may disagree with their teachers, and citizens may express opposition to the actions of the government. If the soup has a fly in it or the meat is too tough to chew, the diner can complain to the waiter. If a teacher is wrong or confusing, a student will say so. If the boss makes a mistake, an employee will politely point it out.

31. Some straight talk about the American **character** must include the admission that Americans have their faults. The extremely competitive nature of Americans is probably their worst fault. Of course, competition isn't always bad. In fact, it promotes excellence by encouraging individuals (and businesses) to try to do their best. But the desire to get ahead of others sometimes causes people to do things that are unkind and even dishonest.

32. Also, Americans admire what is practical, fast, efficient, and new. Sometimes they fail to understand and appreciate cultures that have greater respect for more traditional, leisurely ways of doing things. Conversely, people from other cultures may dislike the practical, hectic American lifestyle.

33. Despite cultural differences, most foreigners give Americans credit for their virtues. Americans are generally viewed as friendly, adaptable, energetic, and kindhearted. Most newcomers to the U.S.A. like Americans, and the feeling is usually mutual. Perhaps the greatest American virtue is a deep interest in new ideas and new people. In a nation of immigrants, the foreigner does not remain an outsider for long.

EXERCISES

I. Comprehension Questions. Answer the following questions on paper or in class discussion.

1. In what ways is the U.S.A. a land of diversity?
2. What is the meaning of the expression *majority rule?* How does it relate to American democracy?
3. Name some important traits of the American character mentioned in this chapter.
4. Do you agree with this chapter's generalizations about Americans? Have you noticed any other American traits that were not mentioned in this chapter?

II. Vocabulary Practice. Pronounce the following words after your teacher, and discuss their meanings. Then use some of them to complete the following sentences. You may need to use the same word twice.

century	geography
character	immigrants
conservative	majority
democracy	materialism
deteriorate	minority
diversity	optimistic
efficiency	overwhelm
entrepreneur	protest
environment	representative
generations	urban

1. The word ________________ means 100 years. The 20th ______________ refers to the 1900s.

2. The American ________________ refers to the behavior, attitudes, and beliefs of the American people.

3. About 94% of today's Americans were born in the U.S.A. The other 6% came here as ________________.

4. An ________________ is a person who owns a business.

5. Most Americans live in or near a big city, so they live in an ______________ environment.

6. The word ________________ means more than half; the word ______________ means less than half.

7. Americans admire ________________. They want to do things as quickly as possible and still do them well.

8. The U.S.A. has great ________________ in its climate, geography, and population.

III. Word Study.

A. Use this chapter and your dictionary to find a definition for each of the following phrases. The numbers in brackets tell the paragraphs the phrases are used in.

   1. middle-class [3] ________________________________

   2. Midwestern [7] ________________________________

3. mid-19th century [17] ______________________________

4. mid-life [18] ______________________________

B. Look up the words *mobility* and *mobile* in your dictionary. In what two ways are Americans mobile?

1. ______________________________

2. ______________________________

IV. Idiom Study. Underline the correct word or phrase to complete each sentence.

1. *Mixed emotions* [1] means a) anger b) many different feelings about the same thing c) surprise and joy.
2. Differences that are *skin deep* [6] are a) only on the surface, but not important b) different colors c) very important.
3. To *take something for granted* [6] means to a) get permission to do it b) take it with you c) expect things to be the way they are.
4. *Out of sight, out of mind* [17] means a) gone but not forgotten b) gone and forgotten c) forgotten but not gone.
5. *Keeping up with the Joneses* [28] means a) having possessions that are as nice as your friends' b) being as educated as your friends c) running as fast as your friends.
6. *Point out* [30] means to a) make someone notice something b) remove something c) write out something.
7. *Straight talk* [31] means a) direct and honest b) a loud conversation c) an insult.

V. Reading Skills.

A. The topic sentence is the most general sentence in a paragraph. It tells the main idea, which the other sentences prove or explain. Reread paragraphs 27, 28, and 30. Then write the first two words of each topic sentence.

(27)________________ (28)________________

(30)________________

B. In class, discuss the many possible meanings of the exclamation, "What a country!" Discuss the meaning of the exclamation point at the end. Now write two more sentences in the same pattern. (Example: What a day!)

1. ______________________________

2. ______________________________

C. In paragraph 33, what does "the feeling is usually mutual" mean? Underline the sentence below that best explains the meaning.

1. Immigrants usually like Americans.
2. Americans usually like each other.
3. Americans usually like immigrants.

D. Complete the following sentences:

1. According to this chapter, Americans like to ______________

______________________________.

2. According to this chapter, Americans hate to ______________

______________________________.

2

MARRIAGE, AMERICAN STYLE

1. Proverbial wisdom tells us that marriage "halves our griefs, doubles our joys, and quadruples our expenses." Today's Americans seem willing to take the bad with the good because the institution of marriage continues to be extremely popular in the U.S.A.

CHOOSING A MATE

2. Although Americans try to be practical in most matters, when they choose a spouse, the decision is usually based upon feelings of love rather than practical considerations. In the United States, parents do not arrange marriages for their children. Teenagers usually begin dating in high school and eventually find marriage partners through their own social contacts. Though parents generally encourage their children to marry someone of the same race and religion, when young adults move away from their parents' home to attend school or work in another city, they often date and then marry people from quite different backgrounds. Marriages between people of different religious or racial backgrounds are increasing. However, marriages between blacks and whites are still rather rare, involving less than 0.5% of the nation's 55 million married couples.

ENGAGEMENT AND WEDDING CUSTOMS

3. Today, Americans marry at an older age than did young adults of the 1960s and 1970s. At the time of his first marriage, the average *bridegroom* (or ***groom,*** for short) is about 26. The average **bride** is 24. When a man and woman decide to marry and announce their **engagement** to their friends and relatives, it is **traditional** for the man to give his fiancée a **diamond** engagement ring. When the engagement period begins, the bride-to-be and her future husband meet each other's relatives, make arrangements for their **wedding** and **honeymoon,** and plan their future together.

4. Very few newlyweds choose to begin married life living with either set of parents. Therefore, during the engagement period, most couples look for their own apartment and buy furniture for their new home. Engagement and wedding gifts help the bride and groom to set up housekeeping. The bride's parents usually give their daughter a *trousseau* of new clothing and linens. Relatives and close friends of the bride often arrange a *shower*—a party just for women at which each guest gives the bride-to-be a gift for her new home. Also, shortly before the wedding, the groom and his close friends and relatives celebrate at an all-male party called a *bachelor* or *stag* party. On this occasion, the groom usually receives gifts.

5. Most wedding customs observed in the United States today originated in other countries and past centuries. Some relate to old **superstitions** about ways to bring the bride and groom good luck and many children. Other customs are ancient symbols of the marital promise of lifelong devotion.

6. The traditional American bride wears a long white gown and a **veil.** (In ancient times, the veil was supposed to protect the bride from evil spirits and to **symbolize** her innocence.) Traditional brides also obey the well-known verse and wear "something old, something new, something borrowed, and something blue." The groom usually wears a **tuxedo** (a fancy suit), which is often rented just for his wedding day. According to custom, the groom should not see the bride's wedding gown before the wedding. Also, on their wedding day, the bride and groom do not see each other until they meet during the **ceremony.**

7. The American wedding is often an expensive affair (average cost: about $10,000). It is usually paid for by the bride's parents, although the groom and his parents help prepare the guest list. The day's festivities begin with the marriage ceremony, which may be held in a church, synagogue, home, or hotel. Guests are seated on either side of an aisle, and the wedding starts with a procession down the aisle. The procession includes the bridal couple and their closest relatives and friends. There are usually bridesmaids and a maid of honor (all wearing matching dresses) and the groom's *best man,* who carries the bride's wedding ring. Walking immediately in front of the bride is a young girl (the *flower girl*), who decorates the bride's path with flower petals dropped from her straw basket. The bride walks down the aisle with her father, who leads her to the altar and "gives her away" to the groom. The bride and groom then face a cleric or judge conducting the service, as the traditional service is recited.

8. The **double** ring ceremony is quite common today, with bride and groom placing **identical** rings on each other's fingers. The ring, a circle with no beginning and no end, is a familiar symbol of unending love and loyalty. It is worn on the fourth finger of the left hand because of a very old (and incorrect) idea that a vein or nerve ran from this finger directly to the heart.

9. Toward the end of the wedding ceremony, the bride and groom promise to love each other "until death do us part." They are pronounced husband and wife, and are invited to kiss each other. Then, the entire wedding procession walks back up the aisle, and the ceremony is over. Often, after a church wedding, guests throw rice, rose petals, or confetti at the newlyweds as they leave the church. Sometimes, the couple's car is decorated with tin cans, paper streamers, or old shoes, along with a "Just Married" sign. The tin cans and shoes are a modern version of the ancient idea that noisemakers will scare away evil spirits and bring the couple good luck. Rice, a common fertility symbol, is supposed to help the couple become parents.

10. After the ceremony, there is a party at which guests enjoy dinner and dancing. During the meal, the wedding cake—a tall, many-layered cake with white frosting—is displayed. Most wedding cakes have a miniature bride and groom or miniature wedding bells on the top. After the meal, the bride and groom cut the cake, and it is served to the guests. Some guests take a slice of cake home with them. If a single woman sleeps with a slice of the wedding cake under her pillow, she is supposed to dream of the man she will marry.

11. Just before the bride leaves the wedding party, she throws her bouquet of flowers to the group of single women at the wedding. Supposedly, the one who catches the bouquet will be the next to marry. At some weddings, the groom throws his bride's garter to the single men. Catching the garter also means an approaching marriage.

12. After the wedding, the newlyweds take a vacation called a *honeymoon*. This word comes from a French phrase that means "month of honey." Some scholars believe the phrase came from an ancient custom for newlyweds to share a drink made with honey every day during the first month of their marriage.

13. Though it is common to get married with a large group of relatives and friends present, it is by no means essential. Some couples simply go to City Hall and have a local judge perform the ceremony. To be legally wed, a couple need only fulfill the requirements set by the state in which the ceremony is performed. Each state prescribes who may get a **license** to marry there. In most states, 18-year-olds can marry without their parents' consent, and 16-year-olds can marry with parental consent. Marriages between first cousins or people more closely related are forbidden in many states. Most states require medical examinations and certificates before issuing a marriage license and refuse licenses to people with certain physical or mental illnesses. Once given a license, the couple then appears before someone authorized to perform marriages (usually a judge or religious leader), and, within a few minutes, they have "tied the knot." Some couples elope to get married without fanfare or to escape parental disapproval. People marrying for the second time often do so in a quiet way, without a large party.

14. Finally, following one last wedding tradition, when the bride and groom first enter their new home as husband and wife, the husband carries his wife across the threshold.

THE CONTEMPORARY AMERICAN MARRIAGE

15. On her wedding day, the radiant American bride is the star of the show. But what happens to her after that? Among married couples in the U.S.A., one finds a wide range of living patterns. Many older couples still have traditional marriages with the man as the *breadwinner* (money-earner) and the woman as the homemaker. But most young women today are not content to be full-time homemakers, identified only as "Joe's wife" and, later, as "Lisa's mother." The Women's Liberation Movement, which swept the country in the 1960s, has changed attitudes and behavior forever. Today's young American woman wants marriage, but she also wants to keep her own identity. She wants what men have always had—a marriage that is important but still allows time for the pursuit of individual goals. The majority of American wives, even those with children, work outside the home. As a result, older ideas that labeled housework, cooking, and child care as "women's work" are being discarded. In the **contemporary** American marriage, the husband and wife share both financial and domestic responsibilities. In most families, the working wife probably still handles the larger share of the housework, cooking, and child care, but she gets more help from her husband than non-working wives.

16. In most households, both husband and wife are happy with this arrangement because it provides a more varied life for both parents and also a higher standard of living for the family. The educated American wife enjoys being out in the working world. Her husband discovers that cooking and child care can be fun on a part-time basis and can bring him closer to his family. Moreover, the two-income family can enjoy a higher standard of living, or, at least, free themselves from the worry of unpaid bills. In the United States today, the family with both parents working full-time has an average annual income of at least $40,000.

17. Of course, problems can develop in the two-income family. If the husband expects his working wife to be the kind of homemaker that his mother was, or if the working wife expects her husband to help her with household chores and he is unwilling to do this, the two-income home can become a battleground.

18. The contemporary American marriage is also characterized by a relationship of equality and a sharing of the decision making. Most American women today will not tolerate a husband who considers himself the boss. The American girl is given freedom and education equal to a boy's. After completing her schooling, she is able to get a job and **support** herself. She does not need to marry for financial security. She is a self-sufficient person and will not accept a submissive role in marriage. She wants a husband whom she can respect, but she does not want to be dominated by him. She wants a democratic household in which she has a voice in making decisions that affect the family. When husband and wife are able to share decision making and respect each other's viewpoints, their marriage is probably closer and stronger than those of past generations. When they battle for dominance, the couple is likely to end up in the divorce courts.

DIVORCE AND ALTERNATIVE LIFESTYLES

19. During the traditional wedding ceremony, the bridal couple promise each other lifelong devotion. Yet, about one out of four American marriages ends in divorce. Since 1940, the divorce rate has more than doubled, and experts predict that, of all marriages that occurred in the 1970s, about 50% will end in divorce. The U.S.A. has one of the highest divorce rates in the world, perhaps even the highest.

20. What goes wrong? The fact that divorce is so common in the United States does not mean that Americans consider marriage a casual, unimportant relationship. Just the opposite is true. Americans expect a great deal from marriage. They seek physical, emotional, and intellectual compatibility. They want to be deeply loved and understood. It is because Americans expect so much from marriage that so many get divorced. They prefer no marriage at all to a marriage without love and understanding. With typical American **optimism,** they end one marriage in hope that the next will be happier. With no-fault divorce laws in many states, it is easier than ever to get a divorce. Some American women stay in unhappy marriages because they don't have the education or job experience to support themselves and their children. But most American women believe that, if necessary, they can make it alone without a husband. All things considered, Americans have little reason to continue an unhappy marriage.

21. Which marriages are most likely to end in divorce? Marriages between people with low incomes or limited education and marriages between teenagers are at greatest risk. The number of divorces between couples with children under the age of 18 is declining, and almost 45% of divorcing couples are childless.

22. When a couple gets divorced, the court may require the man to pay his former wife a monthly sum of money called ***alimony.*** The amount of alimony depends on the husband's income, the wife's needs, and the length of the marriage. If the woman is working and earns a good salary, she may receive no alimony at all. Occasionally, the court decides that a woman should pay her husband alimony. About 10% of American women outearn their husbands. If the woman has totally supported her husband during the marriage, the court may decide that she must continue to support him after the divorce. This is a rather new concept in the United States.

23. If a divorcing couple has children, the court must determine which parent the children will live with and who will provide for their support. In most cases, the children live with the mother, and the father pays child support and has visitation rights. However, it is not uncommon for a father to get full custody or joint custody of his children when this arrangement seems to be in the children's best interest.

24. The high risk of divorce doesn't seem to make Americans afraid to try marriage—again and again. By middle age, about 95% of Americans have been married at least once. About 80% of those who get divorced eventually remarry. Only in Japan is the married proportion of the population as high as it is in the U.S.A. In fact, remarriage and the creation of new families is so common in the United States that one American joke tells of a wife calling to her second husband, "Quick, John! Come here and help me! Your children and my children are beating up our children!"

25. Despite the dominance of the married lifestyle, the number of people choosing alternative lifestyles is increasing, and their behavior is increasingly accepted by the general population. The number of unmarried couples living together rose from about 500,000 in 1970 to about 2.6 million in 1988. Many older people are horrified by the growing trend of unmarried couples living together. However, it is not just an American trend. It's even more common in Europe than in the U.S.A.

26. Another alternative to the traditional marriage is the homosexual relationship. Scientists estimate that about 4% of American men and 1.5% of American women are homosexuals. Many homosexuals live with someone of their own sex, and sometimes these relationships last for many years, with the same loyalty and emotional attachment as in a happy marriage.

HAPPY ANNIVERSARY!

27. Maintaining a good marriage has always been work as well as fun, so it's no wonder that Americans celebrate the completion of each successful year. Married couples celebrate most of their wedding anniversaries rather quietly, perhaps by going out to a romantic dinner for two, or perhaps bringing their children or close friends. But certain landmark anniversaries—especially the 25th and the 50th—are commonly celebrated with big parties. There is a special type of gift that is traditional for each **anniversary** year (paper or plastics for the first, cotton for the second, leather for the third, and so on). However, these categories are often ignored except for the 25th (silver) and the 50th (gold). It is a joyous occasion when a couple celebrates a golden wedding anniversary with their children, grandchildren, and great-grandchildren around them. Reaching this moment is a goal of most young couples when they walk down the aisle as bride and groom.

EXERCISES

I. Comprehension Questions. Answer the following questions on paper or in class discussion.

1. What are some prewedding and wedding customs in the U.S.A.? Compare them to customs in your country.
2. What is the role of the wife in the contemporary American marriage?
3. Why do so many Americans get divorced?
4. When a couple gets divorced, which parent do the children usually live with, and who supports them?

II. Vocabulary Practice. Pronounce the following words after your teacher, and discuss their meanings. Then use some of them to complete the following sentences.

alimony	identical
anniversary	license
bride	optimism
ceremony	superstitions
contemporary	support
diamond	symbolize
double	traditional
engagement	tuxedo
groom	veil
honeymoon	wedding

1. When a man proposes marriage to a woman, it is traditional for him to give her a ________________ ring.
2. In order to get married, the engaged couple must get a marriage ________________ .
3. At the wedding ________________ , the bride wears a white gown and a ________________ , and the groom wears a ________________ .
4. It is ________________ for the bride to throw her bouquet of flowers to the unmarried women at the ________________ .
5. Many ________________ (modern) wedding customs come from old ________________ (unscientific beliefs) about ways to protect the bridal couple from bad luck.
6. After the wedding ceremony, the newlyweds usually take a vacation called a ________________ .

7. When a married couple gets divorced, the man usually pays

_______________ to help _________________ his ex-wife.

8. With typical American _________________, people who get divorced usually marry again.

III. Word Study.

A. Homonyms are words that sound alike but have different meanings and spellings. Pronounce the following two sets of homonyms, and discuss their meanings.

1. I'll, aisle, isle

2. altar, alter

Now underline the correct homonyms in the following sentences.

1. The bride walked down the (aisle, isle) to the (altar, alter).

2. If the bride wants to (altar, alter) her dress or (altar, alter) her wedding plans, (isle, I'll) help her.

B. Very few English words have accent marks. But some words that have come into English from another language keep the accent mark they had in the original language. Look up the words *fiancé* and *fiancée* in a dictionary.

1. What is the difference in meaning?

fiancé ____

fiancée ____

2. What language do they come from? _________________

IV. Idiom Study. Write a definition for each of the following idioms. The numbers in brackets give the paragraphs in which these idioms are used.

1. set up [4] ______________________________
2. best man [7] ______________________________
3. walk down the aisle [7, 27] ______________________________
4. tie the knot [13] ______________________________
5. breadwinner [15] ______________________________
6. make it [20] ______________________________
7. beat up [24] ______________________________

V. Reading Skills.

A. Context clues: Many English words have more than one meaning. To understand them, it is necessary to study the sentence or situation in which they are used. Practice using context clues with the following words from this chapter.

1. In paragraph 3, the word *engagement* means a) a military conflict b) the public announcement of a promise to marry someone c) an appointment to meet someone. ___
2. In paragraph 4, the word *shower* means a) a party b) a rainstorm c) a way to wash yourself. ___
3. In paragraph 4, the word *just* means a) exactly b) immediately c) only. ___
4. In paragraph 11, the word *just* means a) exactly b) immediately c) only. ___

5. In paragraph 20, the word *just* means a) exactly b) immediately c) only. ___

6. In paragraph 15, the word *domestic* means a) not foreign b) a servant c) housekeeping. ___

7. In paragraph 23, the word *joint* means a) a part of the body b) total c) shared. ___

B. Transitional words: Complete each of the following sentences with the appropriate transitional word.

however therefore though

1. He was sick; ________________, he went to the doctor.

2. He was sick; ________________, he came to school anyway.

3. ________________ he was sick, he came to school anyway.

3

AMERICAN FAMILY LIFE

1. Families have existed for about 300,000 years now, continually changing with the times. Still, the lifestyle of the contemporary American family horrifies some foreigners. They describe it this way: "Young children are in day care centers. Teenagers are often in trouble. Mothers are at work. Divorced fathers rarely see their children. Widowed grandparents live alone. Great-grandparents live in nursing homes. Don't American family members love each other and take care of each other?"

2. Yes, they do. The American family still cares about and cares for its members, but in new ways. American children, for example, may spend less time with **relatives** than children did in the past. Nevertheless, families still give children their most important experiences and values, as well as their most enduring relationships.

WHO'S AT HOME?

3. Americans are like most people: when they grow up, they **eventually** leave the family of their childhood and form their own families. About 71% of Americans live with people that they're related to by blood or marriage. Of the 91.5 million households in the U.S.A., 65 million are families. Most other households consist of one person living alone. Only 9% of households are made up of people who are not related.

4. Today's **typical** American family is not the traditional one with Daddy at work, Mommy in the kitchen, and several children playing in the backyard. Approximately 51% of American families have no children under the age of 18 living at home. Because of the high divorce rate and the large number of children born out-of-wedlock, 24% (15 million) of American children live with only one parent, usually their mother. Predictions are that 60% of today's American youngsters will spend at least part of their childhood in a one-parent household.

5. The contemporary American child doesn't have a lot of companionship from brothers and sisters because the average family has only one or two children. With so many women working full-time, five or six million

preteens come home from school to an empty house, while others go to after-school centers to avoid being alone. Because of the high divorce rate and the trend toward having fewer children, the American household is now smaller than it has ever been, down to a statistical average of 2.6 people.

6. Most American children live with their parents at least until they finish high school at age 17 or 18. Then, many go away to college, leaving some parents sad and lonely in their empty nest and others enjoying their release from parental responsibilities. However, many young, single adults stay with their parents during their college years or return home after graduation. The high cost of housing keeps many young adults in their parents' home until they get married.

7. Today's parents cannot even be sure that their married children have moved out forever. After a divorce, adults may return to the parental home temporarily or even on a long-term basis, especially if they are lonely, short of money, or in need of babysitting grandparents.

8. Although adult children sometimes come home to Mom and Dad, middle-aged and elderly people seldom move in with their grown children. Older people take pride in their independence, enjoy their freedom, and do not want to be a **burden** to their children. The telephone, the car, and the airplane keep them in close contact even when they live in different parts of the country.

9. In the U.S.A., it's common for a family to span four generations. In this aging population, the average American is 32 years old, and a newborn baby has a life expectancy of 75 years. About 30 million Americans—12% of the nation's population—are 65 or older, and the nation's over-85 population is increasing rapidly.

10. Senior citizens are often thought of as two different groups—the "young old" (ages 65 to 75) and the "old old" (over 75). The younger senior citizens are often quite active—working part-time, traveling, enjoying leisure activities with friends, and traveling across the country to visit their children and grandchildren.

11. But what about the "old old"? Sometimes, foreigners mistakenly conclude that Americans simply leave their elderly relatives in nursing homes and forget about them. (Actually, only about 6% of today's senior citizens live in nursing homes; however, experts predict that 20% to 25% of Americans alive today will reside in a nursing home at some time in their lives.) For elderly people who are ill or handicapped, a nursing home may be the only alternative because their daughters and daughters-in-law are working, and there is no one home during the day to care for them. Family members usually select a nursing home that is nearby so that they can visit often.

12. In many communities, retirement facilities have been developed to provide living quarters for older people who do not need constant nursing care but who can no longer handle the burden of shopping and cooking for themselves. Other senior citizens choose to move to the *Sun Belt*, one of the southern or southwestern states, where the climate is milder. But wherever they are, they are part of a family that has not forgotten them.

13. The mobility of Americans works against the family unit by sometimes placing thousands of miles between people who once shared the same dinner table. But family members hop into a car or onto a plane to come together for the major turning points in each others' lives. Birthdays, graduations, marriages, anniversaries, and funerals all reunite families. Family parties may be all the more joyous when they bring together relatives who haven't seen each other for a while.

WHERE IS HOME?

14. This nation's 242 million people are overwhelmingly urban. Only one out of every 45 people lives on a farm. The majority of Americans live in or near large cities, but small-town living is still widespread. A suburb (a small community near a big city) offers the advantages of safer, more intimate small-town life with the recreational and cultural facilities (and job opportunities) of the big city nearby.

15. About two-thirds of Americans live in homes or apartments that they own, but many people rent their living quarters. Apartment buildings range from walk-ups containing from two to six apartments to high-rise elevator buildings that may have more than 100 units. Some high-rise apartments are very expensive and elegant, but many are built for moderate or even low-income families. Many apartment buildings are **condominiums** (*condos*), or cooperative apartments (*co-ops*), which means that each family owns the unit it lives in.

16. More than 10 million Americans live in *mobile homes*, living quarters built on wheels. They can be moved, but are generally brought to a site that becomes more or less permanent. Then the wheels are removed, and the home is attached to the ground. Because they cost less than conventional homes, mobile homes are especially popular with young couples and retired couples with a limited income.

17. For the typical American family, home may be at a different place every five or six years. All of this moving deprives the nuclear family (parents and their children) of many relatives and long-time friends living nearby. The nuclear family must now supply the **psychological** support that was once provided in part by aunts, uncles, cousins, and close friends that were right in the neighborhood. Why do Americans move so much? Most moves relate to new job opportunities, but sometimes the American **pioneering** spirit and desire for adventure inspire the move.

18. Where is home? According to the well-known American poet Robert Frost, it is "the place where, if you have to go there, they have to take you in." This definition itself reflects the strong bond that holds American family members together.

19. Unfortunately, for some Americans, home is nowhere. Visitors to the U.S.A. are often shocked to see that, in this generally prosperous nation, many urban areas have people sleeping overnight on park benches, on bus terminal floors, and even on public sidewalks. Some of them are mentally ill, some are drug addicts, and some are simply unemployed and broke. Though it is difficult to estimate the number of homeless Americans, in 1988 between 1.3 and 2 million Americans spent at least one night on the streets, and on any given night about 700,000 were homeless. Americans are quite concerned about this statistic. Many social service organizations try to help these people get back on their feet, and it is hoped that the 1990s will bring solutions to this heartbreaking social problem.

WHO'S THE BREADWINNER?

20. The average family income in the U.S.A. is in the $31,000 range, but it is significantly higher when both parents work full-time. Because there are so many things that American families want, it has become customary for American women to work outside the home. Also, many women pursue careers because they find the working world more interesting than full-time homemaking. This change has caused a revolution in American family life. In 1940, only 15% of married women worked. Today, about 55% do, and, among younger women, the percentage is much higher.

21. In some families, when the father is unemployed or still a college student, the wife may be the one going off to work while the husband is at home with the baby and the housework. But the occupation of *househusband* is usually a **temporary,** not a lifelong, career.

22. When both the mother and father work outside the home, the lives of all the family members change quite a bit. Dad must help out more at home. The older children must be more independent and may be asked to take care of the younger children and help with the housework. The younger children spend less time with Mommy and more time in a day care center, with a babysitter, or with a grandparent. Even with all this help from the family, the working mother often finds that, between her paying job and her job as a homemaker, she is working constantly. Trying to be Supermom, she becomes exhausted and irritable. Some women hire household help in order to manage at home. Others simply do less work around the house. A few nights a week, dinner comes from the carry-out restaurant instead of the oven. Dust lies patiently on the furniture until the weekend. Although working mothers have a lot of responsibilities and very little free time, most of them are happy with their double lives.

23. Do American children **resent** having a part-time mother? Probably not. No doubt, it is hardest on the young child, who may miss Mommy when she's away at work. Older children realize that Mom's salary helps to pay for the things they want—a home computer, a video recorder, a second family car, and so on. In some families, (especially when the father is unemployed or has left the household), the mother's salary pays for the necessities of life. Also, in the U.S.A., it's not uncommon for women to outearn their husbands. Clearly, the desire for material things strongly influences the way American families live. A lot of money is needed not only for things but for experiences as well—summer camp for the kids, a vacation for the family, lessons in music or athletics, religious training, and, most expensive of all these days, a college education.

24. Of course, not all working wives are on the job just for the money. Some women want to work even if the family doesn't need extra income. Many women find homemaking tasks boring and want the stimulation of the working world. This is especially true of college-educated women.

25. Mother's salary helps to support the family, but what about the children's earnings? In the past, children were a **financial** asset. They worked on the farm or elsewhere and contributed to the family's income. Today's American children are a financial **liability.** Except for occasional part-time jobs such as babysitting, shoveling snow, mowing lawns, or delivering newspapers, American children do not work until they are about 15 or 16 years old. Then, many work part time to save for their college education and their own personal expenses. They rarely contribute their earnings to help support the family. The average family spends at least $85,000 to raise a child to the age of 18, which may explain why the majority of young couples plan to have only one or two children.

WHO'S IN CHARGE?

26. No longer do American families live by the rule that "Father's word is law." Today's family tries to be democratic, to give all family members some voice in decision making. Of course, this approach is not always possible, but when parents must make the decision, it is usually a joint one.

27. This democratic approach to family life does not prevent all family **quarrels.** Americans have familiar phrases to describe various types of family arguments. First, there's the *battle of the sexes,* when husband and wife fight for dominance of the family. Then there's ***sibling rivalry,*** competition and jealousy between brothers and sisters. Americans also speak of the *generation gap,* which makes it difficult for parents to understand the attitudes and behavior of their childern and vice versa. Married people often have *in-law problems,* especially when older parents try to control the lives of their married children. But despite all these common family conflicts, family members usually get special consideration just because they're family. Americans often justify special treatment of relatives by quoting the expression "Blood is thicker than water."

28. The whole question of who's in charge becomes much more complicated when there is divorce and remarriage. Sometimes divorced parents don't agree on what's best for their child. Many American children have to adjust to a stepparent living in the home, supervising and disciplining them. When they are tossed back and forth between different authority figures, American children sometimes wonder who's in charge.

29. A small percentage of troubled parents, (especially those who were mistreated by their own parents) physically abuse their children. Child abuse has been much publicized in recent years, and the **publicity** creates a distorted impression of the American family. In general, Americans are very loving, kind, generous, and permissive parents. In fact, some are afraid to say no to their children for fear of losing their love or stifling their personalities. As a result, in some households, the children take over most of the space and make excessive demands upon their parents' time and money. Americans have been accused of creating a child-centered culture, though perhaps this is changing now that both parents are working. Nevertheless, believing that knowledge leads to a successful life, American parents still spend a great deal of their money on their children's education and hobbies.

30. Problems between parent and child usually increase when the children become teenagers and want greater freedom to make decisions for themselves. Parents want to maintain a friendly relationship with their teenagers and also want to guide them toward proper behavior. However, in a society of rapidly changing values, parents and children often disagree about what is important and right. Arguments may concern such **trivial** matters as clothing or hairdos. More important quarrels may arise about school work, after-school jobs, money, career decisions, use of the family car, dating, and sexual behavior.

31. Some parents have serious problems with teenagers who quit school, become alcoholics, run away from home, get involved with gangs, have illegitimate children, or use illegal drugs. Many of these problems are caused by influences outside the family. When one member of a family is in serious trouble, the whole family is affected, and all should become involved in efforts to help. Often, family counselors or special hospital programs assist in this endeavor.

32. Some middle-aged parents joke that worrying about their teenagers is what made their hair turn gray. But the majority of teenagers are "good kids" and grow up into responsible adults.

PARENTHOOD: A CHOICE

33. The making of an American family is not merely an accident these days. Couples who don't want children have access to a wide range of birth control measures and, as a last resort, the option of **abortion,** which has been legal in the U.S.A. since 1973. For people who want children but have medical problems that interfere, modern science has come up with many new techniques to help couples conceive. If none of these work, there is always the route of **adoption.** Because there are relatively few healthy American **infants** available for adoption, some Americans adopt babies or young children from other countries, especially those countries where wars and other tragedies have created **orphans.**

34. However parenting begins, the role of the family in raising a child continues to be what it has always been—a wonderful (and difficult!) experience of lifelong giving, caring, and sharing. As in all other nations, in the United States family life is the basis of individual security and cultural continuity.

EXERCISES

I. Comprehension Questions. Answer the following questions on paper or in class discussion.

1. In the U.S.A., why don't most elderly people live with their married children?
2. Why do so many American women work? Give two reasons.
3. Is the nuclear American family getting bigger or smaller? Why?
4. Do you think that American families are as happy as families in your native country? Why or why not?

II. Vocabulary Practice. Pronounce the following vocabulary words after your teacher, and discuss the meanings. Then use some of them to complete the following sentences.

abortion	psychological
adoption	publicity
burden	quarrel
condominium	relatives
eventually	resent
financial	rivalry
infant	sibling
liability	temporary
orphan	trivial
pioneer	typical

1. If a woman is pregnant and she cannot raise the child, she has two choices: getting an ________________ or giving the baby up for ________________.

2. Physical problems are problems with the body. ________________ problems are problems with the mind.

3. Competition between two brothers or between a brother and sister is called ________________ ________________.

4. The opposite of permanent is ________________.

5. Raising a child costs a lot of money in the U.S.A. Children are a great financial ________________.

6. People who belong to the same family because of either birth or marriage are called ________________.

7. Buying a ________________ is a big ________________ investment, but Americans like to own their own homes or apartments if they can afford it.

8. An ________________ is a child who has no living parents.

III. Word Study.

A. Use your dictionary to find the age range of the following:

an infant________________ a teenager________________

an adult________________

a middle-aged person________________

a senior citizen________________

B. What's the difference between a brother, a half brother, and a stepbrother?________________________________

C. In this chapter, the negative prefix *il-* was used. In your dictionary, find the meaning of the following words:

illegal______________________________________

illegitimate__________________________________

In paragraph 31, *illegitimate children* means a) children that commit crimes b) children whose parents aren't married to each other c) young illegal immigrants. ___

IV. Idiom Study. Underline the correct phrase to complete each sentence. The numbers in brackets give the paragraphs in which these idioms are used.

1. A *turning point* [13] in a person's life refers to a a) problem b) major change c) move to another city.
2. If a mother has no children living at home anymore, she has a) *an empty nest* [6] b) *a Sun Belt* [12] c) *a generation gap* [27].
3. *Supermom* [22] a) works very hard b) is very lazy c) has *an empty nest* [6].
4. A person who is *broke* [19] a) has an injury b) is in charge c) has no money.
5. The *generation gap* [27] refers to a) the number of years between parents and their children b) the difficulty that parents and children have understanding each other c) a space between the front teeth.
6. A *househusband* [21] is a) Supermom b) Superman c) a man who does most of the family's homemaking tasks.
7. The person who is *in charge* [28] a) pays the bills b) makes the decisions c) uses a charge account.

V. Reading Skills.

A. *In the U.S.A., it is common for living family members to span four generations. More children than ever before enjoy the companionship of loving grandparents and great-grandparents.*
According to the preceding sentences, are the following statements *true* or *false?*

___1. *Span* means the distance from one end to the other end.

___2. A generation is probably about five years.

___3. Americans have a short life expectancy.

B. Discuss in class the meanings of the following sentences:

1. paragraph 13, sentence 1

2. paragraph 26, sentences 2 and 3

C. Using context clues, determine the meaning of the word *still* in the following paragraphs:

[1] ____________________

[2] ____________________

D. What does *vice versa* [27] mean? ____________________

Which of the following statements can be completed correctly with *vice versa?*

1. Parents usually love their children and ____________.

2. Cats eat mice and ____________.

3. Children like to watch TV and ____________.

4. Children enjoy playing with dogs and ____________.

4

RELIGION IN AMERICAN LIFE

1. **Diversity** is the main characteristic of religion in the United States. Christianity has always been the major American faith, and 85% of today's Americans are Christian. However, American Christians are divided into many different religious groups including Roman Catholic, the various national **denominations** of the Eastern Orthodox Churches, and hundreds of different Protestant denominations and **sects.** In the U.S.A., there are also many non-Christian religions. Americans are proud of this diversity and of the religious freedom which all these different groups enjoy.

RELIGION AND THE U.S. GOVERNMENT

2. Many immigrants came to the American colonies to escape religious **persecution.** Therefore, it was natural that the nation's founders demanded legal guarantees of religious freedom. The First Amendment to the Constitution forbids the establishment of an official national religion and **prohibits** governmental assistance to religious groups. It also prohibits state or federal interference with religious institutions or practices.

3. This doctrine of *separation of church and state* also means that any institution supported by the federal government and/or a state government must be free from the influence of religion. In American public schools, for example, children do not say prayers. In many communities where Christian symbols once decorated public buildings, citizens have filed lawsuits claiming that the presence of these symbols on public property is unconstitutional. The debate as to exactly what violates separation of church and state is ongoing in the U.S.A. Can a state government provide funds for busing children to parochial (private religious) schools? Should parents who send their children to parochial schools receive tax credits because they are not using the public schools? Can textbooks used in public schools use the word *God?* Can taxpayers' money be spent on Christmas displays? These matters are often debated in legislative bodies and courts of law.

4. **Atheists** (people who do not believe in the **existence** of God) feel that the government must not only be free of the influence of a particular religion; it must also avoid imposing on people the idea of religion itself, the belief that a supernatural being influences human destiny. But the vast majority of Americans have always been believers in God. Therefore, although it may seem inconsistent with the doctrine of separation of church and state, many official American **ceremonies** and documents make reference to God. Sessions of Congress and state legislatures begin with prayers. The national motto (printed on U.S. currency) is, "In God We Trust." The Pledge of Allegiance to the flag declares that the United States is "one nation under God." These examples reflect the basic American attitude—that there is a God, but that people are free to believe in God or not and are free to worship in whatever way they choose.

MAJOR AMERICAN RELIGIONS

5. Exact statistics on the size of various American religious groups are not available; however, in one survey in which American adults were asked their religion, 57% identified themselves as Protestant, 28% as Catholic, and 2% as Jewish. About 143 million people living in the U.S.A. (59% of the population) belong to a church, temple, or synagogue.

6. Protestants are by far the largest religious group in the U.S.A., with a membership of 79 million. American Protestantism is divided into more than 200 different denominations, most with fewer than 50,000 members. Only about 20 Protestant groups **claim** a membership as large as 500,000. The major Protestant bodies, all having memberships in the millions, are the United Methodists, Baptists, Lutherans, Presbyterians, and Episcopalians.

7. Perhaps the greatest influence that Protestantism has had on American life comes from its **philosophy** regarding a person's relationship to his or her work. This philosophy—commonly called the Protestant work ethic—stresses the moral value of work, self-discipline, and personal responsibility. According to this ethic, people prove their worth to themselves and to God by working hard, being honest and **thrifty,** and avoiding luxury, excessive personal pleasure, and waste. The accumulation of wealth is not considered evil unless it leads to a life of idleness and **sin.** The Protestant work ethic has long been associated with capitalism and with American attitudes. The American **emphasis** on hard work, financial success, practicality, efficiency, and self-sufficiency has much in common with the Protestant work ethic.

8. Two interesting Protestant groups founded in the United States are the Mormons and the Christian Scientists. The Mormons (officially known as the Church of Jesus Christ of Latter-day Saints) were organized in New York in 1830. Because it was customary for Mormon men to have more than one wife, they were forced out of several established communities. So they traveled westward and settled in the unpopulated valley of the Great Salt Lake, where they built a thriving community. Then the federal government passed antipolygamy laws and refused to admit Utah as a state until 1896, after the Mormons had discontinued this practice. Today, there are 3.6 million Mormons in the U.S.A. Most of them live in Utah and in eastern Idaho, where they are the major religious sect, but many live in other Western states.

9. The Christian Science Church was founded by Mary Baker Eddy in 1879. Christian Scientists believe that, since people are wholly **spiritual,** healing of sickness results from spiritual understanding rather than from medical treatment. The Christian Science movement now has more than 3,500 churches and societies in at least 57 countries. About two-thirds of these are within the United States.

10. The combined Protestant groups form the largest religious faith in the United States. But Roman Catholicism is by far the largest unified religious body. About 53 million Americans are members of Catholic **congregations.** Since many Catholics send their children to parochial schools, Catholic funds have built thousands of elementary and secondary schools, plus many fine colleges and universities. Catholics have also played a prominent role in American politics, although it was not until 1960, when John F. Kennedy was elected President, that a Catholic held the highest office in the land.

11. The third major religion in the United States is Judaism. Nearly six million Americans are members of Jewish congregations. There are three major denominations in Judaism: Orthodox, Conservative, and Reform. During the Sabbath, observed from sundown Friday until sundown Saturday, Orthodox Jews do not work, and they do not travel, except on foot. Jewish tradition imposes certain dietary **restrictions,** prohibiting pork and certain seafoods and forbidding the serving of milk products at meals which include meat or poultry. Reform Judaism does not impose these restrictions.

12. The Jewish people are few in number in the U.S.A. and worldwide, but their intellectual and cultural contributions have been very great indeed. Among the great 20th-century musicians, for example, are many Jewish violinists, pianists, and composers. American Jews have also been prominent lawyers, judges, and doctors. Twentieth-century thought has been greatly influenced by the original ideas of three European-born Jews: Karl Marx (founder of socialism and communism), Albert Einstein (one of the founders of the atomic age), and Sigmund Freud (founder of psychoanalysis).

ARE AMERICANS RELIGIOUS?

13. The 20th century has often been called a **secular** age. To what extent has this attitude affected Americans? Is religion an important force in their lives or merely a habit and a social convenience? Clearly, large numbers of Americans **disregard** religious teachings that oppose interfaith marriages, divorce, premarital sex, and abortion. Does this behavior indicate a turning away from religious teachings in other areas of their lives as well?

14. Generalizations about what religion really means to Americans are quite difficult to make. Religious outlook varies immensely depending on many factors, including age, social class, economic condition, degree of education, and region of the country. Religious differences seem to be less significant to today's young adults than to their parents and grandparents, judging by the rising rate of interfaith marriages. Religion also seems to have a greater emotional hold on the poor and uneducated than on the rich and educated. In the southern part of the country, sometimes called the *Bible Belt,* church members are generally more influenced by religion than is the rest of the nation.

15. For Americans, as for people throughout the world, religion provides a personal identity, social contacts, and important rituals. Social groups, close friendships, and marriages are most often formed with members of one's own religion. As elsewhere, in the United States religion provides the customs and ceremonies that mark life's most important events—birth, coming of age, marriage, and death.

16. But the question, "Are Americans religious?" also asks if Americans believe in a personal God, are concerned about God's judgment of their behavior, believe in life after death, and feel that their religious beliefs do and should influence the way they live. Recent surveys suggest answers to some of these questions. One study indicated that 95% of Americans believe in God, and only 2% never pray. Nevertheless, the famous pollster George Gallup describes 44% of Americans as "unchurched," meaning that they aren't church members or didn't attend religious services within the preceding six months. Gallup concludes that many people who have not lost faith in God are "turned off" by the lack of spiritual nurturing in their religious institutions. This may explain why some young Americans join cults and spiritual movements outside the Judeo-Christian tradition. All things considered, the influence of an American's inherited religion seems to be decreasing. When Americans need advice, they often consult psychiatrists, psychologists, and other secular counselors rather than their religious leaders.

17. What about belief in the afterlife? Contemporary Americans, like their ancestors, are practical people, less concerned about life after death than about the quality of life on earth. In their endeavor to improve the human condition, Americans have never believed in waiting for God to do the job. In the American outlook, faith in God lives side by side with a strong belief in free will and an admiration for self-reliance. Ben Franklin (the great 18th-century writer, inventor, and statesman) said, "God helps them that help themselves." During World War II, this same idea was expressed in the saying, "Praise the Lord and pass the ammunition." Americans do not believe in simply accepting misfortune and calling it God's will. They count on their own actions to improve the quality of life.

18. Though some evidence indicates a decline in recent decades of the influence of religion in American life, religion reaches large audiences via radio and TV. Weekly audiences of religious TV shows are about 24 million, and radio audiences are probably even larger. Prior to 1960, most religious broadcasting was handled by the major religious groups, and the broadcasting time was given to them free as a public service. Today, many small religious groups buy broadcasting time and use it, not only to preach the word of God, but also to plead for contributions to support their church (and sometimes the preacher's expensive lifestyle as well). Many of these *televangelists* are talented, exciting public speakers. Some have become very famous. Others have become involved in **scandals** after committing the very sins they were preaching against.

19. The 20th century has been a period of great change. Both the advances of science and the horrors of modern history have caused a decrease in religious faith. Scientific insights have explained many of the mysteries once explained only by religion. As a result, for many people, science has become their religion. The history of this century has been a recurring nightmare revealing the frightening depths of people's cruelty to one another. People who have grown up in Communist countries, where God has been officially dead for decades, may wonder how anyone can believe in an all-powerful, positive force that would allow so much evil and suffering to exist in the world. Religious people have several answers. Some say that one cannot blame God for the sins committed by people. Others respond that human beings cannot expect to understand the purposes of the **divine** Creator. Still, despite the effects of modern science and modern history, the concept of God remains. A few years ago, "God is dead" signs and jokes were everywhere in the U.S.A. Today, that slogan seems to be dead, and belief in God is still very much alive. Though most Americans do not let organized religion dominate their lives, God remains an honorary citizen in the U.S.A., welcome in the nation's hundreds of different churches, the recipient of prayers in many different styles and languages.

EXERCISES

I. Comprehension Questions. Answer the following questions on paper or in class discussion.

1. In what ways are religion and government kept separate in the U.S.A.?
2. In what ways is the Protestant work ethic similar to American capitalism?
3. What are the major religions in the U.S.A.?
4. What evidence is there that religion is losing influence in American life?

II. Vocabulary Practice. Pronounce the following words after your teacher, and discuss their meanings. Then use some of them to complete the following sentences.

atheists	persecution
ceremonies	philosophy
claim	prohibit
congregation	restrictions
denomination	scandal
disregard	sect
diversity	secular
divine	sin
emphasis	spiritual
existence	thrifty

1. The idea of life after death refers to a ________________ life rather than a physical life.

2. Polygamy (being married to more than one person at the same time) is illegal in the U.S.A. and is also generally considered a ________________ in most religions.
3. Most Americans believe in the ________________ of God, but those that don't are called ________________.
4. When famous people are discovered doing something illegal and/or sinful, there is a ________________.
5. The 20th century is called a ________________ century in the U.S.A. because religion seems to be declining in importance in people's lives.
6. A person's ________________ of life refers to his or her ideas about the best and the right ways to behave.
7. A religious ________________ is a major division or branch of a particular religion.
8. A ________________ is a group of people who belong to the same church, temple, or synagogue.

III. Word Study.

A. This chapter includes many words with prefixes. Discuss the meanings of the following prefixes and words. The numbers in brackets give the paragraphs in which these words are used.

self-discipline [7]	premarital [13]	interfaith [13]
disregard [13]	misfortune [17]	televangelists [18]

B. This chapter also includes many compound words. Discuss the meanings of the following words.

lawsuit [3]	supernatural [4]
afterlife [17]	lifestyle [18]

IV. Idiom Study. Underline the correct completion for each of the following idioms.

1. *Separation of church and state* [3] a) protects religious freedom b) threatens religious freedom c) limits religious freedom.
2. *The Protestant work ethic* [7] encourages people to a) give a lot of money to the poor b) work hard c) go to church every day.
3. *The Bible Belt* [14] is a) a belt worn by religious people b) a copy of the *New Testament* c) an area of the U.S.A.
4. He is *turned off* [16] by religious rituals. He a) doesn't like them b) won't watch them on TV c) finds them relaxing.
5. *Side by side* [17] means a) two things next to each other b) horizontal c) vertical.

V. Reading Skills.

1. In paragraph 7, what two philosophies is the text comparing?

   ________________ ________________

2. In paragraph 14, which sentence expresses the main idea? Write the first two words of that sentence. ________________

3. Paragraphs 3, 4, 17, and 18 all contain passages in parentheses. Underline these passages, and discuss in class what kinds of information writers often put in parentheses.

4. Reread paragraph 17. What do you think the phrase *free will* means?

   ____

5. Paragraph 19 gives two general reasons why people living in the 20th century might question the existence of God. What are they?

____

6. In paragraph 19, what does the text mean when it says that in Communist countries "God has been officially dead for decades"?

____

5

EATING THE AMERICAN WAY

1. Three square meals a day—that's what Americans are supposed to eat. But, in reality, most add between-meal **snacks** and have a bite five or six times a day. Is this healthy? Americans believe that what they eat is more important than how often. However, the **quality** and the **quantity** of American **consumption** are both matters of concern.

AMERICAN MEALS AND SNACKS

2. The meal that breaks the overnight fast is, of course, breakfast. It is a meal that about 25% of Americans **skip,** either because they're in a hurry or on a diet. Many adults that do eat breakfast have only a small meal, perhaps just orange juice or toast along with the traditional wake-up beverage, coffee. But others eat a real meal in the morning. A complete American breakfast begins with fruit or fruit juice. The main course is generally hot or cold cereal or eggs. The eggs are usually served with toast and perhaps also bacon, ham, or sausages. Other popular breakfast foods are pancakes, waffles, and French toast (bread soaked in a mixture of eggs and milk and then fried), all served with maple syrup.

3. Americans usually eat breakfast between 7 and 8 A.M. By 10:30 or thereabouts, they're ready for their mid-morning coffee break. Most workers are given 10 to 15 minutes off the job to have coffee, a snack, and a chat with coworkers.

4. Most Americans eat lunch between noon and two o'clock. This mid-day meal is eaten away from home more often than breakfast or **dinner.** It is rare for working adults to go home for lunch, and many schoolchildren also eat at school. Some people brown-bag it—that is, they bring food from home in a paper bag. For this purpose, they need a meal that is small and portable. The sandwich meets these requirements. In addition, it is inexpensive and easy to prepare. The sandwich chef needs only two pieces of bread, something moist to smear on the bread (butter, mayonnaise, mustard, or catsup), and some meat, cheese, fish, or poultry to stuff in between. Some popular cold sandwiches are those made with ham and cheese, peanut butter and jelly, sliced chicken or turkey, tuna salad, and roast beef.

5. People who eat lunch in restaurants are more likely to order hot sandwiches. The most popular of these are hamburgers and hot dogs. Hamburgers are patties of chopped meat, usually served in round buns. Hot dogs are 5 to 7-inch sausages (also called red hots, frankfurters, or wieners) served in long, thin buns. The name *hot dog* was inspired (about 1900) by an American vendor who compared the frankfurter to the long-bodied German dog. His *hot dachshund sausages* eventually became simply hot dogs.

6. The sandwich is standard lunchtime fare, but for a bigger meal, the **diner** might add a bowl of soup, a salad, French fried potatoes or potato chips, and a sweet dessert or fruit.

7. Because most people eat lunch around the same time, restaurants are quite crowded between noon and two o'clock. At counters, where customers sit on a row of stools rather than at separate tables, waiters and waitresses can provide faster service. To save time, many people eat in cafeterias, where customers walk by displays of food, place what they want on their trays, and then pay a cashier at the end of the line. Self-service cafeterias handle big crowds quickly and efficiently. Large institutions such as factories, hospitals, and schools often have cafeterias and/or lunchrooms with food-dispensing machines from which customers can purchase soup, sandwiches, drinks, fruit, and sweets. Microwave ovens for heating foods quickly may be set up near these machines. Fast-food restaurants (where customers order food and get it in about two minutes) also do a thriving business at lunchtime.

8. On the other hand, those who want a more leisurely lunch served to them can find many traditional restaurants. At nice restaurants, diners sometimes combine business and pleasure at a *business luncheon*, where work is discussed while eating.

9. The mid-afternoon snack is also an American tradition. Office and factory workers take a second coffee break. Children coming home from school usually head immediately for the refrigerator. In warm weather, ice cream is a popular snack food. It's consumed in cones, bars, and sundaes (with a sweet sauce on top). It is also used in two popular drinks, milkshakes and ice cream sodas.

10. The biggest meal of the day is dinner, served about six o'clock. Dinner may include several courses: an appetizer (consisting of fresh fruit, fruit juice, or a small portion of fish); soup; salad; an entrée of meat, poultry, or fish; and side dishes such as cooked vegetables, rice, or noodles. Coffee or tea and dessert finish off the meal. Most Ameri-

cans prefer a sweet dessert such as cake, pie, or ice cream. Apple pie, served hot with a scoop of ice cream (*à la mode*) or with a **slice** of cheese, is a national favorite, hence the popular expression, "as American as apple pie." Most Americans don't eat all these courses for dinner every evening, but they often do so when eating out or serving guests at home.

11. With lunch and dinner, Americans commonly drink water, fruit juice, beer, coffee, tea, or a carbonated drink called *soda* or *pop*. Though children are urged to drink milk with every meal, many prefer soda or juice instead. Wine is considered festive and is likely to appear on holidays, at celebrations, and when dining out.

12. Since dinner is customarily served early in the evening, the late evening snack is a ritual in most households. Children often have milk and cookies before bedtime. Adults may nibble on fruit or sweets.

13. On weekends and holidays, the meal schedule may vary. On Saturday evenings, many people eat very late dinners, particularly those who dine out. On Sundays, many families have brunch, a meal that combines breakfast and lunch. It is usually served between 11 A.M. and 2 P.M. and includes typical breakfast foods plus cheese, fruit, cake, and perhaps cold fish. Families who go to church on Sunday morning may have their usual weekday breakfast before services and then eat their biggest meal of the day about two o'clock. The main meal of the day is always called dinner, no matter what time it is served. When dinner is eaten in mid-afternoon, a smaller evening meal, called supper, is served around seven o'clock.

14. On Sundays and holidays when the weather is mild, Americans often eat outdoors. They enjoy **picnics** in parks, backyard barbecues (usually featuring charcoal-broiled steaks, hot dogs, or hamburgers) and clambakes.

15. In the U.S.A. as elsewhere, eating is an important part of family life and social activity. In many homes, dinner time may be the only time when everyone gets together and shares the day's experiences. It is also an occasion for inviting friends.

16. Dining out is also an important part of American social life. For single men and women, dates often begin with dinner at a nice restaurant. Married couples often get together in groups to eat out, especially on weekends. In their desire to use time efficiently, Americans may rush through breakfast and lunch, but dinner is usually a more leisurely meal at which enjoyment of food is enhanced by pleasant conversation.

EASY DOES IT!

17. Putting food on the American table is easier now than ever before. More than enough food to feed the nation is produced by about 4% of the population, and paying for it is not a huge burden for most Americans. In 1986, the average household earning about $26,000 spent $60 a week for food, about two-thirds of it for food eaten at home and the other third for eating out.

18. Today's family shopper can go to one store—the nearby supermarket—and find nearly everything the household needs. Believe it or not, the average number of items in today's American supermarket is almost 25,000! In addition to food, supermarkets sell paper goods, cleaning supplies, cooking utensils, cosmetics, common medicines, tobacco products, pet products, books and magazines, flowers and plants, alcoholic beverages, and so on. Many are open until 10 P.M. or later to serve the working public.

19. Not only is shopping quicker and easier than ever before; cooking is, too. Many foods are partly or wholly prepared. A great **variety** of soups and sauces come in cans or in small packages. The cook just adds water, heats, and serves. Other timesavers include mixes for making mashed potatoes, pancakes, cookies, and cakes. To these, the cook adds just two or three **ingredients**—usually butter, milk, and eggs. There are also instant beverages—coffee, cocoa, lemonade, and many others—which are made by adding only water. Many frozen foods are precooked and need only to be heated.

20. Food preparation is fast and easy with a food processor, which can, for example, turn a bunch of carrots into carrot juice with the flick of a switch. In a microwave oven, the American cook can bake a chocolate cake in five minutes or a good-sized turkey in a few hours. Clean-up is speedy, too, with the automatic dishwasher and the garbage disposal at hand. Not all Americans have this equipment, but many do.

21. The ultimate in easy eating is, of course, eating out, and Americans do that quite a bit, in fact about four times a week. American restaurants range from inexpensive fast-food places, to exotic **ethnic** restaurants, to expensive, formal places that serve elegant food in an elegant setting.

22. Most fast-food restaurants are **franchises**—individually owned businesses operating in accordance with guidelines from the company's central management. Fast-food franchises have been very successful in the U.S.A. because they provide quick, inexpensive, tasty meals that can be eaten at the restaurant or taken home. Part of the appeal is the predictability. People know what McDonald's Big Mac or Kentucky Fried chicken is going to taste like, wherever they buy it.

23. For many Americans, ethnic dining means the fun of the unknown. The most familiar of the ethnic **cuisines** are Chinese, Italian, and Mexican. In large cities, there may be dozens of different types of ethnic restaurants. In Chicago, for example, the range of ethnic dining goes, if not from A to Z, at least from A to Y (Arabian to Yugoslavian). In between, there's Armenian, Cuban, Ethiopian, Greek, Indian, Persian, Philippine, Peruvian, Russian, Thai, Vietnamese, and many other national cooking styles. These places serve immigrants who want their own native cuisine, but they also serve Americans looking for a dining adventure.

VARIETY—THE SPICE OF LIFE

24. The ethnic influence affects not only dining out but home cooking as well. Ingredients for ethnic foods are readily available at the supermarkets and specialty stores catering to the needs of the various ethnic communities. The U.S.A. is a nation of immigrants, commonly called a *melting pot* of people from nations **throughout** the world. Therefore, it is not surprising that its cooking pots may contain cuisine from anywhere in the world.

25. Regional food specialties add further variety to the American diet. From New England come wonderful seafood chowders (usually clams or lobsters stewed with vegetables and milk), baked beans, brown breads, and Boston cream pie. Southerners have created delicious recipes for fried chicken, smoked ham, grits (a side dish made with corn meal, milk, and eggs), and fritters (small fried cakes often containing fruit). New Orleans is famous for its spicy Creole cooking, which combines French, Spanish, black, and American Indian cooking styles. The western part of the country has adopted many specialties from Chinese and Mexican cuisines.

26. Because of the nation's varied climate and geography, a great variety of fruits and vegetables are grown in the United States. Americans enjoy fresh tomatoes from Texas, oranges from Florida, and strawberries from California. High-quality fruits, juices, and vegetables are available any time of the year, thanks to modern transportation and freezing techniques.

DEATH BY CONSUMPTION

27. Although there is ample opportunity to get enough food and **nutritious** food in the U.S.A., many Americans eat (or drink) themselves into an early grave. In many countries, especially those in Africa, Asia, and parts of Latin America, people depend on plants for more than two-thirds of their food. In the U.S.A. (as in Europe), meat, fish, poultry, and dairy products make up about 40% of the typical diet, and it is a diet overloaded with harmful fats. Americans also tend to nibble on salty junk foods and sweet desserts, consuming far too much sugar and salt.

28. In recent years, Americans have learned that you are what you eat, that diet affects not only appearance, but also performance, mental state, health, and longevity. As a result, many Americans have increased their consumption of fruits, vegetables, and the less fatty sources of protein (such as fish, grains, and poultry). Still, about 60% of Americans are at least somewhat overweight, including about 13% that are obese (fat).

29. Most overweight Americans have a dual problem—they eat too much and exercise too little. Automobiles, elevators, escalators, power lawn mowers, and many other mechanical devices rob Americans of the physical work they need to burn up the calories they eat. "Everything enjoyable in life is either illegal, immoral, or fattening," complain those who are overweight. In response, the American food industry has produced a wide assortment of foods without sugar, using **artificial** sweeteners which have no food value. In supermarkets, dieters can find low-calorie beverages, ice cream, cookies, jelly, syrup, and canned fruit, as well as low-calorie frozen dinners.

30. Even more serious than overeating are the health and social problems created by consumption of alcoholic beverages, cigarettes, and illegal drugs. About 60% to 70% of Americans drink alcoholic beverages to some extent, about 40% occasionally drink too much, and at least 10 million Americans are alcoholics. Those who engage in heavy drinking damage their own health, cause pain to their families, and are dangerous behind the wheel of an automobile. In recent years, many organizations of private citizens have campaigned to keep drunks off the road by increasing penalties for drunk driving. In almost every state, the minimum legal age for buying liquor, wine, or beer is 21. Nevertheless, American teenagers often become involved in alcohol-related accidents and sometimes become alcoholics.

31. Another way that Americans consume themselves to death is by smoking. About 26% of American adults smoke, and many of them develop serious health problems. The medical expenses and human tragedy caused by smoking are immeasurable. Unfortunately, the political influence of the tobacco industry is so great that although the government urges smokers to quit, it also pays farmers to grow tobacco.

32. One of the greatest concerns of Americans is the large amount of illegal drugs consumed in the U.S.A., especially by teenagers and young adults. For all ages, the average current marijuana usage is about 9%, and about 3% of Americans use cocaine. But, among young adults, the figures are much higher (about 21% using marijuana and 8% using cocaine). The U.S.A., with only 5% of the world's population, consumes about 50% of the world's cocaine. This widespread cocaine usage is of special concern since it is highly addictive. Many people who become *hooked* (addicted) are then forced to become criminals in order to get money to buy this illegal (therefore expensive) substance. The connection between drug usage and crime was recently illustrated by a study of people arrested for various crimes in the Chicago area. They were asked to agree to be tested for drugs. Of those who volunteered, 75% were found to be using illegal drugs. Another recent study indicated that cocaine use by teenagers and young adults is finally beginning to decline. Still, more than half of high school seniors have tried an illegal drug other than marijuana.

33. In dealing with all of these health problems—**obesity,** alcoholism, smoking, and drug **addiction**—Americans often turn to support groups of fellow sufferers. Groups such as Weight Watchers, Alcoholics Anonymous, and Narcotics Anonymous have helped people overcome destructive behavior. With the assistance of professional counselors and the support of a group, Americans work hard to rid themselves of habits that could destroy their health and shorten their lives.

34. At the other end of the health spectrum are people who have great self-control and who consume only what is healthy. Many of them are quite critical (even fearful) of the typical American cuisine. Of course, they **avoid** high-fat and high-salt foods. But, in addition, they worry about the possible health threats from chemicals added to food. Three common sources of these chemicals are pesticides sprayed on plants to keep insects off; additives used in some packaged foods to improve appearance and lengthen shelf life; and drugs fed to beef cattle to improve the quantity and taste of meat. Are these chemicals harmful to human beings? Those that believe they are read labels carefully, avoid foods with preservatives, and do some of their shopping in health food stores (of which there are about 6,000 in the U.S.A.). Defenders of the chemicals say that the quantities used are too small to be harmful, and that discontinuing their use would mean smaller harvests, less prime beef, faster food spoilage, and higher food prices.

35. In the 1960s, people who were afraid of the typical American diet were called health food nuts. Today, Americans realize that these people have had a healthy influence on what is served in American homes and restaurants. As a result of the health food movement, many Americans survey the great variety of good things to eat and then make wiser, healthier choices.

EXERCISES

I. Comprehension Questions. Answer the following questions on paper or in class discussion.

1. In this chapter, what two meals were discussed besides breakfast, lunch, and dinner? Describe when they are eaten and what is eaten.
2. Why is preparing a meal easy for Americans?
3. What are some of the dangerous aspects of American food consumption?
4. How do American meals compare to those in your native country? List some similarities and differences.

II. Vocabulary Practice. Pronounce the following words after your teacher, and discuss their meanings. Then use some of them to complete the following sentences. You may need to use the same word twice.

addiction	nutritious
artificial	obesity
avoid	picnic
consumption	quality
cuisine	quantity
diner	skip
dinner	slice
ethnic	snack
franchise	throughout
ingredients	variety

1. A person who is eating in a restaurant may be called a ______________. He or she may be having breakfast, lunch, or ______________.

2. ________________ is a common problem in the U.S.A. because many Americans eat too much and exercise too little.

3. If you ________________ a meal, you don't eat that meal.

4. A person who is overweight should ________________ eating food with a lot of sugar and fat in it.

5. During a coffee break, many workers have a ________________.

6. In a restaurant, you may order a ________________ of cake or pie. At home, you may nibble on a ________________ of cheese or bread.

7. ________________ the U.S.A., there is great variety in the American ________________ because of various ________________ influences.

8. The word ________________ means *how much*; the word ________________ means *how good*.

III. Word Study.

A. Homonyms are words that sound the same but have different meanings and spellings. In the following sentences, circle the correct homonyms.

1. Americans like to eat (they're; their) lunches quickly because (they're; their) often in a hurry.
2. Let's (by; buy) some (meat; meet) and then (meat; meet) (by; buy) the cashier.
3. I want (to; too) have (some; sum) coffee.
4. Every (Sunday; sundae), I eat a chocolate (Sunday; sundae).
5. Cooking styles (vary; very) a great deal in the U.S., so eating American style is (vary; very) interesting.

6. It's (to; too) late for breakfast and (to; too) early for lunch, so let's go (to; too) a restaurant and have brunch.

B. Sometimes a word from another language enters the English language, accent mark and all. Here are two examples from this chapter. Pronounce these words, and write their meanings.

1. entrée ______________________________

2. à la mode ______________________________

IV. Idiom Study.

A. Write the meanings of the following idioms. The numbers in brackets give the paragraphs in which these idioms are used.

1. a bite [1] ______________________________

2. a coffee break [3] ______________________________

3. brown-bag it [4] ______________________________

4. believe it or not [18] ______________________________

5. and so on [18] ______________________________

6. to become hooked [32] ______________________________

7. shelf life [34] ______________________________

8. health food nut [35] ______________________________

B. Discuss the meanings of *three square meals a day* [1] and *variety is the spice of life* (see heading above paragraph 24), and *into an early grave* [27].

V. Reading Skills.

A. Most paragraphs contain a topic sentence that states the main idea. The topic sentence is more general than the other sentences in the paragraph, and it often suggests the writer's attitude toward the subject. The other sentences in the paragraph support this topic idea by offering examples, reasons, or other evidence. Write down the first two words of the topic sentence in each of the following paragraphs:

[17] ________________

[27] ________________

[33] ________________

B. What is the meaning of the colon (:) used in paragraph 10?

____

C. Discuss the difference between a fact and an opinion. Then mark the following statements *fact* (F) or *opinion* (O).

___ 1. American food isn't healthy.

___ 2. Americans eat more beef than people from many other countries do.

___ 3. Illegal drugs cause an increase in crime.

___ 4. Americans should legalize all drugs.

___ 5. Americans eat too many snacks.

___ 6. Smoking cigarettes is bad for a person's health.

6

AMERICAN ETIQUETTE

1. In the 17th century, King Louis XIV of France gave people who came into his court *une etiquette* (a ticket) containing a list of rules of acceptable **behavior** in his palace. **Fortunately** for immigrants and visitors to the U.S.A., Americans are far less rigid about right and wrong ways to behave.

2. Most American rules of **etiquette** are simply ways to show respect and consideration for others. People who show concern for others are usually considered **polite** even if the words or gestures aren't quite what's expected. The foreign student who addresses a female teacher as "Sir" has made a mistake. But the teacher understands the intention and considers the student well-mannered.

3. There are many books about American etiquette in libraries, but it probably isn't necessary to read any of them. Americans are quite **casual** about **manners** and accept a wide range of behavior as **appropriate.** If you follow the suggestions and warnings in this chapter and your own good judgment, your behavior will probably satisfy even the most **proper** American.

INTRODUCTIONS AND TITLES

4. Making introductions (presenting two strangers to each other) is one of the most common social duties. There are traditional rules for doing this **properly,** but many Americans don't know them, and others don't notice when the rules are broken. When introducing people of different sexes, it's polite to say the woman's name first; for example, "Mrs. Fox, this is my neighbor, Mr. Wolf." But if the man is elderly or famous, then his name or title should be **mentioned** first: "Mr. President, I'd like you to meet my sister, Luisa Rivera." When two people of the same sex are introduced, the older person is named first: "Grandfather, this is my friend, Narish Patel. Narish, this is my grandfather, Mr. Kim." A very formal introduction of someone important often begins, "May I present...?"

5. Appropriate responses to an introduction include "How do you do?", "It's very nice to meet you," or simply an informal, "Hello," often accompanied by a handshake. At one time, only American men shook hands. Today, a woman may also extend her hand to a man for an introduction. Two women do not usually shake hands in a social situation, but they may in a business situation.

6. At the end of a conversation with a new **acquaintance,** it's polite to say, "Good-bye. It was nice meeting you." One might also add some appropriate conclusion that wishes the person a good time or good luck; for example, "Enjoy your visit to our city" or "Good luck with your new job."

7. Proper forms of **address** are often a puzzle to foreigners. In the U.S.A., people in the same general age group tend to get on a first-name basis very quickly. Coworkers, classmates, and neighbors often call each other by first names. But an adult is likely to continue to call doctors, lawyers, teachers, religious leaders, and bosses by their last names. However, it is not polite to call someone by the last name only. Titles that precede the last name include *Mr.* (*mister,* for a man), *Miss* (for a single woman), *Mrs.* (pronounced *missus* and used for a woman who is married, divorced, or widowed), and *Ms.* (pronounced *miz* and used for a woman whose marital status you don't know). Some single or divorced women may prefer the title *Ms.* When in doubt about which title to use when introducing a woman, use her full name without any title at all. To address a man whose name you don't know, use *sir.* (It is **rude** to call him *mister.*) To address a woman you don't know, use *madam* or *ma'am.* Remember that the title *doctor* (Dr.) is used not only for a medical doctor but also for a dentist and for a person with an academic doctorate degree.

8. It is also important to remember that very few titles are used without the last name (family name). Those that can be used alone include *Doctor, Professor,* and some of the titles for religious leaders (such as *Father* or *Rabbi*). It is not correct to address a teacher as *Teacher.*

CONGRATULATIONS, CONDOLENCES, APOLOGIES, AND REQUESTS

9. ***Congratulations*** is a wonderful word that fits a great many happy social occasions. In general, it's polite to say "Congratulations!" (with a lot of enthusiasm in your voice) when a person has accomplished something. The accomplishment may be academic (such as a graduation), vocational (such as a job promotion), or personal (such as the birth of a child or grandchild).

10. When congratulations are in order, it is sometimes also appropriate to give a gift, especially if you are invited to a party to celebrate a particular occasion or accomplishment, such as a birthday, graduation, wedding, or anniversary.

11. When you receive a party invitation, it may say on the bottom *R.S.V.P.*, initials that refer to a French expression meaning *respond, please.* That means you must write or phone to say whether or not you can come. If the invitation says *R.S.V.P. regrets only,* it means that you should respond only if you cannot come.

12. Equal attention must be given to good manners on sad occasions. If you know that an American coworker, classmate, or neighbor has had a recent death in the family, you should express your sympathy (**condolences**). Even if you hate mentioning the sad event, do so. In expressing sympathy, it's a good idea not to use the words *die* or *death* but simply to say, "I was so sorry to hear about your loss" (or "...about your father"). It's also appropriate to send a sympathy card, but if you don't know the mourner's religion, be sure to select one without any religious symbols on it. Most customs regarding mourning relate to the family's religion and vary from one religious group to another, so don't send flowers or food unless you know that these gifts are appropriate.

13. The simple words *I'm sorry* display very good manners in a great many difficult social situations. *I'm sorry* has two main uses: to express your sympathy to someone who has had a bad experience and to express your regret when you have bothered someone or caused a problem. Other useful apologies are *excuse me* and *pardon me,* which mean the same thing. These expressions are appropriate when pushing your way out of a crowded elevator or stopping a stranger to ask directions.

DINING ETIQUETTE

14. If you're invited to an American friend's home for dinner, keep in mind these general rules for polite behavior. First of all, arrive approximately on time (but not early). Americans expect promptness. It's OK to be 10 or 15 minutes late but not 45 minutes late. Dinner might be overcooked and ruined by then. When you're invited to someone's home for a meal, it's polite to bring a small gift. Flowers or candy are always appropriate. If you have an attractive item made in your native country, your host and/or hostess would certainly enjoy receiving that as a gift.

15. Some Americans don't know about the dietary restrictions of various ethnic and religious groups. What do you do if you're served a food that you don't like or cannot eat? Don't make a fuss about it. If your host doesn't say anything about what you aren't eating, then you shouldn't, either. Simply eat what you can and hope that no one notices what you left. If you are questioned, you may have to admit that you don't eat meat (or whatever), but you can also say that you've enjoyed the other foods and have had "more than enough" to eat. Don't make the cook feel obliged to prepare something else for you. Be sure to **compliment** the cook on the food that you enjoyed.

16. Don't leave immediately after dinner, but don't overstay your welcome, either. When your friends seem to be getting tired and running out of conversation, take their behavior as a cue to leave. The next day, call or write a thank-you note to say how much you enjoyed the evening.

17. If you invite someone to join you for dinner in a restaurant, phone the restaurant first to find out if you need a reservation in order to avoid a long wait for a table. To make a reservation, just give your name, the number of people in your group, and the time you plan to arrive. When you invite someone to dinner, you should be prepared to pay the bill and reach for it when it arrives. However, if your companion insists on paying his or her share, don't get into an argument about it. Some people prefer to pay their own way so that they don't feel indebted, and those feelings should be respected. In most American restaurants, the waiter or waitress's tip is not added to the bill. If the service was adequate, it's customary to leave a tip equal to about 15% of the bill. In expensive restaurants, leave a bit more.

18. American table manners are easy to learn by observation. A few characteristics to note: the napkin should not be tucked into the collar or vest but should be placed across the lap; the **silverware** placement is quite different from the European style, but you can't go wrong if you use the piece of silverware furthest from the plate first and work your way in toward the plate as the meal progresses. Before cutting food, some Americans switch their knife and fork to the opposite hands, but it isn't necessary to do this.

MANNERS BETWEEN MEN AND WOMEN

19. In the 1960s, the U.S.A. went through a social revolution commonly referred to as the *Women's Liberation Movement*. One of the goals of this movement was to promote the idea that women are equal to men in their ability to learn and to succeed in almost any occupation. The movement has benefited women in many ways, especially in terms of job opportunity and advancement. But it has also created great confusion regarding manners. Formerly, men were considered the stronger and the dominant sex, so etiquette required them to adopt a protective attitude toward the so-called weaker sex. That meant helping women on and off with their coats, lighting their cigarettes, opening doors for them, allowing them to exit from elevators first, and so on. Today, American women, who outlive men by seven years, do not consider themselves the weaker sex and do not generally feel in need of male protection. Their self-sufficient attitude has led men to wonder whether the traditional etiquette is still appropriate or whether it will, in fact, offend independent, confident American women. Most men continue to perform the traditional courtesies, but both sexes are more casual about them. If a man does not help his date into and out of her chair in a restaurant, no one will think he's rude.

20. Traditionally, when a man invites a woman out on a date, he picks her up at her home, pays all the expenses for the evening, and takes her home at the end of the evening. Prior to Women's Liberation, the woman was expected to sit at home by the phone and wait and hope for the man of her dreams to call her. Today's liberated woman may take the initiative in suggesting an evening together by inviting a man she likes to a party, to a home-cooked meal, or to an evening at the theater. If she does the inviting, she pays for at least part of the evening's expenses. Often, a man and woman who are friends but not romantically involved go out together *Dutch treat*, which means that each person pays his or her own way.

21. Today, many men working in the U.S.A. have a female boss. Men who come from countries in which the woman's place is still in the home may find it difficult to take orders from a woman. But in the U.S.A., 44% of the work force is female, and many women are judges, doctors, company presidents, college presidents, and entrepreneurs. It is important for men to respect a person who holds a position of responsibility and authority, whether that person is male or female. To treat a woman as inferior just because she is female is not only insulting but also out of step with contemporary American culture.

CLASSROOM ETIQUETTE

22. The relationship between student and teacher is less formal in the U.S.A. than in many other countries, especially at the college level. American college students do not stand up when their teacher enters the room. Students are generally encouraged to ask questions during class, to stop in the professor's office for extra help, and to phone if they're absent and need an assignment. Most teachers allow students to enter class late or leave early, if necessary.

23. Despite the lack of formality, students are still expected to be polite and considerate of their teacher and fellow classmates. When students want to ask questions, they usually raise a hand and wait to be called on. But if a professor is giving a formal lecture, that is the wrong time to interrupt with a question. When the teacher or a student is speaking to the class, it's rude to begin whispering to another classmate. When a test is being given, talking to a classmate is not only rude but also risky. Most American teachers assume that students who are talking to each other during a test are cheating.

AMERICAN ATTITUDES

24. Remember that Americans have a democratic outlook, a strong belief that all people are entitled to equal opportunity and equal respect. No one is a privileged being, and no one is worthless. A person who acts very humble and timid may make his or her American friends uncomfortable. On the other hand, a person who acts as if he or she is ruler of the world will have trouble keeping any American friends. A polite but **assertive** manner is what is socially acceptable. So, no matter what your status in relation to the person you're with, feel free to look directly into his or her eyes and speak your true feelings. You have no obligation to say what the other person wants to hear. Occasionally, it is necessary to tell a white lie and compliment your friend on something you don't really like. But, most of the time, you can express your true opinions, and Americans won't mind at all if you disagree with them. Also, you need not worry much about asking inappropriate questions. Americans (like people everywhere) enjoy talking about themselves. Your interest in them will be considered good manners as long as you stay away from questions about three subjects that most American adults don't want to discuss—their age, weight, and income.

LANGUAGE ETIQUETTE

25. Americans are usually tolerant of non-native speakers who have some trouble understanding English. But they become annoyed when a person pretends to understand but doesn't really and then creates problems because of misunderstanding what was said. No one wants soap when he asked for soup. So if you don't understand what is said to you, admit it and politely ask the person to repeat or explain.

26. Second, it is quite rude to converse with a companion in your native language and leave your American friends standing there feeling stupid because they can't understand the conversation. The Americans may also feel that you are talking about them or saying something you don't want them to hear. If you must switch to your native language to explain something to a non-English-speaking companion, at least translate for your American friends so they don't feel left out.

27. Learn just a few more polite English expressions, and you'll be ready to face the world of Americans with **confidence.** The polite response to a compliment about your looks or your work is "Thank you." (A smile and a nod is not enough.) The response to "Thank you" is, of course, "You're welcome." If someone asks, "How are you?", don't give your medical history. Just say, "Fine, thanks. How are you?" Finally, what should you say when someone sneezes? It may not seem **logical,** but the correct response is "God bless you." That's about all there is to it. Now that you've studied this quick overview of manners in the U.S.A., you're ready to be polite in English. Let's hope your American friends will be just as polite.

EXERCISES

I. Comprehension Questions. Answer the following questions on paper or in class discussion.

1. On what occasions should you say "Congratulations!"?
2. How has the Women's Liberation Movement affected American manners?
3. How do American democratic attitudes affect manners?
4. How do American manners compare to those in your country? What are some differences?

II. Vocabulary Practice. Pronounce the following words after your teacher, and discuss their meanings. Then use some of them to complete the following sentences. You may need to use the same word twice.

acquaintance	etiquette
address	fortunately
appropriate	logical
assertive	manners
behavior	mention
casual	polite
compliment	proper
condolences	properly
confidence	rude
congratulations	silverware

1. If you have good manners, then you are ________________ .

2. Rules of ________________ tell people how to behave in different social situations.

3. The word *title* sometimes means the name of a piece of writing, but in this chapter it means polite forms of ________________ (such as *Mr.*, *Dr.*, or *Mrs.*) used before a person's family (last) name.

4. The adverb for the word *proper* is *properly*. We say, "His behavior is ________________ " but "He is behaving ________________ ."

5. The adjectives ________________ and *proper* have related meanings. Both refer to behavior that is considered polite and socially correct for a particular occasion.

6. When someone dies, you should express your ________________ to members of the family.

7. When your friend graduates from college, you should say ________________ to him or her.

8. Americans believe people should not be afraid to ask for the things they want. In other words, people should be ________________. However, in expressing their needs or wishes, they should be ________________, not ________________ to others.

III. Word Study.

A. Write the nouns for each of the following verbs.

behave________________ converse________________

congratulate________________

compliment________________

B. What is the meaning of the word-part *mis-*, as used in *misunderstand* and *misinterpret*? ________________________________

C. Sometimes *-ess* is added to an English noun to change the masculine form to a feminine form, as in *prince* and *princess*. Check the dictionary, and then write the feminine form for each of the following words.

waiter________________ host________________

duke________________ actor________________

IV. Idiom Study. Underline the correct answer to complete each statement. (The numbers in brackets give the paragraphs in which the idioms are used.)

1. *R.S.V.P.* [11] on a party invitation means that you should a) phone the host or hostess to respond b) come on time c) bring your own wine.
2. If you have *run out of* [16] postage stamps, a) you had some before, but you used them all, so now you don't have any b) you have run out to get some c) you have a few left.

3. She *went through* [19] a difficult period in her life. She a) traveled through it b) experienced it c) remembered it.
4. If you and your friend go out for dinner *Dutch treat,* [20] a) you eat Dutch food b) you each pay for your own meal c) the meal is free.
5. If you tell a *white lie,* [24] a) it's not really a lie b) it insults someone c) it doesn't hurt anyone.

V. Reading Skills.

A. Pronouns and possessive adjectives generally refer to a noun that is used earlier in the same sentence or in the preceding sentence.

1. In paragraph 8, sentence 2, what word does *those* refer to?

____

2. In paragraph 9, sentence 1, what word does *that* refer to?

____

3. In paragraph 12, sentence 5, what word does *one* refer to?

____

4. In paragraph 16, sentence 2, what word does *their* refer to?

____

5. In paragraph 19, sentence 5, what word does *them* refer to?

____

6. In paragraph 25, sentence 2, what word does *they* refer to?

____

B. What does the last sentence of the chapter imply about Americans?

____

7

THE AMERICAN ECONOMY

AN EXPLANATION OF CAPITALISM

1. The United States is a capitalistic country. To Americans, **capitalism** is not a political philosophy; it is an economic system. In a capitalistic **economy,** businesses are privately owned and operated. The government's job in the business world is only to protect each part of the economy—big business, small business, workers, and consumers—from abuse. Even such basic needs as transportation and communications are provided by private companies. However, because of the importance of these **services,** the government regulates these industries more than others to make sure that they are operated fairly and safely.

2. In a capitalistic economy, prices vary with changes in supply and demand. In other words, when there are more apples available than people want to buy, the price of apples goes down; when there is a **shortage,** the price goes up. Of course, prices of **goods** and services are also affected by the cost of producing them.

3. Under ideal conditions, a free economy is good for everyone. Workers can choose the career they want to follow; they can change jobs to get higher wages, better working conditions, or professional advancement; and they can unite with other workers to demand better treatment from their employer. Manufacturers and merchants **profit** when their businesses are successful. In order to compete, businesses must operate efficiently, economically, and creatively. Therefore, because of **competition,** customers receive high-quality merchandise at the lowest possible prices.

4. Of course, American capitalism is not ideal. Weaknesses in the system sometimes create problems. Two of these are strikes and monopolies. A **strike** occurs when a group of employees refuses to work until its demands are satisfied. A strike in a vital industry such as transportation can disrupt the entire economy. Companies that depend on trains or trucks to transport raw materials and/or finished products must shut down. Their employees are laid off. When workers' incomes are greatly reduced, they do not spend as much. This, in turn, affects

the income of merchants who usually sell to those unemployed workers. Also, when workers go on strike, the public may be seriously inconvenienced. Strikes can shut down transportation or cut off food or fuel supplies to large areas.

5. A **monopoly** occurs when there is a lack of competition in an industry. This sometimes happens when a company buys its competitors or when it is so powerful that it can sell its products at prices others cannot match. Then the competition is forced to go out of business. When there is inadequate competition in an industry, the public suffers because competition forces companies to keep quality high and prices low.

6. Although capitalism is good for most Americans, in recent years a growing number of people have been unable to share in its benefits. Foreign competition and factory automation have caused many semi-skilled workers who were earning good wages in manufacturing industries (such as automobile production) to lose their jobs. Many of those able to get new employment had to settle for low-paying jobs—for example, in fast-food restaurants or retail stores. At one time, income distribution in the U.S.A. resembled a diamond, with the majority of people in the middle, and the numbers of rich and poor quite small. Today, many economists say that the country is moving toward an hourglass distribution, with a much smaller middle-income group and much larger numbers of rich and poor. Still, most people with marketable job skills can earn a living in the U.S.A., and opportunities for learning marketable skills are plentiful.

7. At one time, capitalism was considered an evil system which brought great wealth to the few by exploiting the majority. But today's American capitalism is good for most workers as well as owners. The majority of poor Americans are those who, because of illness, old age, drug or alcohol addiction, disability, or lack of skills, cannot get full time work at decent wages. To most of the population, capitalism has brought at least moderate **prosperity.** Many Americans who may not consider themselves prosperous can afford more conveniences (such as a car, TV set, and a refrigerator) than the average worker in a communist or third-world country.

STOCKS AND BONDS

8. A capitalistic economy requires capitalists. To some people, the word *capitalist* suggests a wealthy person getting richer by buying and selling **stocks** on Wall Street without producing anything of value or

contributing anything to society. What makes a capitalist? Who are today's capitalists? How do they contribute to the economy?

9. American businesses need huge amounts of money for developing new products, purchasing new equipment and factories, and paying other expenses of doing business. This money is known as *capital,* and much of it comes from **investors** who expect to receive a profitable return on the money that they invest.

10. These investments usually take one of two forms—stocks or **bonds.** People who purchase bonds lend their money to a business in exchange for a fixed rate of return known as **interest.** Stockholders, on the other hand, purchase a **share** of the business and share in the profits of the company by receiving *dividends.* In addition, both stockholders and bondholders hope that the value of their investment will increase. Stocks and bonds are traded on national exchanges where investors can buy and sell them to other investors. Stock prices are usually affected by the profits of the company, the general economic climate, and the outlook for the company in the near future. Bond prices are primarily influenced by interest rates. If interest rates rise, bond prices usually fall and vice versa. Without these investors, the American economy would not be able to grow and produce the goods that consumers want. In other words, a capitalistic economy depends on capitalists to keep it growing.

11. During the past 15 years, there has been a huge growth in the volume of stock and bond sales. In 1970, the value of all stocks traded on stock exchanges was $136 billion. By 1980, that figure had jumped to $522 billion, and by 1987, it was $1.9 trillion. Also, between 1970 and 1987, the number of shares of stock traded on exchanges each year rose from about 4.5 billion to more than 63 billion. On an average trading day, more than 150 million shares of stock change hands on the New York Stock Exchange alone.

12. In 1952, only about 6.5 million Americans were shareholders. Today, more than 50 million individuals own stock. And many more are indirectly involved in the markets through their participation in pensions, credit unions, and insurance plans. In fact, most of the stocks and bonds that are traded are not owned by individuals but by large investors such as banks, insurance companies, pension funds, and mutual funds.

THE CASHLESS SOCIETY

13. In 1987, the gross national product of the United States was more than $4.5 trillion, and each year it increases. (The gross national product is the total value of all goods and services produced in the United States in a year.) Yet, only a small portion of that amount is actually paid for in dollar bills.

14. A very popular method of making payments is by check. People and companies keep money on deposit at their banks. A check is an order for the bank to transfer some of that money to another person (an employee or supplier, for example). The employee can either get cash for a paycheck or deposit it in his or her bank account. Once the check is deposited, the employee can write checks to others to pay bills or purchase goods or services. Those who receive the checks, in turn, deposit them into their bank accounts and write checks to pay their bills. So money is continually circulating without ever being converted into cash.

15. Another way of making purchases without cash is by **credit.** A person wishing to buy an expensive item such as a car or house will borrow the money and pay it back over a period of years. The payments are usually made each month until the amount due has been paid with interest. A car may be paid for over a 5-year period, while paying for a house may take 30 years. These loans enable Americans to buy the things they need and want before they have all of the money to pay for them.

16. For less costly items, credit cards are often used. Credit cards are issued by stores to their regular customers. When a purchase is made, the customer gives the card to the salesperson, who fills out a charge sales slip and returns the card to the purchaser. At the end of each month, the customer receives a bill showing the charge purchases that were made during that period and how much is owed on his or her account. The customer must pay the balance within three or four weeks. If the payment is late, the customer is usually charged interest on the amount owed. Most credit cards permit the user to pay a small portion of the total due instead of paying all of it. In that case, interest is charged on the unpaid balance.

17. Another type of credit card is issued by banks or other financial institutions. (Some of the most widely used are MasterCard, Visa, American Express, and the Discover card.) These cards can be used for purchases at any business establishment that has agreed to accept them. The merchant sends the sales slip to the bank, which pays the amount of the charge (less a discount) to the merchant and then bills the cardholder each month for all charges made. Again, interest is charged on the unpaid balance.

18. The easy availability of credit has given American consumers tremendous purchasing power. But it has also given them huge **debt.** Americans now owe more than $700 billion for credit purchases (not including mortgage loans). Most people pay their debts regularly. But if they have unexpected problems such as the loss of a job, a strike, or an illness, there may not be enough money to make the payments. If payments are not made for several months, the seller may take legal action such as taking back the merchandise (repossession) or suing the debtor in court.

19. If the debtor thinks that there is little chance of debt repayment, he or she may go into the **bankruptcy** courts to be relieved of these debts. If the debtor has any sizable **assets,** these may be sold to partially pay the creditors, but in exchange, the debtor is freed of his or her debts. While this sounds like an attractive solution, it is only available once every six years, and it results in a loss of credit to the bankrupt person. That is, the person will be unable to get loans or credit cards for a long period of time, until he or she can show the ability and willingness to pay debts. About 300,000 individuals each year require the protection of bankruptcy laws. While this is a significant number, it is only 0.125% of the population. Most people pay their bills regularly, and the economy is greatly strengthened by the billions of dollars of credit purchases that are made each year.

RECENT TRENDS IN BUSINESS

20. Many changes in the way businesses operate have occurred over the past 25 years. Some of the most interesting are the increased use of computers; the increase in business ownership, especially by women and minorities; and the growth of franchised businesses.

Computers in Business

21. Although computers have been used by businesses for many years, until recently only large companies could afford to own them. Because of their large size and delicate parts, the earlier computers required specially designed rooms with the temperature and humidity carefully controlled. Highly trained people were required to program and operate them. The 1980s saw a breakthrough in computer development. Small yet powerful machines known as *personal computers* were introduced. They required little maintenance and could be operated by office personnel with a minimum of training. Because of their widespread use, mass-produced programs were developed that could fill the needs of most businesses so that computer users did not have to hire programmers.

22. Today, a business can hardly afford not to have its own computer. Small computers costing less than $2,000 can perform functions such as word processing, recordkeeping, financial projections, budgeting, and mechanical drawing. One rapidly growing use of personal computers is known as desktop publishing. With less than $10,000 in computer equipment, a business can create attractive and inexpensive newsletters or advertising material.

23. Computers are continually being improved to speed up their operations, provide more memory, make them portable and easier to operate, and lower their cost. Software (the instructions that computers need to perform particular functions) is also being improved to enable computers to do more jobs better.

More and More Entrepreneurs

24. Every year, increasing numbers of Americans go into business for themselves. In the 1960s, there were about 7 or 8 million American companies; in 1989, about 19 or 20 million Americans owned their own businesses. Predictions are that by the year 2000 there will be 30 million business enterprises. For those who want to be their own boss, American capitalism provides the exciting (though risky) opportunity to try it.

25. Although American business has long been dominated by male whites, there is a growing trend toward business ownership by women and minorities. This is partly due to the influence of the civil rights and women's movements, which have encouraged these groups to go into fields which offer greater opportunity for advancement. In 1982, women owned about 25% of noncorporate businesses, while members of minority groups owned another 7%.

Franchises

26. A company that has developed a successful business may decide to license other companies to operate similar businesses under the same name. That license is called a **franchise.** The original company is known as the *franchisor,* and the licensed companies are *franchisees.* Each franchisee pays the franchisor for the right to use the franchise name and ideas. The franchisor assists its franchisees in selecting a site for the business, purchasing equipment, learning how to run the business, and so on. Advertising is done on a national basis in the name of the franchise. The franchisor controls the products that its franchisees sell so that the consumers can be assured that their McDonald's hamburger will taste the same whether they buy it in Atlanta, Georgia or Atlantic City, New Jersey.

27. There are more than 500,000 franchises operating with sales of more than $600 billion annually. That is more than one-third of all retail sales in the United States. Although the most well-known franchises are fast-food businesses, franchises also include almost every category of business, such as real estate brokers, automotive parts, and employment agencies.

28. Why do people buy franchises? Buying a franchise is the least risky way to go into business for oneself. The franchise's national reputation, advertising, training program, and business experience give the franchisee a big advantage over independent enterprises. As a result, the failure rate of franchised businesses is only 4%, while most nonfranchised businesses fail within their first five years. These statistics encourage many people with no prior experience in business to invest in a franchise, which will guide them toward success.

29. American capitalism, with all its problems, has proved to be one of the most productive economic systems in history. In a capitalistic system, people try to produce better goods and services because there are financial rewards for doing so. In addition, the freedom of choice that capitalism provides appeals to the independent American character. With few exceptions, no outside power tells an entrepreneur how much to charge for goods or services, and people are free to decide how they will earn and spend their income. The American economy is based upon the belief that every individual knows what is best for himself or herself and must take responsibility for his or her decisions. Risks exist, but so do opportunities for advancement. Most Americans gladly accept both.

EXERCISES

I. Comprehension Questions. Answer the following questions on paper or in class discussion.

1. What does the word *capitalism* mean? Why do Americans like this system?
2. How does the average American invest money in a big business?
3. What are the advantages and disadvantages of buying on credit?
4. What is a franchise?

II. Vocabulary Practice. Pronounce the following words after your teacher, and discuss their meanings. Then use some of them to complete the following sentences. You may need to use the same word twice.

assets	interest
bankruptcy	investors
bonds	monopoly
capitalism	profit
competition	prosperity
credit	services
debt	shares
economy	shortage
franchise	stocks
goods	strike

1. The American ________________ is sometimes called a cashless society because so many people use checks and ________________ cards instead of money.

2. People lend money to a business by buying ________________, or they purchase a share of a business by buying ________________. These people are called capitalists or ________________.

3. A person can buy ________________ of a stock sold on a stock exchange. If that business makes money, the stockholder then ________________ in the profits. (Use the same word in both blanks.)

4. When workers refuse to work because they are not satisfied with their salaries or working conditions, they go on ________________.

5. When there is a ________________ of certain goods or services, the price is likely to go up.

6. A capitalistic economy depends on ________________ to keep prices reasonable and quality high.

7. When one company has all or most of the business in a particular industry, that company has a ________________.

8. People spend money for ________________ (things they buy) and ________________ (care they get).

III. Word Study. Circle the correct word form, noun or adjective, for each sentence.

1. To Americans, capitalism is an (economy; economic) system, not a (politics; political) system.
2. The American (economy; economic) depends on capitalists who invest in businesses.
3. In a (capitalism; capitalistic) economy, businesses are privately owned. (They are not owned by the government.)
4. People buy stocks and bonds because they hope to make a (profit; profitable).
5. Sometimes their investments are (profit; profitable), and sometimes they lose money.
6. People who make a good living are said to be (prosperity; prosperous).

IV. Idiom Study. Match each idiom with its definition by writing the correct number on each line. The numbers in brackets give the paragraphs in which the idioms are used.

1. supply and demand [2]	___ a business that has been permanently closed
2. a free economy [3]	___ without governmental controls

3. laid off [4]	___ operate it
4. shut down [4]	___ closed (usually temporarily)
5. cut off [4]	___ be satisfied with
6. out of business [5]	___ transferred from one owner to another
7. settle for [6]	___ the amount available compared to the amount consumers want
8. change hands [11]	___ told not to come back to work because you're not needed
9. run a business [26]	___ make enough money to pay one's expenses
10. earn a living [6]	___ stop something from getting through

V. Reading Skills. Underline the correct answer.

A. Understanding the main idea:

1. Paragraph 1 says that the American government a) strictly regulates business b) is not allowed to regulate business c) regulates business to some extent.
2. Paragraph 4 implies that a) workers shouldn't go on strike because strikes inconvenience people b) strikes sometimes create problems for the American public c) strikes are one of the benefits of capitalism.
3. Paragraphs 8 through 10 say that a) capitalists are evil b) capitalists contribute nothing to the American economy c) capitalists are an essential part of the economy.

4. According to paragraphs 9 and 10, people who buy stocks and bonds a) hope to make a profit b) are in competition with capitalists c) usually become wealthy.
5. According to paragraph 18, buying on credit a) usually leads to bankruptcy b) can lead to more debt than the consumer can handle c) is something that only poor people do.

B. Words in Context:

1. What does the word *return* mean in paragraphs 9 and 10?

____

2. What does the word *interest* mean in paragraphs 15 and 17?

____

C. Comparisons:

Discuss the diamond and hourglass comparison in paragraph 6. Why is the hourglass income distribution less desirable for Americans in general? ______________________

8

LABOR DAY AND THE AMERICAN WORKER

THE ORIGIN OF THE HOLIDAY

1. The story of Labor Day began in the 19th century with the dream of a carpenter named Peter J. McGuire. McGuire was born in 1852, long before the United States had laws prohibiting child labor. He was the 10th child in a poor family. To help support his brothers and sisters, he went to work in a furniture factory when he was only 11 years old. He grew up to become a carpenter and, **eventually,** the president of a national union of carpenters.

2. McGuire was well-acquainted with both the satisfaction and the suffering that accompanies hard work. He wanted to establish a holiday "to honor the industrial spirit, the great vital force of this nation." At his suggestion, the first Labor Day parade was held in New York City in 1882. In 1894, Labor Day became a federal holiday, and it was quickly adopted by all of the states.

3. Labor Day, celebrated on the first Monday in September, is still an occasion for parades to honor workers. In addition, because the holiday also marks the end of the summer vacation period for many people, it is often the time for an outing to the beach, a picnic in the park, or a barbecue in the back yard. Since this holiday provides a three-day weekend for most workers and for students, many people use it to enjoy a few last summer days relaxing outdoors.

THE ROLE OF LABOR UNIONS

4. On Labor Day, when Americans celebrate the good fortune of the American worker, they are really honoring the achievements of labor **unions.** A labor union is a group of workers doing the same general type of work (a craft union) or employed in the same industry (an industrial union) who form an organization in order to **negotiate** effectively with management. There are unions for miners, musicians, public employees (teachers, policemen, and so on), janitors, nurses, plumbers, factory workers, construction workers, employees in the transportation industries, and dozens of other occupational groups.

5. Unions are democratic institutions that have elected leaders (some paid and some **volunteers**) who try to carry out the group's goals. Goals and decisions of the group are decided by a majority vote of the membership.

6. For more than 100 years, American unions have been representing workers. During the early years, there were many violent **incidents** because management considered unions illegal and tried to prevent workers from organizing. Later, unions became so powerful that federal laws were required to control union **abuses.** Today, unions are an accepted part of the workplace. In 1987, about 17% of the nation's workers (about 17 million employees) belonged to unions.

7. Unions have made great strides in getting employees greater job **security,** higher wages, a shorter work week, extra pay for overtime work, paid vacations, sick leave, health insurance, pension plans, and safe, sanitary working conditions. As a result of union efforts, many laws have been passed that protect and help workers. Today, most workers are covered by a federal minimum hourly wage ($3.80 in 1990). Federal laws **prohibit** employers from discriminating against workers because of race, religion, sex, age, or physical handicap. Federal law also requires most employers to pay their employees at least time-and-a-half (1 1/2 times their hourly rate) when they work overtime. Unions have also fought the abuse of child labor. In most states, children under the age of 14 are not allowed to hold jobs, though there are some **exceptions** to this restriction. For example, children are allowed to work part time to deliver newspapers or work as entertainers.

8. Thanks to organized labor, the American worker is one of the best paid and best cared for in the world. The chart on page 90 lists some of the major gains unions have made.

9. In attempting to achieve its goals, a union may employ the most powerful weapon that it possesses: the **strike.** A strike occurs when union members decide not to return to work until their employer gives in to some or all of their demands. Workers on strike ***picket*** their employer by walking back and forth in front of their place of business, carrying signs stating their complaints. (The custom of picketing has also been adopted by other protest groups to make known their disapproval of particular policies of government or industry.)

10. In spite of the gains that unions have made for workers, in recent years the American labor movement has been losing membership, both in its percentage of the work force and in actual numbers of members. Labor unions have always been strongest in construction, manufacturing, mining, and transportation industries. In recent years, because of the automation of American factories and the shifting of many factories to foreign countries, the number of blue-collar employees in general has

Gains for Workers

This chart shows how average working hours and other conditions have changed in the United States since the 1880's.

	1880	Today
Length of workday	10 hours	8 hours or less
Length of workweek	6 or 7 days	5 days
Overtime pay	Almost none	At least one-and-a-half times normal pay
Paid vacations	Almost none	2 to 4 weeks a year
Paid holidays	Almost none	10 a year
Hospital insurance	Paid for by individuals or unions	Provided by most employers

greatly declined. In fact, white-collar workers now make up about 55% of the American work force.

11. Still, unions are very important in the U.S.A. Many nonunion members are affected by the collective bargaining agreements between labor and management. Moreover, labor unions are active politically. Though the American labor movement does not have its own political party, as in some other countries, union leaders influence legislation and government policy by **lobbying** (talking to legislators in the state capitals and in Washington, D.C.). In an election year, most candidates want the support of organized labor, so they must be concerned about the needs and interests of unions. There are more than 40 national unions with membership exceeding 100,000. About 80% of all American unions are affiliated with a federation called the AFL-CIO (an organization which combined the American Federation of Labor and the Congress of Industrial Organizations). This federation has a great deal of political influence. Its president is the nation's most important labor leader.

PROTECTION FOR THE AMERICAN WORKER

12. Most American workers have some protection against sudden stoppage of income. If workers are *laid off* through no fault of their own, they may be **eligible** for *unemployment* ***compensation***—temporary payments from the government—until they find another job. Another way in which workers can protect their paychecks is by purchasing insurance that guarantees the family a regular income if the breadwinner(s) cannot continue working because of injury, illness, or death.

13. The most widespread type of financial protection is a federal program called *Social Security.* About 37 million people (approximately one out of seven) receive Social Security **benefits.** More than 90% of U.S. workers (employees and self-employed persons as well) are required to participate in this program. Self-employed people pay contributions quarterly. Employees' contributions are **deducted** from their paychecks each payday. For most workers, the employee contribution is about 7% of their wages; the employer contributes an equal amount. A record of the lifetime contributions credited to each worker is maintained by the government under the worker's Social Security number.

14. A worker must contribute to the fund a specified **length** of time in order to be eligible for Social Security benefits. The amount of money received depends on the individual's average earnings during his or her working years. However, workers with low lifetime earnings collect benefits proportionally greater in relation to their contributions than do those with higher lifetime earnings.

15. Workers who **retire** usually begin receiving monthly Social Security checks at age 65. Retired workers may choose to begin receiving payments a few years earlier, but then the amount received each month is smaller. A person does not have to stop working completely to collect a full Social Security check. However, if earnings exceed a certain amount (about $8,000), the Social Security benefits may be reduced.

16. The U.S. Department of Labor has many agencies and programs that help promote employment, especially its employment service. It also provides funds to state and local governments to train people who have no marketable job skills. The Department of Labor also enforces laws that protect workers and collects statistics about the ever-changing American workplace.

THE AMERICAN WORKER TODAY AND TOMORROW

17. For most Americans, Labor Day is an occasion to pause and count their blessings. The United States is the most prosperous nation in the world. Its unemployment rate (about 5%) is the lowest in the Western World. The average family income (about $31,000) **enables** most families to live comfortably, own a car, and buy a huge array of appliances that save work and provide entertainment. But in the midst of prosperity for the majority, about 33 million Americans (14% of the population) live below what the federal government considers the poverty level (an annual income of $5,500 for one person or $11,200 for a family of four). Among these poor people are many who cannot find employment and who are living on welfare payments. About nine million Americans who work part time or full time are still poor, because a worker earning minimum wage makes only about $8,000 a year, even working full time, and that places the worker below the poverty level if he or she is supporting more than one person.

18. Most poor American adults fall into one or more of the following categories: the elderly retired, the physically or mentally ill, unskilled workers, the uneducated, the unemployed, and nonwhites. Although federal or local funds provide for the elderly, the disabled, and the unemployed, benefits are small, so the person living solely on an allowance from the government must budget very strictly. The severe economic problems of minority groups become apparent when one looks at a breakdown of the unemployment rate for 1986: it was 6% for whites, 11% for Hispanics, and almost 15% for blacks. For black teenagers, it was almost 41%. In the North and West, poverty tends to be concentrated in the cities, while in the South most poverty is rural. The poor, whoever and wherever they are, need job training to enable them to work in fields where jobs are available and the pay is adequate.

19. Though not everyone is prosperous in the U.S.A., on the whole the American economy has managed to adjust well to enormous changes in its work force during the 20th century. In 1900, about 20% of American women worked. Today, more than 55% of women are employed, and they make up about 44% of the work force. Also, since 1900 the percentage of employed men age 65 or older has fallen from about 65% to about 15%. Social security and other retirement benefits, compulsory retirement rules, and early retirement **incentives** have combined to discourage people over 65 from continuing to work. At the other end of the age spectrum, more young Americans are attending college now and are, therefore, beginning full-time employment at a later age. As a result, the number of years that the average American works full time has shrunk quite a bit since 1900. Another major change during this century has been the decline of farm workers. The percentage of farm workers has fallen from 40% to about 4%, and the percentage of other blue-collar workers has also declined. The majority of American employees are now white-collar workers. This trend has been continuing in recent years. From 1981 to 1985, about 11 million adult workers lost their jobs because of factory closings and cutbacks. Meanwhile, the number of jobs in service occupations—especially in the computer fields—has been growing rapidly.

20. What does the U.S. Department of Labor predict regarding the American work force at the end of this century? In the year 2000, the work force will be older and made up of more women and minority workers. There will be even fewer people employed in manufacturing and even more in service-producing fields. There will be many more jobs for people with educational preparation, while the number of jobs requiring little training will grow only slightly or perhaps decrease. The labor force is expected to increase from 117 million in the mid-1980s to about 139 million by the year 2000, which suggests that, at the turn of the century, Labor Day celebrations will be bigger and better than ever.

EXERCISES

I. Comprehension Questions. Answer the following questions on paper or in class discussion.

1. What was the original purpose of Labor Day? How is it often celebrated today?
2. What are some benefits that unions have earned for workers?
3. What types of income protection do most American workers have?
4. Today's American workers spend fewer years working full time than their parents and grandparents did. Why?

II. Vocabulary Practice. Pronounce the following words after your teacher, and discuss their meanings. Then use some of them to complete the following sentences.

abuses	length
benefits	lobbying
compensation	negotiating
deducted	picket
eligible	prohibit
enable	retire
eventually	security
exception	strike
incentives	unions
incident	volunteers

1. Labor ________________ are organized groups of workers who do the same type of work or who work in the same industry.
2. ________________ are people who work for no pay.
3. Many Americans ________________ at age 65.
4. Striking workers often ________________ their employers, carrying signs expressing their complaints.
5. The amount of ________________ a retiring worker receives depends on the ________________ of time he or she has worked and the salary earned.
6. Social ________________ provides disability protection and a pension after retirement.
7. Union representatives often get together with employers and try to write a contract that satisfies both sides. This process is called collective bargaining or ________________.
8. Labor unions ________________ workers to negotiate more effectively with employers.

III. Word Study.

A. Discuss the meaning of the prefix *de-* in the following words: *deduct, decline, decrease.* Can you think of other words with this prefix? What meanings does this prefix have?

____

B. Match each word with its definition by writing the correct number on each line.

1. employee	___	person, business, or institution that hires workers
2. employer	___	a worker who has a boss
3. self-employed	___	work, a job
4. unemployed	___	a person who operates his or her own business
5. employment	___	not working

IV. Idiom Study. Underline the phrase that best completes each sentence. The numbers in brackets give the paragraphs in which the idioms are used.

1. The idiom *carry out* [5] is used here to mean a) take outside b) bring home c) do or accomplish.
2. The expression *time-and-a-half* [7] refers to a) music b) a higher rate of pay for working overtime c) working half the usual time.
3. The term *organized labor* [8] refers to a) workers who organize their assignments well b) workers who join a union c) workers who do hard physical work.
4. *Gives in* [9] means a) refuses to accept b) stops arguing and does what someone else wants c) gives workers a raise in pay.
5. *Blue-collar workers* [10] a) come to work wearing a suit and tie b) are usually college-educated, professional people c) often work in factories.
6. *White-collar workers* [10] a) are all professional people b) usually work in offices c) wear uniforms to work.
7. A worker gets *laid off* [12] when he or she a) is lazy or dishonest b) is not needed c) quits the job.
8. In paragraph 20, the *turn of the century* means from a) 1899 to 1900 b) 1999 to 2000 c) 2000 to 2099.

V. Reading Skills.

A. Reread the paragraphs indicated to look for specific information.

1. In paragraph 10, "*in spite of* the gains that unions have made" means a) because of the progress of unions b) although unions have made progress c) if unions make progress.
2. Paragraph 10 says that automation caused a) an increase in the number of factory workers b) a decrease in the number of factory workers c) an increase in union membership.
3. Paragraph 11 says that unions a) have their own political party b) have no effect on the lives of nonmembers c) can influence the outcome of elections.

B. Reread paragraph 20, and then complete the following chart:

Predictions for the Labor Force in the Year 2000

MAY INCREASE	MAY DECREASE
1. ________________	1. ________________
2. ________________	2. ________________
3. ________________	
4. ________________	
5. ________________	
6. ________________	

9

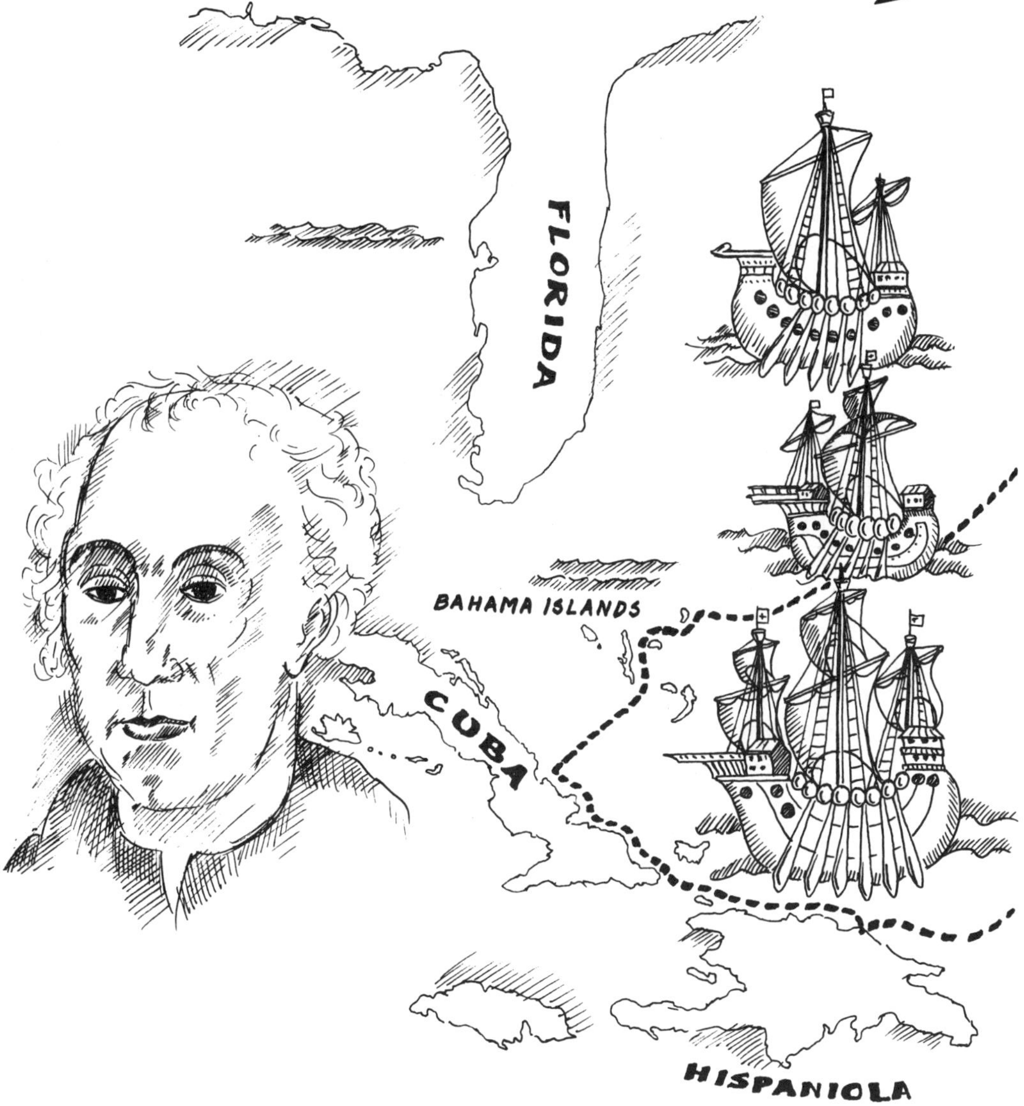

COLUMBUS DAY

THE STORY OF COLUMBUS

1. Throughout most of the United States, Columbus Day is celebrated on the second Monday in October. The holiday honors Christopher Columbus, who is commonly called the discoverer of America. All of North and South America and some cities in Spain and Italy honor this brave explorer, although we know now that he was not the first European to land in the New World. Historians are convinced that Leif Ericson, a Viking seaman, touched the coast of North America in 1000 A.D.—almost 500 years before Columbus's first **voyage.** But Leif Ericson's expedition did not affect world history since it did not lead to mass **migrations** and the development of the Americas. On the other hand, Columbus's voyages opened the Western Hemisphere to millions of European settlers.

2. Christopher Columbus was born in Italy in 1451. He grew up in Genoa, an important Italian seaport. As a boy, he helped his father, a wool-weaver. While he wove, he dreamed of a life at sea. When he was about 19, Columbus began making sea voyages. In 1477, his travels brought him to Lisbon, Portugal, where his brother owned a map-making shop. Columbus stayed in Lisbon, joined his brother's business, and married a Portuguese girl. To please his wife, Columbus gave up his career as a sailor and became a map-maker. But when his wife died shortly after their son was born, Columbus began to think of the sea again.

3. During the 15th century, the Portuguese were looking for a sea **route** to the Indies. (At that time, the name *Indies* referred to India, China, the East Indies, and Japan.) They wanted to bring gold, jewels, spices, perfumes, and silks from the **Orient** back to Europe. When brought by land, these riches had to be loaded on camels and carried across **deserts.** Travelers were often attacked, and valuable goods were stolen. It would be easier, faster, and safer to import these **luxuries** by sea.

4. The Portuguese had tried to reach the Orient by sailing around Africa. Columbus thought he had a better route. He believed that a ship could reach the East by sailing west. Columbus made only one impor-

tant mistake: he underestimated the size of the earth. He never guessed that the huge **continents** of North and South America were between Europe and Asia.

5. Columbus was *not* trying to prove that the world was **round.** The educated people of his time already knew that. Columbus was simply looking for a short sea route to the East. He promised **wealth** and new territory to the king who would provide funds for his expedition. He also wanted **fame** and wealth for himself if his expedition succeeded.

6. The King of Portugal refused to pay for Columbus's explorations because the court's experts advised against it. As a result, in 1485 Columbus and his young son Diego went to Spain to ask King Ferdinand and Queen Isabella for ships and sailors. The queen was **sympathetic.** She put Columbus on the royal payroll but could not equip him for the voyage while the Spanish were fighting the Moors. Columbus waited. His red hair turned gray. He developed arthritis. He used up his savings, and his coat and shoes became so full of holes that he had to stay indoors when it rained.

7. Finally, in 1492, the Spanish conquered Granada. Isabella was able to give more thought to Columbus's idea. King Ferdinand did not want to spend the money because the recent wars had been very expensive, so Isabella offered to pawn her jewels to finance the trip. But this sacrifice was not necessary. The treasurer of Spain supplied most of the funds from the national treasury and from his own savings. The total investment, for which Columbus had waited seven years, was the equivalent of just $14,000!

8. For his first voyage, Columbus had three ships: the *Pinta*, the *Niña*, and the *Santa Maria*. The entire **crew** of all three ships numbered about 87. The ships had good compasses but no instruments to measure distance. Fortunately, Columbus was able to **navigate** by looking at the stars.

9. The ships sailed from the Canary Islands on September 6, 1492. The crew lost sight of land on September 9. Then the ships sailed straight west for three weeks, the longest anyone had ever sailed in one direction without seeing land. The sailors were frightened. They knew that the world was round, and they were not afraid of falling off the edge. But they were afraid that the winds from the east would keep them from reaching their **destination** and that they would die at sea. The crew begged Columbus to turn back; there were even whispers of **mutiny.**

10. On October 10, everyone agreed to sail on for three more days and then turn around if no land was seen. Columbus was optimistic. He had noticed some birds flying overhead and some seaweed on the water's surface. He felt certain that land must be nearby.

11. Before dawn on October 12, just 36 days after leaving the Canary Islands, the sailors were overjoyed to see white sand shining in the moonlight. Columbus's ships were approaching an **island** in the Bahamas, an island which Columbus named San Salvador.

12. When the ships landed, the sailors were greeted by strange-looking people who wore no clothes. Because Columbus thought he had landed on an island in the Indies near Japan or China, he called these natives *Indians*. To this day, we refer to the islands which Columbus discovered and explored as the *West Indies,* and we call the **descendants** of the people he found there *American Indians* (or *Native Americans*).

13. The three ships spent only a few days at San Salvador. Then they sailed on to Cuba and Haiti, where the Santa Maria was wrecked. On January 16, 1493, the Pinta and Niña set sail for Spain. The voyage home was extremely rough, but Columbus was a brilliant navigator. On March 15, his ships arrived safely in Palos, Spain.

14. Columbus was a great national hero when he returned from this first expedition, but his popularity did not last. He made three more trips to explore the West Indies and South America. Some Spanish settlers remained in the new land to form a colony called *Hispaniola* (where Haiti and the Dominican Republic are now located). These settlers had expected to find huge supplies of gold and other riches. Instead, they found primitive living conditions, strange foods, hard work, and constant danger. They blamed Columbus for their disappointment. Many went back to Spain and complained about him. Others stayed and rebelled against his leadership. The King and Queen sent a representative to settle the trouble in Hispaniola. The representative put Columbus and his brother in chains and sent them back to Spain for trial. When they arrived in Spain, the King and Queen freed them, but Columbus was replaced as governor of Hispaniola.

15. In a final attempt to regain his good name and wealth, Columbus began his fourth and last voyage. He left Spain in the spring of 1502 and returned in the winter of 1504. Before Columbus could appear in court, Queen Isabella died. In great pain from arthritis, Columbus went to King Ferdinand to request the money and titles which he had been promised. The King turned down his request.

16. During his last years, Columbus was a forgotten man with few friends and very little money. He was in much pain and scarcely able to move because of his arthritis. He died in 1506 at the age of 54.

17. Although he was unappreciated during his lifetime, Columbus today is an international hero. Columbus is admired for his courage, self-confidence, and **persistence.** In school, many children **memorize** a

famous poem by Joaquin Miller about Columbus. The closing lines explain what Columbus **symbolizes** to the hemisphere he discovered:

He gained a world: he gave that world
Its grandest lesson: "On! Sail on!"

AMERIGO VESPUCCI

18. If Columbus is considered the most important European discoverer of the Western Hemisphere, then why are citizens of the U.S.A. called *Americans* and not *Columbians?* And who were the continents of North and South America named after? These are questions that newcomers to the United States often ask, especially on Columbus Day.

19. Columbus's name appears many times on a map of the Western Hemisphere. Several cities in the U.S.A. are named after him, as is the Columbia River, one of the chief rivers in the U.S.A. and Canada. The nation's capital city is called Washington, D.C., with the initials standing for *District of Columbia*. But the continents are named after Amerigo Vespucci, another Italian explorer, who made at least two (and possibly four) voyages to the Americas, the first only a few years after Columbus's first voyage in 1492. Vespucci's 1499 voyage was undertaken for Spain and led by a Spanish explorer. It brought Vespucci to Brazil, Venezuela, and Hispaniola. Then, in 1501, he sailed to Brazil again, this time with the ships of a Portuguese captain. This voyage convinced him that he had reached a new continent.

20. In 1502, Vespucci wrote a letter about his explorations to the famous Italian banker and art-lover, Lorenzo Medici. This letter, entitled *Mundus Noves* (*New World*) was translated into many languages and published in many European countries. Its fame established Vespucci's reputation as a famous explorer and as the discoverer of the New World. There is evidence that Columbus, during his third voyage to the Western Hemisphere in 1498, realized that he was not in Asia but was exploring a new continent. When he actually set foot on the mainland of South America for the first time, Columbus wrote in his journal, "I believe that this is a very great continent which until today has been unknown." He called the continent *Other World*. Still, there is no evidence that Columbus disputed Vespucci's claim to being the discoverer of the Western Hemisphere.

21. In 1507, a German map-maker who had read Vespucci's writings became the first person to use the name *America* to describe the area that Columbus and Vespucci had explored. During his lifetime, Vespucci received the rewards that Columbus had always wanted and never attained: Vespucci was well-known and highly respected. He was given important governmental positions. But after Vespucci's death, people made a surprising discovery about this so-called great explorer. He was not all he claimed to be. First of all, he was certainly not the first European to reach the New World. Second, he was not (as he had claimed) the leader of the expeditions he was on but probably only the navigator of one of the ships. Therefore, it is appropriate that, although the continents of the Western Hemisphere were named for Amerigo Vespucci, he is the forgotten explorer, while Columbus's achievements are honored annually throughout the Western Hemisphere and in some European cities as well.

EXERCISES

I. Comprehension Questions. Answer the following questions on paper or in class discussion.

1. Why is Christopher Columbus remembered today? What did he accomplish by his explorations?
2. Why did the Europeans of the 15th century want to find a sea route to the Orient?
3. Why did Columbus call the inhabitants of the New World *Indians?*
4. What sort of a person was Columbus? Describe his character. Relate your answer to the two lines of poetry quoted in paragraph 17.

II. Vocabulary Practice. Pronounce the following words after your teacher, and discuss their meanings. Then use some of them to complete the following sentences.

continents
crew
descendant
desert
destination
fame
island
luxuries
memorize
migration
mutiny
navigate
Orient
persistence
round
route
symbolize
sympathetic
voyage
wealth

1. The earth is ________________, so it is called a sphere, a globe, or a ball.
2. The ________________ refers to the Far East.
3. Columbus's first ________________ to the New World occurred in 1492.
4. Columbus landed on an ________________ in the Bahamas.
5. Columbus thought that he had reached the Orient, but he had actually discovered the Western Hemisphere, the ________________ of North and South America.
6. Columbus wanted ________________ and ________________. He got neither during his lifetime, but now, almost 500 years after his death, he is famous all over the world.
7. Today, students ________________ a famous poem about Columbus. This poem is about Columbus's ________________, his refusal to give up his dream.
8. Expensive jewelry and expensive cars are often considered ________________.

III. Word Study.

A. Draw a vertical line between the two parts of the following compound words. Then write a definition of each word. The numbers in brackets give the paragraphs in which these words occur.

underestimate [4] ______________________________

nearby [10] ______________________________

seaweed [10] ______________________________

overhead [10] ______________________________

moonlight [11] ______________________________

overjoyed [11] ______________________________

lifetime [17] ______________________________

undertaken [19] ______________________________

B. The following words all begin with a prefix. On the line next to each word, write the meaning of each prefix.

international ______________________________

unappreciated ______________________________

retell ______________________________

import ______________________________

hemisphere ______________________________

explore ______________________________

C. Discuss the differences in meaning between *famous* and *popular*.

IV. Idiom Study.

1. What does *New World* [1] mean? ______________________________

2. What does *Old World* mean? (Look it up in a dictionary.)

____

3. What does *gave up* [2] mean?______________________

4. What does *named after* [18] mean?______________________

V. Reading Skills.

A. Map reading:

1. On a map of the world, trace Columbus's first voyage from the Canary Islands to the Bahamas.

2. On the map, find Haiti and the Dominican Republic. What colony did Columbus establish in this area?______________

B. Words in context: Circle the correct word or phrase.

1. In paragraph 2, what does the word *became* mean? a) came to visit b) started to be c) needed d) talked to
2. In paragraph 3, what does *15th century* mean? a)the 1500s b) the 1400s c) 1,500 years ago d) the year 1500 A.D.
3. In paragraph 3, the word *Indies* means a) Europe b) the West Indies c) the Orient d) Indians.
4. In the 16th century, the term *New World* [1] referred to a) the United States b) the Eastern Hemisphere c) any country that an immigrant moved to d) the Western Hemisphere.
5. In paragraph 14, sentence 1, what does the word *last* mean? a) final b) at the end c) continue d) opposite of first

C. Inference:

In paragraph 21, what is implied by the phrase *this so-called great explorer?*

____

D. The concept of irony:

1. Irony is an important concept in many literary works and in life as well. What does it mean?______________________

2. What is ironic about Columbus's life compared to Vespucci's?

____

10

HALLOWEEN

A TYPICAL HALLOWEEN SCENE

1. It was a cool autumn evening. Mrs. Brown was sitting in her living room, reading. Suddenly, there was a loud knock on her door, then two or three more knocks. Mrs. Brown put the safety chain on her door. Then she opened it a little and looked out. There stood three children wearing **masks** and **costumes**. When they saw her, they all shouted, "Trick or treat! Money or eats!"

2. Mrs. Brown dropped a candy bar into each child's bag. Then she said to one boy, who was wearing a big hat, high boots, and a holster with a toy gun in it, "What are you?"

3. "A **cowboy**," he answered.

4. "I'm a **ghost**," shouted another child hidden under a white sheet.

5. "And I'm a **skeleton**," said the third child. "My bones shine in the dark." The "skeleton" was wearing a black suit with white bones painted on it.

6. "Thanks for the candy," shouted the children as they ran off to ring another doorbell.

7. "You're welcome," said Mrs. Brown. "Have fun. And don't play any **pranks**."

THE ORIGINS OF HALLOWEEN CUSTOMS

8. Every year on October 31, Halloween scenes like this occur **throughout** the United States. American children love to dress up in costumes and go trick-or-treating. If an adult refuses to supply a treat—candy, cookies, fruit, or money—the children may play a trick. Typical Halloween pranks are soaping windows, writing on doors with crayons, overturning garbage cans, sticking pins into doorbells to keep them ringing, and spraying shaving cream on cars and friends.

9. Masquerading, begging, and many other Halloween **customs** are now mainly for the amusement of children. But hundreds of years ago, these customs were performed quite seriously by adults as part of their religion.

10. The name *Halloween* is a short way of saying *All Hallow's Eve*, which means the night before the Roman Catholic holiday of *All Saints' Day*. Although Halloween got its name from a Christian festival, its customs are of pagan origin. They come from two different sources: an ancient Celtic festival in honor of Samhain, lord of death, and a Roman festival in honor of Pomona, goddess of gardens and orchards. The Halloween colors, black and orange, suggest both ideas: death and **harvest.**

11. The spooky part of Halloween comes from the Celts, who occupied the British Isles and northern France during ancient and medieval times. The Celts worshiped gods of nature. They feared the coming of winter, associating it with death and **evil spirits.** Every year on October 31, the last day of the year on the old pagan calendar, the Druids (Celtic priests and teachers) built huge bonfires to scare away the bad spirits of evil and death. They threw animals and crops from the harvest into the fire as gifts for the evil spirits. The Celtic people also dressed in ugly, **scary** costumes in order to resemble the evil spirits they feared. The Celts believed that, if they disguised themselves this way, the spirits wouldn't harm them. Supposedly, on this evening, ghosts rose from their graves and **witches** rode through the air on broomsticks or black cats. Also, the spirits of dead relatives and friends were expected to return to earth for a visit. The Druids built bonfires on hilltops to guide these spirits back home.

12. From the Druid religion, then, come the custom of masquerading and the symbols of Halloween: ghosts, skeletons, devils, witches, black cats, and owls. The jack-o'-lantern is also of Celtic origin. It was an Irish custom to **hollow** out turnips and place lighted candles inside them to scare evil spirits away from the house. In the United States, the native **pumpkin** is used to make a jack-o'-lantern. First, the pulp and seeds are removed. Then holes are cut in the hollow pumpkin to make the eyes, nose, and mouth. A candle is put inside, and the jack-o'-lantern is placed by the window.

13. The Irish also introduced the trick-or-treat custom hundreds of years ago. Groups of farmers would travel from house to house asking for food for the village's Halloween party. They would promise good luck to **generous** contributors and threaten those who were **stingy**.

14. The Druid holiday of Samhain contained many elements of a harvest festival. This part of the celebration became even more significant after 55 B.C. when the Romans invaded England and brought with them their harvest festival of Pomona. Thereafter, nuts and fruits—especially apples—became part of the Samhain ceremonies. Today, at Halloween time, Americans honor the harvest by displaying cornstalks and pumpkins, eating nuts, autumn fruits, and pumpkin pies, and playing games with apples. One of the most popular Halloween games is bobbing for apples. In this game, apples float in a large tub of water. One at a time, children bend over the tub and try to catch an apple in their mouths without using their hands.

15. The Druid religion lasted longest in Ireland and Scotland, and Halloween was most important in these two countries. In the 19th century, Irish immigrants brought their Halloween customs to the United States. Today, Halloween is much more important in the United States than it is in Great Britain.

CELEBRATING HALLOWEEN TODAY

16. Although Halloween is celebrated most enthusiastically by children, adults sometimes get into the act, too. College students and other adults may attend **masquerade** parties or participate in Halloween parades. Places of business are often decorated with jack-o'-lanterns, **scarecrows,** and witches. And sometimes a serious, hard-working adult employee will arrive at the office dressed as a tube of toothpaste or a garbage can. No one is too old to enjoy the fun of surprising friends by doing a little creative costuming.

17. Part of the fun of Halloween is to get scared "out of your wits," as Americans say. This can easily be done by visiting a **haunted** house. Supposedly, haunted houses are inhabited by the spirits of dead people. These spirits keep trying to scare away living residents or visitors so that the spirits can enjoy their afterlife (which really means a life after death) in peace. Why do spirits hate the living? For one thing, the living always want to clean up and brighten their surroundings, while ghosts and skeletons prefer to decorate their homes with dust, cobwebs, spiders, and darkness. These days, it's hard to find a genuine haunted house. But every year shortly before Halloween, many charitable organizations create them. They hire actors to dress up in scary costumes and hide inside. Customers pay a few dollars each to walk through these dirty, creaky places and have "ghosts" surprise them with a loud "Boo!," and "skeletons" clang chains in their ears. Children usually love these haunted houses, but sometimes their parents are scared to death!

18. For those that have no haunted house nearby, another way to share a good scare is to go with friends to see a horror movie or rent one and watch it on videotape (in a dark room, of course).

19. Most American children have a wonderful, exciting day on Halloween. If Halloween falls on a school day, they bring their costumes to school and spend the last few hours of the school day with spooks instead of with books. After school and perhaps on into the evening, they go trick-or-treating. Often, there's a party at a friend's home or at the local community center. At most Halloween parties, prizes are given for the best costumes. Bobbing for apples, telling fortunes (predicting the future), playing scary games, and snacking on caramel-covered apples, candy, apple cider, and pumpkin pie are all part of the fun. Some communities build a bonfire, reminiscent of the Celtic celebrations in the Middle Ages. The children may sit around the bonfire telling scary stories while roasting hot dogs or toasting marshmallows. Halloween, which began hundreds of years ago as an evening of terror, is now an occasion of great fun. It is certainly one of the favorite holidays of American children.

20. However, a note of warning is needed. Halloween is a time when children become overexcited and careless, and it is a time when care is especially needed. Parents should set up rules for children to follow before they go out trick-or-treating. Here are a few good ones:

1. Children should go trick-or-treating in groups, never alone.
2. Children should never go inside the house or apartment of a stranger but should wait outside the door for their treat.
3. Younger children should go with older children or with an adult.
4. Children should be reminded not to destroy or damage someone's property.
5. Even older children should stop trick-or-treating by 8 P.M.
6. Children should not eat any treat that is not wrapped and sealed.

Parents should inspect candy to be sure that it hasn't been tampered with. There have been occasional incidents of mentally disturbed people putting harmful ingredients into Halloween candy.

21. On Halloween night, adults should be careful, too. Note that Mrs. Brown (the woman at the beginning of this chapter) did not completely unlock her door until she was sure that her unexpected visitors were children. Robbers sometimes take advantage of the casual, open-door Halloween spirit to gain access to strangers' homes.

EXERCISES

I. Comprehension Questions. Answer the following questions on paper or in class discussion.

1. What do American children do on Halloween?
2. What kind of a holiday was Halloween hundreds of years ago?
3. At a Halloween party, what are some of the games that children play? What foods do they eat?
4. What are some of the dangers of Halloween?

II. Vocabulary Practice. Pronounce the following vocabulary words after your teacher, and discuss their meanings. Then use some of them to complete the following sentences.

costumes	masquerade
cowboy	prank
custom	pumpkin
evil	scarecrow
generous	scary
ghost	skeleton
harvest	spirit
haunted	stingy
hollow	throughout
masks	witches

1. If you give a trick-or-treater a penny, you are ________________.

   If you give the child 50¢, you are very ________________.

2. At Halloween ________________ parties, the people cannot recognize each other because the guests wear ________________ over their faces.

3. On Halloween, it is an American ________________ for children to dress up in funny ________________.

4. The Halloween colors, orange and black, relate to the holiday's two major themes, which are ________________ and death.

5. The word *spooky* means like a ghost or ________________ . These words refer to the soul of a person who has died. Ghosts, spirits, and spooks are invisible (cannot be seen) because they have no bodies.

6. A ________________ helps a farmer's harvest because it scares away birds and animals that might eat seeds or crops.

7. To make a jack-o'-lantern, you must take the insides (the pulp and seeds) out of a ________________ and then cut a face into the orange shell.

8. A child dressed up as a ________________ wears a big, wide hat and toy guns. A child dressed up as a ________________ wears a white sheet.

III. Word Study.

A. Label each item listed to tell which Halloween theme it symbolizes. Write D for darkness and death, and write H for harvest. If an item relates to both themes, write D and H.

witch ___	ghost ___	scarecrow ___
owl ___	apple ___	skeleton ___
pumpkin ___	jack-o'-lantern ___	haunted house ___

B. Underline the correct word or phrase to complete each sentence.
1. A jack-o'-lantern is (hallow, hollow, solid, yellow).
2. On Halloween, children wear (customs, costumes, pranks, tricks).
3. A Halloween (witch, with, which, ghost) is an evil woman who wears black clothing and rides through the sky on a broomstick.
4. A scarecrow (scares birds, scares people, is stingy, scares away ghosts and skeletons).

IV. Idiom Study. Underline the correct phrase to complete each statement. The numbers in brackets give the paragraphs in which these idioms are used.

1. The saying *trick or treat; money or eats* [1] means a) I'd like either a trick or a treat. b) Give me a treat, and I'll play a trick on you. c) Give me a treat, or I'll play a trick on you.
2. In the U.S.A., a jack-o'-lantern [12] is made from a) an apple b) a pumpkin c) a turnip.
3. Bobbing for apples [14] is a) fun b) scary c) spooky.
4. *Scared to death* [17] means that a) someone died of fear b) someone is very frightened c) someone is afraid of dying.
5. *Telling fortunes* [19] means a) predicting what will happen to someone in the future b) telling scary stories c) telling people how to make money.

V. Reading Skills.

A. Making inferences: Sometimes a writer does not tell readers something directly but merely implies (suggests) an idea. Careful, alert readers notice these implications (suggested ideas). When readers figure out what a writer is suggesting, they *infer* or *make inferences* about the meaning.

1. In paragraph 1, what does the text imply by saying, "Mrs. Brown put the safety chain on her door"?

____

2. Can you make inferences about why some adults don't like Halloween? What kinds of behavior does it encourage?

____

____

3. If you live in the U.S.A., what does the text imply that you should buy before Halloween?

____

B. Understanding quotation marks: Reread paragraph 5.

1. What do the quotation marks in sentences 1 and 2 tell you?

____

2. Why are there quotation marks around the word *skeleton* in sentence 3? ______________________________

11

THANKSGIVING AND THE AMERICAN INDIANS

THANKSGIVING: ORIGIN AND CUSTOMS

1. In the United States, the fourth Thursday in November is called Thanksgiving Day. On this day, Americans give thanks for the **blessings** they have enjoyed during the year. Thanksgiving is usually a family day, celebrated with big dinners and happy **reunions.**

2. The first American Thanksgiving was held in Plymouth, Massachusetts in 1621. The people of Plymouth had come to America from England in 1620. In their native land, they had been called Puritans because they wished to purify the Church of England by reforming church ceremonies and clerical clothing to conform with their belief in a simple style of worship. Eventually, some of them decided that they could not change the Church of England, so they formed their own churches. When English officials began to **persecute** them, they fled to Holland.

3. Several years passed. The Puritans living in Holland were again threatened by religious persecution as well as by war. They were also unhappy that their children were speaking Dutch instead of English. Once again, they thought of moving. This time they considered America. In an unsettled land, they would finally be free to live as they chose. Also, the idea of bringing Christianity to a distant part of the world appealed to them. Some English merchants agreed to pay for their journey in return for a share of the profits produced by the new colony. So, after traveling back to England, a small group of Puritans, together with some other passengers, set sail for the New World. The Puritans began to call themselves *Pilgrims* because of their wanderings in search of religious freedom.

4. It was September of 1620 when their ship, called the *Mayflower*, left England with 102 men, women, and children on board. This was the worst season of the year for an ocean crossing, and the trip was very rough. Yet, during the voyage, the travelers suffered only one death. Since there was also one birth aboard ship, the Mayflower was still carrying 102 passengers when, after 65 days at sea, it landed in Provincetown Harbor, inside the tip of Cape Cod, Massachusetts.

5. The Pilgrim leaders knew that, in order to **survive**, every society needed to establish and enforce rules for proper behavior. So 41 men aboard the Mayflower held a meeting to choose their first governor and sign the Mayflower Compact, the first formal agreement for self-government in America.

6. For about a month, the Pilgrims lived aboard ship and sent out a small group of men to explore the coastline of Cape Cod Bay. At Plymouth, the men found a harbor with excellent fishing, some cleared land, cornfields, fresh water, and a high hill that could be fortified. The men went back to the Mayflower and reported their discovery. A few days later, the Mayflower sailed across Cape Cod Bay to Plymouth Harbor. Coming ashore in their small boat, the Pilgrims landed (according to tradition) on a large rock later named *Plymouth Rock.* This was the beginning of the second permanent English settlement in America.

7. The Pilgrims were not trained and equipped to **cope** with life in the **wilderness.** During their first winter, they suffered tremendously. Hard work, diseases, bitterly cold weather, and insufficient food killed about half of them. By the end of this terrible first winter, only about 50 Plymouth colonists remained alive.

8. One spring morning in 1621, an Indian walked into the little village of Plymouth and introduced himself in a friendly way. Later, he brought the Indian chief, Massasoit, who gave gifts to the Pilgrims and offered help. The Indians of Massasoit's **tribe** taught the Pilgrims how to hunt, fish, and grow food. They taught the Pilgrims to use fish for fertilizer when growing corn, pumpkins, and beans. Because of this help from the Indians, the Pilgrims had a good harvest.

9. Governor William Bradford was following an ancient tradition when, in the fall of 1621, he established a day of thanksgiving to God. The governor also decided to use this religious occasion to **strengthen** the friendship between the Pilgrims and their Indian neighbors. So he invited Chief Massasoit and his braves to share the Thanksgiving feast.

10. The Indians gladly accepted and sent deer meat for the feast. The Pilgrim men went hunting and returned with turkey and other wild animals. The women of Plymouth prepared delicious dishes from corn, cranberries, squash, and pumpkins.

11. The first Thanksgiving dinner was cooked and served out-of-doors. Although it was late autumn, huge fires kept the hosts and guests warm. Massasoit and 90 Indians joined the Pilgrims for the first Thanksgiving feast. The celebration lasted three days! On the first day, the Indians spent most of the time eating. On the second and third days, they wrestled, ran races, sang, and danced with the young people in Plymouth Colony. The holiday was a great success.

12. Many of the traditions of the modern American Thanksgiving come from that first Thanksgiving celebration. Today's Thanksgiving turkey is much like the ones that were hunted in the forests around Plymouth. Squash and corn, which were also harvested by the early Pilgrims, appear on the Thanksgiving table. Pumpkin pie is a traditional Thanksgiving dessert.

13. Every year, about 500,000 Americans take a journey into early American history by visiting Plymouth, a modern city that respects its past. In Plymouth Harbor, sightseers tour *Mayflower II,* a recently built ship similar to the original Mayflower. They see the famous Plymouth Rock. Then they spend a few hours walking through a reproduction of the original Pilgrim village. Modern Americans take great pride in these courageous ancestors who had so little by today's standards, but who were thankful for receiving the things they valued most—a good harvest and the freedom to live and worship as they pleased.

A FAMOUS PILGRIM STORY

14. In 1858, Henry Wadsworth Longfellow, a famous American poet, wrote a long poem about the Pilgrims of Plymouth Colony. He called it "The Courtship of Miles Standish."

15. Captain Miles Standish came to America with the Pilgrims, but he was not a Puritan. He was a soldier. Many times, he saved the Pilgrims from being killed by hostile Indians. Although he was very brave in battle, Standish was timid with women. After his wife died, he was lonely and wanted to marry a Puritan girl named Priscilla Mullens. But he was too shy to ask her. Instead, he asked his best friend, John Alden, to **propose** marriage for him.

16. Never were two friends so different. Standish was a short, stocky, middle-aged man. John Alden was a young man and very handsome. While Standish was a man of action, Alden was a scholar. In only one way were these two men alike: they both loved the same girl!

17. Poor John! He also loved Priscilla, but he wanted to be a loyal friend. Hiding his own feelings, he went to Priscilla and asked her to marry Miles Standish. He told her what a kind man the captain was. He talked about Standish's bravery in battle and fine family background. When John finished talking, Priscilla gave a surprising answer. Her reply is now very famous. She said, "Why don't you speak for yourself, John?"

18. John was too loyal to Standish to take Priscilla's advice. Instead, he returned to his friend and told him exactly what Priscilla had said. The captain became very angry and shouted, "You have **betrayed** me!" A short time later, he left for an Indian battle without saying good-bye to John.

19. While the captain was gone, John and Priscilla grew to love each other more and more. However, John would not ask to marry her because he did not want to be an unfaithful friend. Then a message arrived saying that Standish had been killed in battle. After that, John proposed marriage to Priscilla.

20. As the wedding ceremony ended, the guests were surprised and terrified to see a familiar figure standing in the doorway, a figure they thought was a ghost. It was Captain Miles Standish! He hadn't been killed after all. Standish was dressed in armor, but he had not come to fight. He had come to **apologize** to his friend and ask forgiveness for his anger. At the end of the story, John, Priscilla, and Miles were reunited as friends.

AMERICAN INDIANS OR NATIVE AMERICANS

21. Today, the people once called *American Indians* prefer to be called *Native Americans,* a name that reminds the world that they were the first people to live in the Americas. On Thanksgiving Day, when Americans remember the Pilgrims, they also recall how much these earliest Americans helped the European **settlers** and how much Native American culture has contributed to modern American life.

22. The first and most famous Indian friend of the white settlers was a young princess named Pocahontas. She was only 12 years old when English settlers came to Jamestown, Virginia in 1607. Captain John Smith, one of these early colonists, wrote that he owed his life to Pocahontas, who threw her arms around Smith to prevent her father, the chief, from killing him. Pocahontas was a frequent visitor to the English fort and often brought gifts of food and other necessities. Despite her many kindnesses to the settlers, at the age of 17 she was kidnapped by them to guarantee the good behavior of her tribe. The following year, Pocahontas married one of the colonists and later traveled with him to England, where she was introduced to British society. While in London, she died of smallpox at the age of 21. She had a son from whom many **prominent** Virginians claim descent. Her life story is well known to most Americans.

23. Of all the Indians' gifts to the settlers, food was probably the most valuable. Indian foods and methods of planting, hunting, and fishing enabled settlers to survive in their new home. Two of the most important **crops** in the world—corn and white potatoes—were first planted by American Indians, who also introduced the settlers to more than 80 other foods, including the sweet potato, pumpkin, squash, peanut, tomato, banana, pineapple, and avocado.

24. The Native Americans showed the settlers how to cook these unfamiliar plants to make grits, hominy, popcorn, succotash, and tapioca. Cacao (for chocolate), chicle (for chewing gum), and tobacco were also among their crops. Many of the drugs which Indians extracted from plants (such as cocaine, a pain reliever) are still being used (and sometimes abused) today.

25. Indians also helped the settlers by introducing them to Indian **utensils,** clothing, trails, and methods of transportation. Native American inventions adopted by American settlers included hammocks, canoes, dog sleds, toboggans, pipes, rubber balls, snowshoes, moccasins, parkas, and ponchos.

26. The influence of Indian cultures on the European settlers is evident in American English. In the Western Hemisphere, thousands of mountains, lakes, rivers, cities, states, and countries have Indian names—*Chicago, Massachusetts, Oregon, Mexico, Nicaragua,* and *Peru,* to mention just a few. Indian words in the English language include *skunk, moose, tobacco, succotash, squash,* and hundreds of others.

27. Although the Indians helped the European settlers in many ways, because they both wanted the same land, they became **enemies,** and the result was a shameful history of bloodshed and cruelty. The Indians were doomed to defeat since the settlers had guns, while the Indians fought mostly with bows and arrows. Also, the settlers were able to unite, while the Indians were divided into hundreds of different tribes which were hostile to each other. The settlers did not appreciate Indian culture and considered the Indian an inferior savage, so they didn't feel guilty about cheating the Indians and taking their land.

28. As early as 1786, the United States government began setting aside special territories (called **reservations**) for Indian resettlement. The Indians were pushed onto land that was considered undesirable, mostly in the Southwest and the Northwest. During the mid-19th century, they were confined to these reservations and forbidden to leave without a permit. When Columbus discovered the New World in 1492, there were about 700,000 Indians living in the area that later became the U.S.A. By 1890, as a result of poverty and poor living conditions, the Indian population in the United States had decreased to about 240,000.

29. In the 1920s, American treatment of Indians began to improve. As a result, the population grew. Today, there are about 1.5 million Native Americans living in the U.S.A., including the Aleuts and the Eskimos of Alaska. The majority live in or near the federal reservations, but they are, of course, free to leave. Most Indians live in the Southwest—Arizona, Oklahoma, New Mexico, and California. However, a number of tribes are in the Northwest—North Dakota, South Dakota, Wyoming, and Montana. There are also dozens of small Indian communities along the East Coast.

30. On the reservations, traditional Indian customs, languages, and styles of dress have survived. **Tourists** visit these reservations to observe the Indian way of life. Various tribes make baskets, pottery, woven blankets and rugs, wood sculpture, beadwork, and silver jewelry with turquoise stones. Most Indian products have attractive, colorful designs. Because of their beauty and fine, durable workmanship, these goods are often purchased by tourists.

31. On or off the reservation, Native Americans are one of the most deprived and most unhappy of minority groups in the United States. Their education, income, housing, and health are all far below national averages. To improve the quality of life for Indians, the federal government's Bureau of Indian Affairs spends millions of dollars each year. In recent years, it has also responded to Indian insistence on more administrative control of their own affairs.

32. In search of greater prosperity, some Native Americans choose to leave the reservation and find jobs and homes in the cities. The federal government is eager to help those who wish to assimilate, and every year increasing numbers of Indians try it. But many Indians have trouble adjusting to a highly **competitive** capitalistic and materialistic culture. Their attitudes and values are quite different from those of mainstream U.S.A. For example, Indian cultures teach that the land and its produce are not the property of any individual but belong to the group. Also, Indians are not competitive. In school, for example, Indian children try to assist rather than outdo one another. However, the contemporary American society can learn much from the ideas of ancient Indian cultures. For example, modern problems in the field of **ecology** illustrate the timeless wisdom of traditional Indian reluctance to disturb the balance of nature.

33. After two centuries of suffering, Native Americans are finally finding more opportunities for a good life in this land that was once their own, among people to whom they have given so much.

EXERCISES

I. Comprehension Questions. Answer the following questions on paper or in class discussion.

1. Why did the Pilgrims want to come to America?
2. What were the two main purposes of the first Thanksgiving?
3. How do Americans celebrate Thanksgiving today?
4. What are some of the American Indian influences on American words, foods, and clothing?

II. Vocabulary Practice. Pronounce the following words after your teacher, and discuss their meanings. Then use some of them to complete the following sentences.

apologize	propose
betray	reservations
blessings	reunions
competitive	settlers
cope	strengthen
crops	survive
ecology	tourists
enemies	tribe
persecute	utensils
prominent	wilderness

1. When you step on someone's toes, it is polite to ________________ (say that you're sorry).
2. The Pilgrims gave thanks to God for the ________________ (the good things) that they had received.
3. The modern Thanksgiving is a time for family ________________.
4. Many ________________ come to visit American Indian ________________ every year.

5. When the Pilgrims arrived in America, the land was still an unsettled ________________.

6. The Pilgrims met Indians that became their friends, not their ________________.

7. The American Indians taught the ________________ from Europe how to plant many new ________________ (such as corn and potatoes) and how to make many new ________________ (such as snowshoes and sleds).

8. The Indians helped the Pilgrims to survive and to ________________ with life in the New World.

III. Word Study.

A. Write the noun form of each verb. (Use a dictionary for help, if necessary.)

agree________________	explore________________
assist________________	persecute________________
celebrate________________	suppress________________
contribute________________	survive________________

B. What are the two meanings of the prefix *re-*? ________________

____

What does *re-* mean in the words *reproduction* and *reunion?* ______

C. Studying words with multiple meanings:

1. What does *rough* mean in paragraph 4?

____

What other common meaning does it have?

____

2. What does *propose* mean in paragraph 15?

____

What other, more general, meaning does it have?

____

3. What does *reservation* mean in the section about American Indians? ______________________________

What does it mean in a restaurant?

____

4. What is the general meaning of *pilgrim?*

____

Why did the Puritans begin to call themselves *Pilgrims?*

____

____

IV. <u>Idiom Study</u>. Underline the correct meaning of each idiom. The numbers in brackets give the paragraphs in which these idioms are used.

1. *In return for* [3] means a) instead of b) in exchange for c) in time for.
2. You can *spend* [11] a) money and time b) food and money c) happiness and time.
3. When you *take pride* [13] in your work, you a) take it home b) feel that it's good c) take time doing it.
4. If you *take* your friend's *advice* [18], you a) take pride in him or her b) take his or her possessions c) do what he or she suggests.
5. John Smith *owed his life* [22] to Pocahontas because a) she protected him from death b) she was his mother c) he owed her a lot of money.

V. Reading Skills.

A. What was Priscilla implying when she asked, "Why don't you speak for yourself, John?" [17] ______________________________

B. Reread the chapter quickly, looking for the following factual information:

1. What was the name of the Pilgrims' ship? ________________
2. In what year did the Pilgrims arrive in America? __________
3. Whom did Priscilla marry? ________________
4. Approximately how many American Indians live in the U.S.A. today? ________________

C. What is the difference in meaning between *Native Americans* and *native Americans*? ______________________________

____

____

D. In paragraph 27, sentence 1, the word *they* is used twice. What does *they* refer to? ______________________________

E. Using context clues, guess the meaning of *assimilate* (paragraph 32, sentence 2). ______________________________

12

THE WINTER HOLIDAY SEASON

MERRY CHRISTMAS!

1. The winter holiday season is the most festive time of the year in the United States. Students from elementary school through college have about two weeks' vacation, beginning shortly before Christmas and ending soon after New Year's Day. Many families go away for the holidays, but those who stay home have fun, too. There are many parties to celebrate the birth of Christ and the arrival of the new year.

2. Christianity, the major religious faith in the United States, the Western Hemisphere, and the world, is based upon the teachings and life of Jesus Christ. There are about one billion Christians worldwide. They believe in Jesus' ideas of equality, care for the weak, forgiveness, and love and kindness to all. They also believe that Jesus Christ was the son of God, and that he was sent to earth to save the human race. The name *Jesus* means *Savior* or *Help of God.* The name *Christ* means *anointed one,* someone set apart for special honor.

3. Jesus was born in Bethlehem in ancient Judea. No one knows exactly when Jesus was born. The year 1 A.D., from which most modern **calendars** are dated, is supposed to be the year of his birth, but historians now know that he was actually born several years before that time. No one knows the exact date of his birth either, but Christians have celebrated it on December 25 since the fourth century. This date was selected so that Christmas would replace the pagan celebration of the beginning of winter.

4. In the United States, the spirit of Christmas arrives about a month before the holiday itself. Late in November, street lights and store windows are decorated with the traditional Christmas colors of red and green. Santa Claus, shepherds, **angels,** and Nativity scenes appear in shop windows. Winter scenes with snowmen, **sleds**, skaters, and skiers **decorate** cards and windows.

5. The manufacture and sale of Christmas items is big business. Stores depend on Christmas shoppers for about one-fourth of their annual sales. Smart shoppers buy their gifts far in advance, before the Christmas rush makes shopping a chore. Christmas is expensive. To earn extra money for gifts, in December many Americans get part-time jobs delivering mail or selling gifts, trees, **ornaments,** or greeting cards. Many people make monthly bank deposits in special Christmas accounts so that they will have enough money for a nice Christmas.

6. Although Americans enjoy the commercial gaiety of Christmas, the most beautiful and meaningful parts of the holiday occur at home and in church. Many families go to church on Christmas **Eve** and Christmas morning. After services, they gather around the tree and open their gifts. Then they sit down to enjoy a traditional Christmas dinner—turkey or ham, sweet potatoes, vegetables, and cranberry sauce. Dessert is usually fruit cake, plum pudding, or mince pie.

7. Most of the Christmas customs which Americans enjoy today are **variations** of traditions brought here by European immigrants. These are some of the most popular customs:

8. *Exchanging Gifts.* The first Christmas gifts were those that the three Wise Men brought to the infant Jesus. In the United States, it is customary to **exchange** gifts with family members and close friends. Both children and adults get Christmas presents, although children usually get many more.

9. *Receiving Toys from Santa Claus.* Many American children believe that on Christmas Eve, Santa Claus, (a fat, jolly man who wears a red suit, red hat, and long white beard) slides down their chimney to bring them gifts. According to the story, Santa Claus flies through the air in a sleigh (a fancy sled) pulled by eight **reindeer.** Several days or weeks before Christmas, children tell Santa Claus what toys they want by writing him letters or visiting him in a local department store. Then, on Christmas Eve, many youngsters lie awake listening for Santa and his sleigh. Some children even leave him a snack of milk and cookies.

10. Where did this **legend** come from? *Santa Claus* is the American name for St. Nicholas, a generous fourth-century bishop who lived in what is now Turkey. It was his custom to go out at night and bring gifts to the poor. After his death, his fame spread throughout Europe. Dutch immigrants brought the idea of St. Nicholas (whom they called *Sinter Klaas*) to the United States, where the name was **mispronounced** and finally changed to *Santa Claus.* Then, 19th-century American artists and authors changed St. Nick's appearance and created the roly-poly man in red that we know today. Santa's sleigh and reindeer came from an old Norse legend. So today's Santa Claus is really a blend of several different cultures.

11. *Hanging a Stocking near the Chimney.* As in Great Britain, American children hang stockings by the fireplace, hoping that Santa will fill them with candy and toys.

12. *Decorating the Home with Evergreens.* The winter custom of decorating homes and churches with **evergreens** began in ancient times. Branches of fir or spruce were thought to bring good luck and **guarantee** the return of spring. The early Germans believed, for example, that in winter evil spirits killed the plants and trees and caused green leaves and flowers to disappear. They felt that bringing evergreens into their homes would protect them from the spirit of death.

13. Germans of the 16th century probably started the custom of decorating trees. In the 19th century, the idea spread throughout Europe and the United States. Now, at Christmastime, decorated trees stand in about two-thirds of American homes. The modern American tree is usually covered with colored balls and strings of colored lights. The star on top represents the star in the East which guided the three Wise Men to Bethlehem.

14. In ancient times, a branch of mistletoe was hung over doorways for good luck. Today the custom continues, but now it is for fun. Anyone standing under the mistletoe is likely to be kissed.

15. The poinsettia plant is another familiar Christmas decoration. Its star-shaped red leaves are an ideal symbol of the holiday. This plant is native to Central America and Mexico. It is named for Dr. Poinsett of South Carolina, who first created a variety that could be grown in the U.S.A.

16. *Singing Christmas Carols.* In the early days of the Christian Church, the bishops sang **carols** on Christmas Day. Now, everybody sings them. Soloists and choirs on the radio, on TV, in church, and in school all help fill the winter air with beautiful music. Copying an old English custom, many Americans join with friends and walk from house to house singing the traditional songs of Christmas.

17. *Sending Christmas Cards.* The custom of sending Christmas cards began in London in 1843 and came to the United States in 1875. Today, most Americans (Christians and non-Christians) send dozens of Christmas cards or season's greetings to relatives, friends, and business associates.

18. *Christmas Performances.* Three Christmas traditions are beautiful theatrical performances that people of all religions enjoy. One of these is *The Messiah*, an oratorio written by the German composer George Frederick Handel and performed by a chorus, orchestra, and solo singers. Another classic work performed annually during the Christmas season is the Russian composer Peter Ilich Tchaikovsky's ballet *The Nutcracker*. It is a favorite with children because it tells the delightful story of a little girl's Christmas dream about her toys. Finally, there is the story *A Christmas Carol* by the 19th-century English author Charles Dickens. It is traditionally performed as a play (sometimes with music) and tells the tale of a character named

Ebenezer Scrooge. Scrooge is a selfish, lonely, rich, old man who, with the help of ghosts from his past, present, and future life, learns to understand and regain the spirit of Christmas—the spirit of caring for and sharing with others.

HAPPY HANUKKAH!

19. While Christians brighten the winter with Christmas color and lights, American Jews (together with Jews throughout the world) celebrate their Festival of Lights—Hanukkah. This holiday celebrates the **triumph** of religious freedom. In 168 B.C., the Syrian King conquered Judea and tried to force the Jews to worship pagan gods. Three years later, a small group of Jews defeated the powerful Syrian armies.

20. When the Jews recaptured Jerusalem and rededicated their Holy Temple, they relit the eternal lamp. One day's supply of oil—all that was left—burned for eight days, until fresh oil was available. In memory of this **miracle,** Jews celebrate Hanukkah for eight days and light candles in a special candleholder called a *menorah.*

21. The date of Hanukkah is determined by the Hebrew calendar, but the holiday always occurs in December. So, for Americans of both Christian and Jewish faiths, the year ends in a spirit of joy.

HAPPY NEW YEAR!

22. "Ring out the old, ring in the new," wrote Alfred Lord Tennyson, the 19th-century English poet. And that's exactly what Americans do every December 31. New Year's Eve is a time for noise and fun. At midnight, bells ring, horns blow, and friends exchange kisses. Everyone stays up late to celebrate the arrival of another year.

23. At home or in restaurants, most Americans spend the holiday drinking and dining with friends. One popular New Year's Eve drink is **eggnog,** made with eggs, milk or cream, nutmeg, and sugar. Throughout the Christmas season, eggnog (to which adults may add rum or brandy) is a familiar party beverage. Champagne—the drink that symbolizes a celebration—is often served for the midnight toast on New Year's Eve.

24. One of the noisiest and most crowded of New Year's Eve celebrations takes place in New York City at Times Square. Huge crowds gather there, and millions of Americans across the country join them via TV. The new year arrives earlier on the East Coast than in other parts of the country because the United States spans four time zones. When midnight comes to New York, it is 11 P.M. in Chicago, 10 P.M. in Denver, and only 9 P.M. in Los Angeles.

25. New Year's Eve festivities often continue until two or three o'clock in the morning. Many people travel from one party to another to celebrate with several different groups of friends.

26. New Year's Day has traditionally been the occasion for starting new programs and giving up bad habits. People talk about turning over a new leaf. Many Americans make New Year's **resolutions,** promising to improve their behavior. Typical New Year's resolutions are to spend less money, give up smoking, begin a diet, or control one's temper.

27. From ancient times to the present, New Year's customs have been connected with saying good-bye to the past and looking forward to a better future. Although the theme of the holiday has not changed much from one century to the next, the date of the celebration has been changed many times. The ancient Egyptians started their year on September 21, while the ancient Greeks began theirs on June 21. The old Roman calendar contained only 10 months, and New Year's Day was March 1. In 46 B.C., Julius Caesar introduced an improved calendar containing two additional months, January and February. January was named for the Roman god Janus, whose name comes from the Roman word for *door.* Like a door, Janus looks both ways; he is usually shown with two faces, one looking backward and the other forward. Julius Caesar's calendar, called in his honor the *Julian* calendar, was revised in 1582 by Pope Gregory XIII. This *Gregorian* calendar is the one in use today.

28. All Americans celebrate New Year's on December 31 and January 1, but Chinese-Americans and Jewish-Americans also celebrate their own special New Year holidays. Although the Chinese have officially adopted the Gregorian calendar, many still celebrate the New Year holiday established by China's ancient lunar calendar more than 4,000 years ago. The 15-day Chinese New Year begins with *Yuan Tan* and concludes with the Festival of Lanterns, held at the time of the full moon between January 21 and February 19. During this period, Chinatown sections in major American cities look very festive, with paper and glass lanterns decorating the houses and colorful paraders marching in the streets.

29. *Rosh Hashanah* (which means *head of the year*) is the traditional Jewish New Year. It occurs in September or October. Unlike the American New Year, Rosh Hashanah is a very solemn holiday, marking the beginning of 10 days of penitence called the *High Holy Days*. These days are set aside for self-appraisal, **repentance,** and the making of vows to be a better person in the coming year.

30. To Americans of all races, religions, and national origins, the closing of one calendar year and the opening of another is a serious, yet happy occasion. We review the past with **nostalgia.** We judge ourselves and promise to improve. And we look forward to a new beginning with renewed hope.

EXERCISES

I. Comprehension Questions. Answer the following questions on paper or in class discussion.

1. What is the Christian interpretation of the life of Christ? How does this viewpoint compare to the way members of other religious groups think of their first spiritual leader?
2. How does the idea of giving gifts relate to the Christmas story and the holiday spirit?
3. What is the main idea of Hanukkah?
4. Will you make a New Year's resolution this year? What will it be?

II. Vocabulary Practice. Pronounce the following words after your teacher, and discuss their meanings. Then use some of the words to complete the following sentences. You may need to use the same word twice.

angels	miracle
calendar	mispronounced
carol	nostalgia
decorate	ornaments
eggnog	reindeer
Eve	repentance
evergreens	resolutions
exchange	sled
guarantee	triumph
legend	variation

1. Christians consider Jesus the son of God and the Virgin Mary, so his birth is considered a ________________.

2. People________________ the Dutch name *Sinter Klaas,* and it became *Santa Claus.*

3. The modern________________ is supposed to date from the year of Christ's birth, but Christ was actually born several years before 1 A.D.

4. During the Christmas season, Christians________________ their homes with________________, including Christmas trees, wreaths, and mistletoe.

5. Some people decorate Christmas trees with colorful glass ________________.

6. Santa Claus travels in a fancy________________ called a sleigh that is pulled through the sky by eight________________.

7. On Christmas Day, people________________ gifts. At midnight on New Year's________________, they________________ kisses.

8. New Year's________________ are promises to improve oneself in some way.

III. Word Study. The letters *ch* are usually pronounced as in the words *child* and *cheese*. But, in some words, *ch* is pronounced like a *k* and in others like *sh*. Say the following words after your teacher:

[*CH*]	[*K*]	[*SH*]
chore	chorus, choir	champagne
chimney	school, orchestra	Chicago
church	Christmas, Christ	Michigan
China	ache, character	machine

IV. Idiom Study. Underline the correct completion for each sentence. The numbers in brackets give the paragraphs in which these idioms are used.

1. The *Christmas rush* [5] refers to the a) shoppers b) churchgoers c) carolers.
2. *Roly-poly* [10] means a) fat b) jolly c) slender.
3. *Season's greetings* [17] are usually sent to a) Santa Claus b) relatives, friends, and business associates c) strangers.
4. *Turning over a new leaf* [26] means a) buying a new poinsettia plant b) decorating your home with some new evergreens c) improving your behavior.
5. When you *look forward to* [30] an event, you a) expect and want it to happen b) fear it c) shop for it.

V. Reading Skills.

A. Reading for facts and ideas:

1. Most American Christmas customs originated in a) the U.S.A. b) other countries c) Bethlehem.
2. Christ was born a) on December 25, 1 A.D. b) several years before 1 A.D. c) in the Fourth century A.D.
3. Christmas is celebrated by a) all Americans b) Christians throughout the world c) Christians and Jews everywhere.
4. Which would not be a good New Year's resolution? a) I'll spend more time with my family. b) I'll stop smoking cigarettes. c) I'll buy some groceries tomorrow.

5. The year 500 A.D. is about a) 1,500 years ago b) 500 years ago c) 2,500 years ago.

B. Reading fractions: Find the fractions in the paragraphs listed and write their numerical form.

[5]________________ [13]________________

Write the percent (%) for each fraction.
Examples: ¼ (one-fourth) 25%; ⅕ (one-fifth) 20%.

⅔ (two-thirds) ______________

½ (one-half) ______________

¾ (three-fourths) ______________

⅖ (two-fifths) ______________

13

HOLIDAYS HONORING TWO GREAT PRESIDENTS

1. George Washington and Abraham Lincoln are the only American presidents whose birthdays are widely celebrated as legal holidays. Why are these two presidents especially honored? The answer is that, without their wise leadership, the United States of America would probably not **exist** today. Both men lived during **critical** periods in American history, and both met the challenge of their times with great courage and **wisdom.** Washington faced the dangers of being a **revolutionary** to help the British colonies win their **independence** from England. Less than 100 years later, Lincoln **declared** war on the Southern states to keep the young nation from dividing in two.

2. But Washington and Lincoln are remembered not only for their political accomplishments. Both men are American heroes, symbols of traits and ideals which are much admired by the nation they helped to build.

GEORGE WASHINGTON

3. George Washington, commonly called the father of his country, was born in 1732. The son of a wealthy Virginia planter, he was privately educated and trained to be a surveyor. But as an officer in the French and Indian War, he became interested in military leadership.

4. In 1759, Washington married a widow named Martha Custis, who later became famous as a gracious hostess in the first president's home. After his marriage, he returned to his Virginia plantation, Mount Vernon, to live the life of a gentleman farmer. He also became involved in **colonial opposition** to British **policies** in America.

5. By 1775, relations with England had become so bad that the colonists were ready to fight for their independence. The Continental Congress named Washington commander in chief of the revolutionary army. His job was very difficult. His army was small, poorly fed, and inadequately clothed. The men suffered greatly during terribly cold winters. While begging for more men and supplies, Washington had to fight the Revolutionary War with poorly equipped, untrained soldiers. He never asked for and never received any salary for the job he performed. In fact,

he often spent his own money to buy clothing for his men and send aid to their families. Washington brought to the battlefield great military ability and a noble character.

6. Washington was the first man not a king whose birthday was publicly celebrated during his lifetime. Before the colonies declared their independence, celebrations honoring the birthdays of British rulers were customary. After the Declaration of Independence, the American people **ignored** royal birthdays and began instead to celebrate General Washington's birthday. This custom started in 1778 during the army's cold, snowy winter at Valley Forge, when one of the military bands marched to Washington's headquarters and played for him.

7. When the war ended in 1783, Washington eagerly returned to Mount Vernon. But his peaceful retirement was interrupted when he was **unanimously** chosen first president of the United States. He took office in 1789 and was reelected in 1792. In 1796, he refused a third term and retired from political life. He died two years later and was buried at Mount Vernon, which one million tourists visit every year. Shortly after his death, Washington was praised in these famous words: "First in war, first in peace, and first in the hearts of his countrymen."

8. To the American people, Washington symbolizes dignity, statesmanship, and, above all, honesty. The famous cherry tree story, which was invented by Washington's first biographer, has become a lesson in morals for all American schoolchildren. The story goes like this: When George Washington was about six years old, his father gave him a hatchet, which the little boy loved to play with. One day, he tried the edge of his hatchet on his father's favorite young cherry tree and did enough damage to kill the tree. Next morning, his father noticed the damage and ran into the house shouting, "George, do you know who killed that beautiful little cherry tree...in the garden?" George's famous reply was, "I can't tell a lie, Pa, you know I can't tell a lie. I cut it with my hatchet." His father, pleased with the boy's courage and honesty, quickly **forgave** him.

9. Because of this story, traditional desserts on Washington's Birthday are cherry pie or a log-shaped cake decorated with cherries. Washington's Birthday is a legal holiday throughout the U.S.A. It is celebrated on the third Monday in February. In some states, this date is called *Presidents' Day* and **honors** both Washington and Lincoln.

ABRAHAM LINCOLN

10. Although Americans admire George Washington, the greatest of all American heroes is certainly Abraham Lincoln. Why? Basic to the

American philosophy is the idea that a person who is honest and hardworking can achieve success no matter how humble his or her beginnings. Lincoln is a perfect example of a self-made man.

11. Lincoln was born on February 12, 1809 in a log cabin in Kentucky. His parents were uneducated and poor. Although Lincoln eventually became a lawyer, he had very little formal education. But he did have a brilliant mind and great moral strength. He had the courage to do what he felt was right, no matter what the **sacrifice.** In 1860, shortly before the Civil War began, he said, "Let us have faith that right makes might; and in that faith let us to the end, dare to do our duty as we understand it."

12. Elected to the presidency in 1860 and reelectd in 1864, Lincoln was the first successful presidential candidate nominated by the Republican Party. During his term in office, the American Civil War was fought. The issues were slavery and secession. In the agricultural Southern states, Negroes forcibly brought from Africa were used as slaves to grow tobacco and cotton and do housework. In the industrial North, where there were only small farms, the economy had little use for large numbers of agricultural workers. Northerners disapproved of slavery as being inhumane. In order to protect their right to keep slaves, the Southern leaders decided that the Southern states should secede from the Union and form a separate nation—the Confederate States of America.

13. Lincoln felt that the Union had to be saved. In 1860, the United States was the only important democracy in the world. Self-government would be proved a failure if the nation could be destroyed by a minority of its own citizens. Lincoln chose to lead the country into a **civil** war rather than allow the South to secede.

14. In 1858, Lincoln had said, "A house divided against itself cannot stand. I believe this government cannot **endure** permanently half slave and half free." In 1860, the United States was, indeed, "a house divided." There were 33 states at that time. Eighteen of them did not allow slavery, and 15 of them did. During the Civil War, 11 states fought for the Confederacy (Virginia, North Carolina, South Carolina, Georgia, Florida, Tennessee, Alabama, Mississippi, Arkansas, Louisiana, and Texas). On the Union side there were 23 states, after a section of Virginia, wanting to remain in the U.S.A., separated from the rest of the state and became West Virginia. Seven Western territories also fought on the Union side. Among the states that bordered the North and the South, some sided with the Confederacy and others with the Union. For some, it was a difficult decision. Kentucky and Missouri, for example, remained in the Union, but secessionist groups within these states set up their own state governments and sent representatives to the Confederate Congress.

15. The Civil War began in April of 1861, only a few months after Lincoln's inauguration as president. It began when Lincoln declared **secession** illegal and sent military troops to keep federal possession of a United States government fort located in the Charleston, South Carolina harbor. In terms of human suffering, the Civil War was the most costly war the United States has ever been involved in. Emotionally, it was quite painful, too, often breaking up friendships and even families when loyalties were on opposite sides. About one million soldiers were killed or wounded. The death toll, from **battle** or from disease, totaled more than 500,000. By the end of the war, the economy of the South was in ruins, and a great deal of property had been destroyed. On April 9, 1865, General Lee, the Confederate commander in chief, surrendered to General Grant, the Union commander. It took until May 26 before the word reached all of the generals in the field, and the battle between the North and the South was finally over.

16. During the war, Lincoln issued the famous Emancipation Proclamation, declaring all slaves in the Confederate states to be free. After the war, the Thirteenth Amendment to the Constitution was adopted. It freed all slaves throughout the nation.

17. Because he was an excellent writer who could express his beliefs clearly and with great emotional force, Lincoln was able to make Northerners understand why they were fighting a civil war. Parts of his speeches are still memorized by schoolchildren because they express in beautiful language the highest **ideals** of American democracy.

18. In 1863, while dedicating a national cemetery in Gettysburg, Pennsylvania, Lincoln concluded his shortest and most famous speech with the following wish: "...that this nation, under God, shall have a new birth of freedom, and that government of the people, by the people, for the people shall not perish from the earth."

19. On April 14, 1865, less than a week after Lee's **surrender,** Lincoln attended a theatrical performance at Ford's Theatre in Washington, D.C. Shortly after 10 P.M., a gunshot rang through the crowded auditorium. John Wilkes Booth, a well-known actor and Southern sympathizer, had shot the president in the head. Lincoln was carried unconscious to a neighboring house, where he died early the following morning.

20. Because Lincoln had spent most of his adult years in Illinois, his body was brought back to his home state and buried in Springfield. Now there is a huge monument above the spot where Lincoln, his wife, and three of their four sons are buried.

21. In about 30 states, Lincoln's Birthday is a legal holiday, celebrated on February 12 or on the first or third Monday in February. Most of the Southern states do not celebrate Lincoln's birthday.

22. The names and faces of both Washington and Lincoln are an important part of American culture. Washington is the only president for whom a state is named. And, of course, on the other side of the country lies the nation's capital city, also named *Washington.* Throughout the U.S.A., cities, towns, streets, schools, bridges, and other structures are called *Washington* or *Lincoln.* In Washington, D.C., beautiful monuments have been dedicated to these national heroes. Portraits of them decorate the walls of many public buildings. Moreover, portraits of Washington and Lincoln (like those of other presidents) appear on the front of U.S. coins and bills. Washington's picture is on the quarter and the $1 bill; Lincoln's is on the penny and the $5 bill. To Americans, the faces of Washington and Lincoln are as familiar and inspiring as their courageous deeds.

EXERCISES

I. Comprehension Questions. Answer the following questions on paper or in class discussion.

1. Why did the 13 American colonies fight the Revolutionary War? Who was the enemy?
2. What were Washington's two important jobs, one for the colonies and one for the newly formed U.S.A.?
3. What were the two main causes of the American Civil War?
4. If Washington and Lincoln had never lived, would the U.S.A. be different? In what ways?

II. Vocabulary Practice. Pronounce the following words after your teacher, and discuss their meanings. Then use some of them to complete the following sentences.

battle
civil
colonial
critical
declared
endure
exist
forgave
honor
ideals
ignore
independence
opposition
policies
revolutionary
sacrifice
secession
surrender
unanimously
wisdom

1. George Washington was ________________ chosen the first president of the new nation.
2. A ________________ war is fought to make a complete change in the government. A ________________ war is fought between two parts of the same country.
3. Soldiers who fight in wars must sometimes ________________ their lives in order to protect their country.
4. When the colonies won their war against England, they won their ________________, their right to be a separate country.
5. Northern ________________ to slavery was one of the main causes of the American Civil War.
6. Washington and Lincoln were men of great ________________ and honor.
7. Beautiful monuments in Washington, D.C. ________________ the memory of these two great presidents.
8. In the story about George Washington and the cherry tree, the boy's father ________________ his son for disobeying him.

III. Word Study.

A. Write the noun for each verb. Use a dictionary for help, if necessary.

accomplish________________ oppose________________

exist________________ rebel________________

retire________________ revolt________________

secede________________ surrender________________

B. Distinguish between these look-alike words. Underline the correct word to complete each sentence. Then read the sentences aloud in class.

1. Sometimes soldiers become frightened and run away or (desert; dessert) from the army. A (desert; dessert) is a dry, sandy area. Cherry pie is a traditional (desert; dessert) on Washington's Birthday.
2. The word *separate* is both an adjective and a verb. The verb has a long *a* sound in the final syllable. Before the Civil War, the Southern states wanted to (separate; separated) from the rest of the United States and become a (separate; separated) country. When they seceded or (separate; separated) from the Union, they called themselves the Confederate States of America.
3. The word *face* can be a noun or a verb. Washington and Lincoln both (facing; faced) difficult decisions. Today, their (face; faces) are familiar to all Americans.
4. The Civil War led to a great deal of (human; humane) suffering. The war was fought because people in the North thought that slavery was not (human; humane).

IV. Idiom Study. Answer the following questions about expressions used in this chapter. The numbers in brackets give the paragraphs in which the idioms are used.

1. Why is George Washington called the father of his country [3]?

____

2. Why is Lincoln called a self-made man [10]?

____

3. What does the term *legal holiday* [1] mean?

____

V. Reading Skills.

A. Making inferences:

1. The famous cherry tree story illustrates which two character traits? a) strength and humility b) courage and honesty c) wisdom and dignity
2. The Lincoln quotation "Let us have faith that right makes might" [11] means a) If we are strong, we will also be morally right. b) If we are morally right, that will give us strength. c) Right and might are really the same.
3. Explain Lincoln's famous figure of speech: "A house divided against itself cannot stand." a) What two things was he comparing? ______________________

   b) What was he predicting? ______________________

   ____
4. Why do you think Lincoln's birthday is not celebrated in the Southern states? ______________________

B. Understanding punctuation:

1. Note the use of three dots in paragraph 8 and paragraph 18. This is called an *ellipsis*. What does it mean? ______________

   ____

14

MINOR HOLIDAYS

1. From February through June, Americans celebrate five minor holidays which are important because of the light-hearted enjoyment they bring. These holidays do not provide a day off from work or school. Still, they are festive occasions, involving customs which are bright threads in the fabric of American culture.

VALENTINE'S DAY

2. Valentine's Day is a festival of **romance** and **affection**. The holiday is another interesting **combination** of pagan and Christian influences. Some of the day's customs probably came from an ancient Roman holiday called *Lupercalia*, which honored Juno (the goddess of women, marriage, and childbirth) and Pan (the god of nature). During the Lupercalia festival, young women dropped poems bearing their names into a large vase. Each young man picked a name from the vase to find his sweetheart for that year.

3. During the Middle Ages, church leaders wanted to relate this pagan holiday to Christianity, so they renamed it after a Christian saint and moved the holiday from February 15 to February 14, the feast day of St. Valentine. Since there were eight St. Valentines in the early centuries of Christianity, no one is sure which one the holiday is named after. But historians think that it was a third-century Christian martyr, a young man who was imprisoned in Rome for refusing to worship pagan gods. According to legend, before Valentine was beheaded on February 14, he restored the eyesight of his jailer's blind daughter. Then he sent her a farewell letter signed, "From your Valentine." This phrase is now a common expression of affection that appears on many of the holiday's greeting cards.

4. Perhaps another reason that February 14 was selected as a holiday for lovers was that the ancient Romans believed that birds began to mate on this date.

5. Early in February, card shops, drugstores, and department stores begin displaying a wide variety of greeting cards called **valentines**. Most of them are **illustrated** with the symbolic red **heart**, which stands for love.

Many also show a picture of Cupid with his bow and arrow. (In Roman **mythology**, Cupid was the son of Venus, the goddess of love. According to legend, if Cupid's arrow hit a person, the **victim** would fall in love.) Some valentines are very fancy—decorated with paper lace, scented satin, feathers, ribbons, or bows. Some contain affectionate verses, while other simply say, "Be my Valentine." There are special valentines for various family members, sweethearts, and friends.

6. Grammar-school children usually buy packages of small, inexpensive valentines to give to classmates and teachers. Sweethearts and married couples may exchange more expensive cards, along with small gifts. Men often give flowers or candy (in a red, heart-shaped box) to their girlfriends or wives.

7. No one knows exactly when the custom of sending valentine cards began, but some historians think it started around 1400. It was brought to the United States by the earliest English settlers and became very popular during the mid-1800s. Today, Americans probably send more valentines than people in all other countries combined. In the U.S.A., more than 850 million valentine cards are sold each year.

ST. PATRICK'S DAY

8. St. Patrick's Day honors Ireland's patron **saint,** the beloved religious leader who, in the latter part of the fourth century, brought Christianity to a pagan nation. Americans of Irish descent celebrate the anniversary of his death on March 17.

9. Strangely enough, the patron saint of Ireland was not Irish either by birth or **heritage.** Born in what is now Scotland or England, he was the son of Roman citizens. When he was 16 years old, he was captured by pirates and brought to Ireland, where he was sold as a slave. He spent six years in slavery in Ireland. During this time, he saw the Irish worshipping idols and dreamed of bringing them Christianity. When he escaped, he went to France, where he studied religion and later became a monk. He eventually returned to Ireland, where he **preached** Christianity and established more than 300 churches.

10. St. Patrick is the favorite saint of the Irish, who tell many stories about his kind **deeds** and **miraculous** powers. He is even given credit for driving the snakes out of Ireland!

11. In the United States, St. Patrick's Day is celebrated with parades, church services, banquets, and the wearing of the green. St. Patrick used the three-leaf clover, (the **shamrock**) to explain the Trinity, which refers to the unity of the Father (God), the Son (Jesus), and the Holy Ghost (the Holy Spirit). Today, green cloth shamrocks and green clothing are worn by people of Irish descent on St. Patrick's Day.

12. In New York City, Boston, Philadelphia, Chicago, and Atlanta, (all cities with large Irish populations), there are spectacular St. Patrick's Day parades. The marchers wear native Irish costumes and carry colorful banners and flags. Bands play familiar songs about Ireland. Observers crowd the sidewalks to watch the fun and sing or hum along with the marchers. In Chicago, as part of the celebration, the Chicago River is dyed green!

APRIL FOOLS' DAY

13. April Fools' Day is the first day of April. The fun of the holiday is to play silly but harmless jokes on family members, coworkers, and friends. A victim of one of these pranks is called an *April **fool.***

14. This holiday began in France. When the French first adopted the Gregorian calendar in 1564, some people continued to use the old calendar and to celebrate New Year's Day on April 1. These people were called April fools. The custom of playing tricks on this day became popular in France and then spread to many other countries. April Fools' jokes are as **ingenious, humorous,** or **cruel** as the people who perform them. Here are some typical pranks:

- calling the zoo and asking to speak to Mr. Lion;
- putting salt in the sugar bowl;
- setting the clocks back an hour;
- saying to a friend, "Oh my. You have four big holes in your coat–buttonholes"; and
- tying a string to a wallet, leaving the wallet in the middle of the sidewalk, and then, when the victim bends down to pick it up, pulling it out of reach.

15. In the United States today, April Fools' jokes are played mostly by children, who enjoy the holiday very much.

MOTHER'S DAY AND FATHER'S DAY

16. Mother's Day is celebrated on the second Sunday in May. On this occasion, Mother usually receives greeting cards and gifts from her husband and children. The best gift of all for an American Mom is a day of **leisure**. The majority of American mothers have outside jobs as well as homemaking responsibilities, so their typical working day often extends well into the evening. The modern employed homemaker enjoys the traditional Mother's Day custom of breakfast (or brunch) cooked by her family and served to her on a tray in bed. Later in the day, it's also traditional for the extended family group to get together for dinner, either in a restaurant or in one of their homes.

17. Flowers are an important part of Mother's Day. Mothers are often given a **corsage** or a plant for the occasion, particularly if they are elderly.

18. Father's Day is celebrated throughout the United States and Canada on the third Sunday in June. The holiday customs are similar to Mother's Day. Dad also receives greeting cards and gifts from his family and enjoys a day of leisure.

EXERCISES

I. Comprehension Questions. Answer the following questions on paper or in class discussion.

1. What do Americans exchange on Valentine's Day?
2. Who was St. Patrick, and why is he the favorite saint of the Irish?
3. What do people do to celebrate April Fools' Day, Mother's Day, and Father's Day?
4. In your native country, do people celebrate any of the holidays discussed in this chapter or any holidays with similar customs?

II. Vocabulary Practice. Pronounce the following words after your teacher, and discuss their meanings. Then use some of them to complete the following sentences. You may need to use the same word twice.

affection	ingenious
combination	leisure
corsage	miraculous
cruel	mythology
deeds	preach
fool	romance
heart	saint
heritage	shamrock
humorous	valentine
illustrated	victim

1. Valentine's Day is a holiday about ________________ and ________________ .

2. Cupid, the young boy who can make people fall in love, is a character from Roman ________________.

3. The red ________________ that we see on most valentine cards is not the same shape as the human heart.

4. The ________________ is a plant, a three-leaf clover, that is worn by people of Irish descent on St. Patrick's Day.

5. If someone tricks you on April Fools' Day, then you are the ________________ of that person's joke.

6. Some April Fools' Day tricks are ________________ (funny), some are ________________ (clever), and some are ________________ (unkind; hurtful).

7. On Mother's Day, it is common to give Mother a gift, a greeting card, perhaps also a ________________ to wear, and, most important, a day of ________________.

8. Mother's Day and Father's Day are occasions for showing ________________ to one's parents.

III. Word Study.

A. The abbreviation *St.* means *saint.*

What does *saint* mean, as it is used in this chapter? ____________

____

What related meaning does *saint* have? If someone says, "My mother was a saint," what does this mean?

____

B. What do American children call their parents? (See paragraphs 16 and 18 for help.)

Mother______________ Father______________

C. What does *myth* mean? ______________________

What does *mythology* mean? ______________________

In class, discuss other words that end in *-ology*.

IV. Idiom Study. Underline the correct phrase to complete each sentence. The numbers in brackets give the paragraphs in which the idioms are used.

1. Tom was hit by Cupid's arrow [5] means that a) Tom fell in love b) Tom had a bad accident c) Tom was an April fool.
2. *Be my Valentine* [5] means a) send me a valentine b) love me or be my friend c) help me.
3. The red heart *stands for* [5] love. In this sentence, the idiom *stands for* means a) supports or stands up for b) symbolizes c) captures.
4. The wearing of the green [11] is done by people of Irish descent on a) Valentine's Day b) St. Patrick's Day c) Mother's Day.
5. Today, people are called *April fools* [13] if they a) don't know the date of New Year's b) are stupid c) fall for a trick that someone plays on them. (Note: A person falls *in* love [5] but falls *for* a trick.)

V. Reading Skills.

A. Which of the following were real people, and which were mythological characters? Put an *R* after the real people and an *M* after the mythological characters.

1. Cupid___
2. St. Patrick___
3. Pan___
4. Juno___
5. St. Valentine___
6. Venus___

B. Reread paragraph 1.
What are the customs of these minor holidays compared to?

____

Why do you think these five holidays are called minor?

____

C. Compare the words *latter* [8] and *later* [16]. Then underline the correct words to complete these sentences:
I like both coffee and tea, but I'd prefer to have the (later; latter) now.
I'll have some coffee (later; latter).

D. Advertisements and store window decorations remind Americans of all the holidays discussed in this chapter. Why? Which holidays encourage Americans to buy things?

____

Which types of businesses profit?______________________

____

E. What do the following things symbolize?
a red heart______________________________
Cupid______________________________
a shamrock______________________________
a corsage______________________________

15

EASTER AND PASSOVER

EASTER AND RELATED HOLIDAYS

1. Easter, one of the most important Christian holidays, got its name and many of its customs and **symbols** from a pagan festival. This ancient holiday honored Eostre, the goddess of springtime and sunrise. Her name came from the word *east,* where the sun rises. Every spring, northern European people celebrated the festival of Eostre to honor the awakening of new life in nature. Later, Christians related the rising of the sun to the **Resurrection** of Christ and to their own spiritual rebirth. (According to the *New Testament,* on Easter Sunday, Jesus Christ, who had died on the cross and been placed in his tomb, came to life again.)

2. The **Crucifixion** (the death of Christ on the cross) occurred in the spring. The Last Supper, which took place the day before the Crucifixion, was a traditional Jewish *Passover* feast. The early Christians celebrated Easter on the same date as Passover. But they were not happy with this date because they wanted Easter to fall on a Sunday every year, and Passover did not. For some time, Easter was celebrated on different dates in different places. Finally, in 325 A.D., a group of church leaders solved the problem with the help of **astronomers.** They decided that Easter should be celebrated on the Sunday following the first full moon after March 21. The full moon was important because, many years ago, it helped to **guide** travelers who wished to join friends and relatives at big Easter festivals.

3. Many modern Easter symbols came from pagan times. The egg, for example, was a **fertility** symbol long before the Christian era. The ancient Persians, Greeks, and Chinese exchanged eggs at their spring festivals. In Christian times, the egg took on a new meaning, symbolizing the tomb from which Christ rose. The ancient custom of dyeing eggs at Easter time is still very popular with American children.

4. The Easter bunny also came from pre-Christian times. The rabbit, a very fertile animal, was a natural symbol of new life. Today, children enjoy eating candy bunnies and listening to stories about the Easter bunny, who brings Easter eggs in a fancy basket.

5. Traditionally, the meats associated with Easter are lamb and ham. Both of these meats have had symbolic meaning since ancient times. In the *Old Testament*, Abraham used the lamb as a **sacrifice** after God ordered him not to kill his son Isaac. The lamb has always been a part of the Passover tradition. For Christians, the lamb symbolizes the sacrifice of Christ. For thousands of years, the pig has been a symbol of good luck. On Easter Sunday, smoked or cooked ham is the traditional main course in both Europe and the United States.

6. Easter is a happy time. The continual rebirth of physical life on earth symbolizes the eternity of spiritual life. But the deeper meaning of Easter is a **profound paradox.** The story of Christ implies that for all Christians the beginning of eternal life is physical death.

7. Christians **observe** several holidays in remembrance of the last days of Christ and his Crucifixion. *Shrovetide* is the English name for the three or four days preceding Lent. The idea of Lent (observed by some Christian churches) is for people to give up certain pleasures and perhaps make some sacrifices in remembrance of the suffering of Christ. Shrovetide was a time for enjoying oneself before the Lenten period of self-denial. Years ago, when Lenten restrictions were much stricter than they are today, Shrovetide was celebrated everywhere with parties, games, dances, and feasting. It is still **carnival** season in many European countries.

8. The last day of Shrovetide is called *Shrove Tuesday* or *Mardi Gras* (French for *Fat Tuesday*). In the United States, a few Southern cities have elaborate Mardi Gras celebrations. The most famous one occurs in New Orleans, Louisiana. The New Orleans Mardi Gras lasts six days and includes torchlight parades, beautiful floats, marching bands, and masked costume balls. Thousands of tourists come to see this event.

9. Lent begins with Ash Wednesday. On this day, when a Catholic approaches the church altar, the priest makes the sign of the cross on his or her forehead with special ashes. Lent lasts for 40 weekdays before Easter Sunday. It honors the 40 days that Jesus spent alone in the desert, fasting and **praying**.

10. Palm Sunday, the beginning of Holy Week, recalls the day that Jesus rode into Jerusalem on a donkey, with the people cheering and spreading palm branches on the path before him.

11. Maundy Thursday (Holy Thursday) comes three days before Easter. It is in remembrance of Christ's Last Supper with his followers. *Maundy* means a command. At the Last Supper, Jesus commanded his followers to love one another.

12. Good Friday, the saddest of Christian holidays, recalls the Friday of the Crucifixion. It is a day of mourning. The name is probably a variation of *God's Friday*. Current American Good Friday customs **include** attending church services and eating hot cross buns, which are popular throughout Lent.

13. Easter Sunday begins early for many Americans. Many people attend sunrise services, a custom brought to this country by European settlers. Easter is a family day. After services, relatives get together for Easter dinner.

14. It is an almost **universal** custom to wear something new on Easter. This tradition was a part of pagan spring festivals. It also reflects the early Christian custom of new white Easter robes for the newly baptized. Many American cities have Easter parades, and people enjoy the return of warmer weather by walking outdoors to display their new spring clothes.

PASSOVER

15. Passover, the festival which Jesus was celebrating at the Last Supper, is still one of the most important Jewish holidays. It is a tribute to freedom, reminding Jews of their liberation from slavery in ancient Egypt.

16. According to the Old Testament, almost 4,000 years ago the Hebrews (Jews) were slaves in Egypt. The men were used as workers to build great Egyptian monuments. When Moses asked Pharaoh, the ruler of Egypt, to let the Hebrews make a religious pilgrimage, Pharaoh refused. For this refusal, God punished Egypt with a **series** of horrible **plagues.** The last and worst plague was the death of every Egyptian firstborn son. The Hebrews escaped this punishment by putting the blood of a lamb on their doorposts. The Angel of Death passed over households so marked. Thus, the holiday is called *Passover.*

17. After this final plague, Pharaoh agreed to release the Hebrews. Then he changed his mind and sent his soldiers after them. Another miracle—the parting of the Red Sea—allowed the Hebrews to escape from their Egyptian pursuers.

18. While preparing to flee from Egypt, the Hebrews ate flat bread (called *matzos*) because there was no time to wait for their **dough** to rise. Today, Jews all over the world observe Passover and eat matzos in memory of the **hardships** their ancestors suffered. Orthodox and Conservative Jews outside Israel observe the holiday for eight days, Reform Jews and Israeli Jews for seven.

19. Passover, like all Jewish holidays, begins after sunset. On the first and second nights of the holiday, Jewish families have a special feast called a **seder.** At this holiday dinner, they sing songs, say prayers, and retell the story of the escape from Egypt. On the seder table, there is always wine, a sacramental beverage that is part of most Jewish religious services.

Foods that symbolize the story of Passover are also used in the religious ceremony. In addition to the matzos (called the bread of affliction or suffering), there is a bitter herb (often a horseradish root) to recall the bitterness of a life of slavery. There is also an apple, nut, and wine mixture, which symbolizes the mortar that the Jewish slaves used when they were forced to build Egyptian monuments.

20. The Passover story of escape from slavery is, to many Christians, a foreshadowing of humanity's **release** from sin through the death and Resurrection of Christ. Thus, in many ways the spring holidays of Easter and Passover remind us of the common heritage of Christians and Jews the world over.

EXERCISES

I. Comprehension Questions. Answer the following questions on paper or in class discussion.

1. According to the New Testament, what happened to Jesus Christ on Good Friday and on Easter Sunday?
2. What are some popular Easter customs in the U.S.A. today?
3. What does the Jewish holiday of Passover celebrate? In what ways is it related to Easter?
4. Some of the customs of Easter originated with pagan spring holidays. In your native country, are there any holidays celebrating the arrival of spring? If so, what are some of the customs?

II. Vocabulary Practice. Pronounce the following words after your teacher, and discuss their meanings. Then use some of them to complete the following sentences.

astronomers	plagues
carnival	pray
Crucifixion	profound
dough	release
fertility	Resurrection
guide	sacrifice
hardships	seder
include	series
observe	symbols
paradox	universal

1. The Easter egg and the Easter bunny are ________________ of ________________ (the ability to create new life).

2. A ________________ is a statement that seems to contradict itself but really doesn't.

3. The ________________ refers to the death of Christ on the cross, and the ________________ refers to his coming to life again.

4. A ________________ idea is one that is very deep; it has many levels of meaning. It is also a serious and important idea.

5. The Egyptians allowed the Jews to leave Egypt after Egyptian families suffered the ________________ of a series of ________________.

6. The Passover holiday begins with a religious service and dinner called a ________________.

7. In ancient times, the full moon provided enough light to ________________ travelers to Easter celebrations.

8. Both Christians and Jews ________________ to God to express thanks and to ask for guidance, help, and understanding.

III. Word Study.

A. Match the opposites by writing the correct number on each line.

1. ancestor	___ celebrate
2. fast	___ descendant

3. include ___ sunset

4. mourn ___ feast

5. profound ___ trivial; on the surface

6. sunrise ___ exclude; pass over

B. Studying the homonyms *die/dye, altar/alter,* and *morning/mourning:* Complete each sentence by underlining the correct homonym. Note: die (dying, died); dye (dyeing, dyed)

1. According to the *New Testament,* Jesus Christ (died; dyed) on the cross.
2. (Dying; Dyeing) Easter eggs is fun.
3. In the U.S.A., many women (dye; die) their hair.
4. The church (alter; altar) is in the front of the church.
5. If your new dress is too big on you, you can (alter; altar) it.
6. Many Christians go to church on Easter (morning; mourning).
7. Good Friday is a day of (morning; mourning) in remembrance of the Crucifixion of Christ.

C. Studying prefixes meaning *before*:
The prefixes *fore-*and *pre-*both mean *before.* Discuss the meanings of the following words in this chapter:

forehead precede foreshadowing pre-Christian times

IV. Idiom Study. Underline the best choice to complete each sentence. The numbers in brackets give the paragraphs in which the idioms are used.

1. "They wanted Easter *to fall on* [2] a Sunday" means a) occur on b) drop on c) not happen on.
2. The *full moon* [2] looks like a) a circle b) a half-circle c) a crescent.
3. *Mardi Gras* [8] is a French name for a) a day of the week b) a celebration before Lent c) a day of mourning.
4. On Easter Sunday, relatives *get together* [13]. That means they a) get some gifts b) stop arguing c) spend the day with each other.
5. If your teacher *passes over* [16] you in class, he or she a) calls on you to speak b) doesn't call on you to speak c) walks above you.

V. Reading Skills.

A. Using context clues: Circle the correct word or phrase.

1. In paragraph 1, *spiritual rebirth* means a) giving birth to a spirit b) renewing one's religious faith c) becoming a ghost.
2. In paragraph 2, the date 325 A.D. refers to a time a) before the birth of Christ b) after the birth of Christ c) before 325 B.C.
3. In paragraph 7, *observe* means a) to look at carefully b) to notice c) to celebrate.
4. In paragraph 9, *fasting* means a) doing something quickly b) not eating c) praying with great speed.
5. In paragraph 18, *dough* means a) money b) uncooked bread c) a female deer.
6. In paragraph 18, the verb *rise* means a) to increase in amount b) to come to life again c) to stand up.
7. In paragraph 3, the verb *rose* means a) came to life again b) stood up c) a kind of flower.

B. Studying paradoxes: Which of the following statements are expressed in a paradoxical manner? Circle the paradoxes.

1. He likes to work hard because he enjoys his work.
2. The hardest work can sometimes be the most fun.
3. Playing it safe can be very dangerous.
4. Your life will be dull if you never take risks.

C. Using capital letters:

1. In this chapter, why are the following words capitalized?

Egypt ____

Jews ____

Passover ____

God ____

2. Discuss other uses of capital letters that you noticed in this chapter.

16

PATRIOTIC HOLIDAYS

1. In addition to the birthdays of Lincoln and Washington, Americans celebrate four other **patriotic** holidays: Memorial Day, Veterans Day, Flag Day, and Independence Day.

MEMORIAL DAY

2. Memorial Day, originally established to honor the Civil War dead, now honors all Americans who served in the military and gave their lives for their country. Unofficially, the holiday has been extended beyond its military connection to become a day of general **tribute** to the dead. On Memorial Day, cemeteries are crowded with families who come to place flowers on the **graves** of their loved ones.

3. Shortly after the bitter and bloody Civil War between the North and South, the women of Columbus, Mississippi decorated the graves of both Confederate and Union soldiers, thus honoring the war dead who were their enemies along with their defenders. Northerners were touched by this **gesture** and saw it as a symbol of national unity. In 1868, Decoration Day—now called Memorial Day—became a legal holiday.

4. In most states, Memorial Day is celebrated on the last Monday in May. Some Southern states observe a Confederate Memorial Day in memory of the soldiers who fought in the Confederate army. The date of this holiday varies from one state to another.

5. The military origin of Memorial Day is evident in the parades and customs which mark the occasion. Military exercises are held at Gettysburg National Military Park in Pennsylvania and at the National Cemetery in Arlington, Virginia.

VETERANS DAY

6. Veterans Day, like Memorial Day, is a **solemn** occasion honoring men and women who have served in the military. Originally, the

holiday was called *Armistice Day*. It was established by President Wilson in 1919 to commemorate the signing of the **armistice** (on November 11, 1918) which brought an end to World War I. In 1954, President Eisenhower signed a bill changing the name of the holiday to Veterans Day and extending its **significance** so that it now honors American **veterans** of all wars. It reminds us of the tragedies of war and is celebrated as a day dedicated to world peace. The holiday is celebrated on November 11 throughout the U.S.A.

7. On Veterans Day, the flag is displayed, and veterans march in parades in many communities. Special services are held at the Tomb of the Unknown Soldier in Arlington National Cemetery. To Americans, the Unknown Soldier symbolizes everyone who died in defense of the U.S.A.

FLAG DAY

8. Flag Day, June 14, is the birthday of the American flag. On this date in 1777, the Continental Congress adopted a resolution stating that the flag of the new nation should have 13 **horizontal stripes** (seven red ones and six white ones) to symbolize the 13 colonies and 13 white **stars** arranged in a circle to symbolize the unity and equality of these colonies.

9. This **original** design was created by George Washington and two other revolutionary leaders. In 1776, after the colonies had declared their independence, Washington and two other men were asked to design a national flag. The colors they chose were red for courage, white for liberty, and blue for **loyalty**. According to American legend, they brought a drawing to Betsy Ross, a young widow who was an excellent **seamstress**. She followed their design exactly, except for suggesting that the stars be five-pointed, not six-pointed. Because she made the first American flag, Betsy Ross's name is still well-known to Americans. Her little home in Philadelphia has been preserved as a monument, and tens of thousands of tourists visit it each year.

10. The American flag has been redesigned many times since Betsy Ross made the original. Today, the flag still contains 13 stripes in honor of the original colonies. But now there are 50 stars (one for each state) arranged in nine rows, alternating with six stars in one row and five in the next. Because of its design, the American flag has been nicknamed the *Stars and Stripes*.

11. In school, children memorize and often **recite** the following Pledge of **Allegiance** to the flag:

> I pledge allegiance to the flag of the United States of America and to the Republic for which it stands, one Nation under God, indivisible, with liberty and justice for all.

Americans recite this pledge with the right hand held over the heart to show devotion to the flag and to the nation that it represents. The country's national **anthem**, "The Star Spangled Banner," is also a tribute to the flag. It is sung at the opening of most public **gatherings**.

INDEPENDENCE DAY

12. Independence Day, our most important patriotic holiday, celebrates the birth of the nation. In 1776, the 13 American colonies were in the midst of their Revolutionary War against Great Britain. On the Fourth of July of that year, the Continental Congress adopted the Declaration of Independence—a document which declared the colonies free and independent states. It is the signing and the significance of this document that Americans remember on July 4th. On this date in 1976, Americans celebrated, with lavish festivities, the bicentennial (200th anniversary) of this historic **document.**

13. The Declaration of Independence was written by Thomas Jefferson, who later became the young nation's third president. Its most famous paragraph sums up the ideals of Americans from colonial days to the present:

> We hold these Truths to be self-evident, that all Men are created equal, that they are endowed by their Creator with certain unalienable Rights, that among these are Life, Liberty, and the Pursuit of Happiness—That to secure these Rights, Governments are instituted among Men, deriving their just Powers from the Consent of the Governed.

14. Since Independence Day is a summer holiday and a day off from work for almost everyone, many families enjoy picnics or beach outings on that day. The occasion is also commemorated by colorful and noisy **fireworks** displays, parades, and, in some communities, patriotic speeches. The flag is flown, and red, white, and blue ribbons are used for decoration at public ceremonies. Throughout the nation, church bells ring in memory of the Philadelphia Liberty Bell that first announced American independence.

EXERCISES

I. Comprehension Questions. Answer the following questions on paper or in class discussion.

1. Two of the four holidays discussed in this chapter are birthday celebrations. Which are they, and what do they celebrate?
2. Why do some of the Southern states have a separate Memorial Day holiday?
3. Of the four holidays discussed in this chapter, which two seem the most similar to you? Why?
4. Why does the U.S.A. have these patriotic holidays? Do they serve any purpose?

II. Vocabulary Practice. Pronounce the following words after your teacher, and discuss their meanings. Then use some of them to complete the following sentences.

allegiance	original
anthem	patriotic
armistice	recite
document	seamstress
fireworks	significance
gathering	solemn
gesture	stars
graves	stripes
horizontal	tribute
loyalty	veterans

1. When you are standing up, your body is vertical. When you are lying down, you are in a ________________ position.
2. A country's national ________________ is a special song that expresses love of one's country.
3. Memorial Day is a ________________ (serious) holiday in honor of the dead.

4. The Declaration of Independence is a very important ________________ in American history.

5. People who were in one of the branches of military service are called ________________.

6. When they ________________ the Pledge of Allegiance to the Flag, Americans place the right hand over the heart, a ________________ that shows love and respect for the flag and the nation.

7. Noisy and colorful ________________ are a traditional part of an Independence Day celebration.

8. Today's American flag has 13 ________________ and 50 ________________.

III. Word Study.

A. Discuss the meanings of these related words: *memorial, memory, remember, memorize,* and *commemorate.* Which one means the same as the verb *recall?* ________________

B. Look up the word *grave* in a dictionary. Write down two meanings:

as a noun ____;

as an adjective ____.

IV. Idiom Study. Underline the phrase that best completes each sentence. The numbers in brackets give the paragraphs in which the idioms are used.

1. Members of the military who *gave their lives for their country* [2] were probably a) killed in battle b) in the military until they retired c) veterans.
2. "Northerners *were touched by* [3] this gesture" means that a) the Southerners held their hands b) the Northerners had emotional feelings about the event c) Northerners were frightened by the event.
3. When you *mark an occasion* [5], you a) write the date on your calendar b) do something special in honor of the occasion c) forget about the occasion.
4. The *Stars and Stripes* [10] is a nickname for the a) Fourth of July holiday b) American flag c) Declaration of Independence.

V. Reading Skills.

A. Reread paragraphs 8 through 10, and then mark each of the following statements true (T) or false (F).

___ 1. The American flag has more white stripes than red stripes.

___ 2. Betsy Ross designed the first American flag.

___ 3. Today's American flag looks exactly like the one that Betsy Ross made.

___ 4. Today's American flag has 50 five-pointed stars.

B. Reread the Pledge of Allegiance to the Flag in paragraph 11. What does the person reciting it promise to do?

____

C. Paragraph 13 quotes a difficult but very famous part of the Declaration of Independence. The following exercise uses vocabulary from this quote. Match each word with its definition by writing the correct number on each line.

1. self-evident ___ rightful

2. secure ___ obvious; easy to see

3. endowed ___ given

4. instituted ___ getting

5. deriving ___ protect and keep

6. just ___ created; established

According to paragraph 13, what is the purpose of a government?

____

Where does the U.S. government get its powers?

____

17

A NATION OF IMMIGRANTS

1. In 1958, a young senator from Massachusetts published a book called *A Nation of Immigrants.* He was a wealthy and well-known American whose great-grandfather had come to the United States as a poor Irish immigrant. The author's name was John F. Kennedy, later the 35th President of the United States.

2. In his book, Kennedy pointed out, "Every American who ever lived...was either an immigrant himself or a **descendant** of **immigrants.**" This nation of more than 244 million was built by about 57 million immigrants and their descendants. They came from everywhere, bringing the skills, ambition, and courage to **convert** a vast wilderness into a great industrial nation.

3. From 1820 to 1987, about 36.7 million immigrants came from Europe, 6.2 million from Asia, and 11 million from the Americas. What made all these people leave their homelands to come to a **foreign** country? Said President Kennedy, "Three strong forces—religious **persecution,** political **oppression,** and economic hardship—provided the chief **motives** for the mass migrations to our shores." Whatever their reasons, this influx of people who came to live in the U.S.A. represents the largest migration that the human race has ever known.

IMMIGRATION BEFORE INDEPENDENCE

4. Today's American Indians call themselves *Native Americans,* but in reality they were not natives here. Rather, they were the area's earliest immigrants. They came to the Western Hemisphere from Asia more than 20,000 years ago. By the 15th century, there were 15 to 20 million Indians in the Americas. Perhaps as many as 700,000 were living within the present limits of the United States when Columbus discovered the New World (the Western Hemisphere) in 1492.

5. During the 1500s, French and Spanish explorers visited the New World. But the first Europeans who came to stay were English. The first **permanent** colony in the U.S.A. was established in Jamestown, Virginia in 1607 by 104 British colonists. In 1620, a second British colony, consisting of 102 people, was founded in Plymouth, Massachusetts. These were the beginnings of a nation that, by 1988, had grown to 244 million.

6. In 1790, the white population of the 13 original states totaled slightly more than three million. About 75% of these first Americans were of British ancestry; the rest were German, Dutch, French, Swiss, and Spanish. The British gave the new nation its language, laws, and philosophy of government.

IMMIGRATION FROM 1790 TO 1920

7. American independence did not immediately stimulate immigration. Between 1790 and 1840, fewer than one million foreigners entered the country. But between 1841 and 1860, more than four million arrived. They came primarily from Ireland, England, Germany, and France. Potato crop failures in Ireland stimulated Irish immigration. Germans came to escape economic and political difficulties. During the last half of the 19th century, many Scandinavians came, attracted by good farmland. The Industrial Revolution and the Westward Movement gave new immigrants a **vital** role in the nation's economic development. Employers who needed factory workers and landowners who wanted tenants for western lands sent agents to Europe to "sell" America. Agents of steamship lines and railroad companies attracted thousands of immigrants with fabulous stories about the land of opportunity.

8. Immigration took another great leap after 1880. Between 1881 and 1920, 23.5 million **aliens** were admitted. Nearly 90% of these newcomers were from Europe. After 1882, the government kept Asian immigration to a minimum because American workers feared that new Asian immigrants would threaten their jobs and lower their wages.

9. In the 1890s, the sources of European immigration began to shift. Between 1881 and 1890, 80% of American immigrants had come from Northern and Western Europe. By 1911, 77% were coming from Southern and Eastern Europe–Italy, Russia, Austria-Hungary, Romania, Bulgaria, Greece, and areas that later became Poland and Czechoslovakia. Many of those from Russia, Romania, and Poland were Jews **flee**ing religious persecution.

IMMIGRATION SINCE 1920

10. During World War I, immigration declined due to traveling difficulties. After the war, Europeans once again began crowding aboard ships to the United States. But American industry no longer needed them. During the 1920s, Congress passed the first **quota** law that limited the number of European immigrants.

11. From 1930 to 1945, legal limits and World War II kept immigration to a minimum. When the war ended, immigration rose sharply because entrance was allowed to millions of people left homeless by the war. Special legislation admitted large numbers of displaced persons, **refugees,** and orphans, as well as war brides. From time to time since then, the United States has lifted immigration **restrictions** to accommodate refugees and ease suffering in other parts of the world. In 1958, thousands of Hungarians were admitted, and in the early 1960s, because of the revolution in Cuba, more than 150,000 Cubans entered the U.S.A. To relieve crowded conditions in Hong Kong, several thousand nonquota Chinese were also permitted entry. In 1979, the United States admitted more than 20,000 Vietnamese refugees per month. In the late 1970s and 1980s, many thousands of Russian Jews were also allowed to enter.

12. At present, there is a ceiling on immigration, allowing for 270,000 immigrants to be admitted to the U.S.A. annually, no more than 20,000 from any one country. However, during the 1980s, the number of immigrants actually admitted each year always exceeded 500,000 because certain categories of applicants were excluded from the numerical limitations. These exemptions included the parents, spouses, or minor children of U.S. citizens.

13. Immigration restrictions may seem cruel to those who are living in difficult circumstances elsewhere, but they have become necessary because, in the 20th century, the United States' population has grown at a very rapid rate. In 1915, the population reached 100 million. Forty-two years later, it had **doubled.** A higher birth rate, lower infant mortality, and longer life expectancy had all combined to cause this population explosion. Today, Americans are having smaller families. However, the population is continuing to increase, and about 28% of this growth comes from immigration. Therefore, strict limits on immigration seem likely to continue.

14. Who are today's immigrants? They are vastly different from earlier groups. Clearly, the ethnic make-up of the United States is changing. From 1981 to 1985, immigration from Europe dropped to 11% of the total legal immigration, while Asia provided about 48% and Latin America about 35% of legal immigrants. In addition, about three-quarters of the illegal immigrants (about 500,000 per year) come from Latin America. If the current trends continue, experts predict that, by the year 2020, about 35% of Americans will be minority group members, primarily black,

Hispanic, or Asian. Looking even further ahead, by 2090, descendants of non-Hispanic European whites will be in the minority in the U.S.A.

THE HISPANIC POPULATION

15. About 19 million people living in the U.S.A. (about 8% of the population) belong to a Spanish-speaking ethnic group and name Spanish as their first language. These people are called *Hispanics* (or *Latinos*). Hispanics form the second largest cultural minority in the United States, after the nation's 30 million blacks. The Hispanic population is younger than the national average, and their birth rate is higher, so they are the most rapidly growing minority group in the country. In the 1980s, the Hispanic population grew about 34% while the non-Hispanic population grew about 7%. As a result, Hispanics are becoming an increasingly important cultural and political force.

16. The three largest Hispanic groups in the U.S.A. are the Mexicans, Puerto Ricans, and Cubans. Mexican-Americans, numbering about 12 million, are the largest of these three. About 70% of Mexican-Americans live in Texas and California, with nearly a million in Los Angeles alone. New Mexico, Arizona, and Colorado also have large Mexican populations.

17. Mexicans have an important place in American history. They helped establish Los Angeles and many other settlements that later became major American cities. Also, they taught important methods of farming, mining, and ranching to Americans who settled in the West. When the Mexican-American War ended in 1848, the peace treaty gave the United States more than 525,000 square miles of territory in the Southwest, for which Mexico was paid $15 million. Mexicans living in this area were automatically granted American citizenship. Because of these Mexican-Americans, California, New Mexico, and Colorado all entered the union as **bilingual** states.

18. Between 1910 and 1930, nearly two million Mexicans immigrated to the U.S.A. During this period, the term *Chicano* became a form of **insult** to Mexican-Americans. Today, it is the name Mexican-Americans use to refer proudly to themselves.

19. The island of Puerto Rico is located about 1,000 miles southeast of Florida. In 1878, during the brief Spanish-American War, the United States won Puerto Rico (along with Guam and the Philippine Islands) from Spain. Puerto Rico has remained part of the United States ever since. Puerto Ricans are American citizens, and they can travel to and from the nation's mainland without immigration restrictions. About 2.5 million Puerto Ricans live on the mainland, the majority in or near New York City.

20. In its relationship with the United States government, Puerto Rico has what is called *commonwealth status*. It receives protection and assistance from the federal government but has some local authority over its internal affairs. Puerto Ricans who live on the island cannot vote in the nation's elections nor do they pay federal income taxes. Among Puerto Ricans, there is disagreement about political goals for the island. Some are satisfied with the commonwealth status, some advocate statehood, and others want the island to become independent.

21. Cuban immigrants and their children make up the third largest group of Hispanics. About one million Cubans now live in the United States. Most of them came here as exiles during or after 1959, when Fidel Castro took over the Cuban government and the country became Communist. Most of the Cubans in the United States live in Southern Florida, Puerto Rico, New York City, and New Jersey. The Cuban population is largely middle-class. Many of these immigrants are educated people with backgrounds in professions or business. As a result, they have had more economic success in the U.S.A. than many other Hispanics.

22. Two other sizable Hispanic groups in the U.S.A. are the Colombians and the Dominicans (from the Dominican Republic). Colombians are probably the largest group of South Americans living in the U.S.A., numbering about 50,000. Altogether, there are about 2.2 million immigrants from Central and South America.

23. In the U.S.A., Hispanics as a group have many problems. Because of lower levels of education, difficulties with English, and **discrimination,** they hold fewer jobs in the professions and management and earn less money than the average American. In addition, they hold relatively few positions in government. National Hispanic organizations are working to unite the various Latino groups, expand their educational and vocational opportunities, and increase their voter registration and political power.

ILLEGAL ALIENS AND THE NEW IMMIGRATION LAW

24. Illegal aliens are people living in the U.S.A. without proper authorization. Many entered the country by sneaking across the border. Others came on temporary student or visitor visas and did not leave when their visas **expired.** Most illegal aliens want to stay in the U.S.A. because employment opportunities are so much greater than in their native country. Since illegal aliens try hard not to be discovered by the government, it is impossible to get an accurate count of them. Recent estimates have ranged from 2.5 million to as high as 12 million.

25. In 1986, the United States government adopted a new law affecting illegal aliens—the Immigration Reform and Control Act. This law was designed to accomplish two main goals: 1) to allow illegal aliens who had been living in the country since January, 1982 to gain legal status if they applied by May 4, 1988; and 2) to discourage others from coming into or staying in the country illegally by making it difficult for undocumented people to find employment. The law prohibits American employers from hiring illegals and provides for severe penalties—fines and even imprisonment—if they do so. This new law has helped large numbers of formerly illegal aliens to become legal residents. But it also forces employers to check on all prospective employees who look or sound foreign to be sure that they have documents allowing them to work. This may discourage some employers from hiring any immigrants.

THE MANY CONTRIBUTIONS OF IMMIGRANTS

26. This nation of immigrants is rapidly becoming a nation of native-born citizens. Today, the number of foreign-born in the United States makes up only about 6% of the population, and only 11% of Americans are the children of immigrants. The days of mass immigration are probably over. But the influence of the movement will never be erased. Americans have adopted many of the customs and ideas of the immigrants as their own. President Kennedy explained it this way: "...each wave of immigration left its own impact on American society; each made its distinctive 'contribution' to the building of the nation and the evolution of American life."

27. The wide variety of immigrant groups in the United States has given the nation great industrial diversity. Germans, Scandinavians, and Poles share the credit for turning millions of acres of wilderness into productive farmland. Scandinavians also helped to develop the lumbering industry, along with Canadians. The Swedes built the first log cabins. The Swiss brought clock-making and cheese-making skills. The English were experienced in the handling of horses, cattle, and sheep. The Greeks, Italians, Portuguese, and Spanish grew citrus fruits and grapes. Italians started the wine industry. Chinese and Irish laborers built the first railroad that spanned the nation.

28. In addition to their skills, immigrants brought their native customs and beliefs—political and social theories, religions, academic traditions, holidays, festivals, sports, arts, hobbies, foods—and by doing so, they greatly enriched American culture. The Germans introduced the Christmas tree, kindergarten, and the symphony orchestra. The Dutch brought the art of growing tulips, ice skating, bowling, and golf. The French taught Americans elegant continental cooking and dancing. Italians brought their talents in painting, sculpture, and architecture. The Irish firmly established the Catholic Church as an English-speaking institution (originally, on this continent, it was French), introduced parochial schools, and built many Catholic colleges. The Irish also became active in politics and organized the first big nationwide labor union.

29. The American diet has also been delightfully affected by various immigrant groups. The Dutch taught Americans to make waffles and donuts. The Germans brought hamburgers and sausages. Italians introduced Americans to pizza, spaghetti, minestrone, and ravioli. Americans also enjoy Swiss cheeses and fondue, Irish stew, Chinese chow mein, Mexican tacos, Indian curries, Russian caviar, Middle Eastern shish kebab and yogurt, British Yorkshire pudding, Danish pastry, French chocolate mousse, and Turkish coffee. These are just a few of the foreign foods frequently on American dinner tables.

30. The United States has often been called a melting pot because immigrants from all over the world come to the U.S.A. and become one people with a common culture and a common loyalty. But the United States has never been a melting pot in the sense that it melted away all recollections of another way of life in another place. On the contrary, immigrants from the same country tend to settle in the same neighborhoods and establish their native religious and cultural institutions. Most immigrant parents try to teach their children the language, traditions, religious customs, and moral outlook that is their heritage. Some of these traditions are handed down from one generation to another. Many cities and communities have ethnic festivals (featuring food, music, games, and arts and crafts) to bring together people who share a common national heritage. Some festivals are sponsored by one group (for example, people of Italian, Irish, or Polish descent), but others include people from dozens of different cultures. These events remind Americans that the nation is not really a melting pot at all. In fact, in recent years, people have begun to call it a salad bowl. Why? In a salad, many different elements are combined into a whole, but each ingredient also retains its individual identity. That is what happens to people of different cultures when they become American citizens.

31. In spite of the nation's immigrant tradition, it still isn't easy being a newcomer to the U.S.A. Often, there is conflict between the ideas of the old country and those of the new country. Learning English is, for many, a very difficult task. Finding a good job in this highly technological nation is another challenge. Nevertheless, despite the need for tremendous adjustments, most immigrants learn to love their adopted land and to live happily in it. Some of the most **patriotic** Americans are those who have lived and suffered elsewhere. The U.S.A. has given many people a sense of hope and safety that they never had before. In return, immigrants have made immense contributions to their new country. Undoubtedly, the U.S.A. has been strong and prosperous largely because it is a nation of immigrants.

EXERCISES

I. Comprehension Questions. Answer the following questions on paper or in class discussion.

1. Who were the first American immigrants, and where did they come from?
2. What did British immigrants give to the U.S.A.?
3. What are the three main reasons that immigrants have come to the U.S.A.?
4. What do you think are the two main ideas of this chapter? See if you and your classmates agree.

II. Vocabulary Practice. Pronounce the following words after your teacher, and discuss their meanings. Then use some of them to complete the following sentences.

alien	insult
bilingual	motive
convert	oppression
descendant	patriotic
discrimination	permanent
doubled	persecution
expires	quota
flee	refugees
foreign	restriction
immigrants	vital

1. Immigrants often come to the U.S.A. after they ________________ from their native country because of religious or political problems.
2. People who leave their native land and come to live in the U.S.A. are called ________________ or ________________ residents.
3. When a visitor's visa ________________, the visitor to the U.S.A. is supposed to leave the country.
4. ________________ are people who come to the U.S.A. for safety. If they returned to their native country, they might be imprisoned or killed.
5. There is now a ________________ or limit on the number of people who can enter the U.S.A. as permanent residents each year.
6. Two of this chapter's vocabulary words mean *pain, hardship,* or *suffering*. These words are ________________ and ________________.
7. From 1915 to 1947, the population of the U.S.A. increased from 100 million to 200 million. In other words, the population ________________.
8. People who love their country and are loyal to it are called ________________.

III. Word Study. Use an English dictionary to find the meaning(s) of the word or word part that each group of words shares. Write the definitions in the space provided, and discuss the meanings of the words in class.

1. **refuge, refugee**____

2. **migrate,** im**migrant**_____________________________________

3. **linguis**tic, bi**lingual**____________________________________

4. **descend, descend**ant_____________________________________

5. **ex**ile, **ex**emption, **ex**ceed, **ex**clude, **ex**plosion, **ex**pand

   ____

IV. Idiom Study. Use the following five phrases to complete the sentences. The numbers in brackets give the paragraphs in which the idioms are used.

New World [4]	melting pot [30]
land of opportunity [7]	old country [31]
population explosion [13]	salad bowl [30]

1. An immigrant's homeland is sometimes referred to as the

   __________________ .

2. Because American citizens are from many different countries, the U.S.A.

   has been called a __________________ or a __________________ .

3. The number of people living in the U.S.A. increased a great deal in

   a short time. This was called a __________________.

4. The continents of North and South America were called the

   __________________ .

5. To attract Europeans to the U.S.A., the country was advertised as

   a __________________, where workers could find good jobs.

V. Reading Skills.

A. Using context clues: Many words in English have more than one meaning. To understand what you read, you need to study the context in which a particular word appears. Think about the meanings of the words and sentences that surround a word you don't know. Consider the following words from this chapter:

1. The word *declined* sometimes means *refused* (said no). But what does it mean in paragraph 10? ______________________

2. The word *admit* sometimes means to agree that you did something wrong. But what does *admitted* mean in paragraph 11?

____

3. The word *minor* sometimes means *unimportant*. What does it mean in paragraph 12? ______________________

4. The word *ceiling* usually means the top surface of a room. What related meaning does it have in paragraph 12?

____

B. Understanding sentence patterns:

1. Reread paragraph 20, sentence 3. Do Puerto Ricans living on the island pay U.S. income tax? ______________

2. Reread paragraph 25. Find the words *if they do so*. What does *so* refer to? ______________________

18

THE BLACK AMERICAN

1. Today's black Americans are descendants of African Negroes who were brought to the United States by force and sold into slavery. After slavery was **abolished, segregation** in the South and **discrimination** in the North kept blacks second-class citizens for almost another century. Conditions have greatly improved for black Americans during the past 30 years. Among this nation's 30 million blacks are many successful, important, and famous people. However, as a group, blacks remain a disadvantaged minority. Their **struggle** for equal opportunity has been won in the courts of law, but they are still struggling for the respect and prosperity that most other Americans enjoy.

SLAVERY—FROM BEGINNING TO END

2. In the 15th century, Europeans began to import **slaves** from the African continent. The discovery of the Americas increased the **demand** for cheap labor and therefore increased the slave **trade.** During the next 400 years, slave traders **kidnap**ped about 15 million Negroes from Africa and sold them into slavery. When the American Civil War began in 1860, there were about 4.5 million Negroes in the United States, most of them slaves.

3. The vast majority of Negro slaves lived in the South, where they worked in cotton, tobacco, and sugar cane fields. Most were uneducated, although a few were taught to read and write. Their African religious practices were discouraged, and they were converted to Christianity.

4. The slaves suffered greatly, both physically and emotionally. They worked long hours in the fields. They lived in crowded, primitive houses. Some were the victims of cruel masters who abused them. Often, slave owners separated Negro families by selling a slave's husband, wife, or child. *Uncle Tom's Cabin,* a famous novel about Southern slavery, emphasized these evils. The book aroused so much antislavery sentiment in the North that Abraham Lincoln said to its

author, Harriet Beecher Stowe, "So you're the little woman who wrote the book that made this great war."

5. The "great war" that Lincoln was talking about was, of course, the American Civil War, sometimes called the War between the States. Slavery was the **underlying** cause of this war. The agricultural South depended on slave labor to work the fields of its large **plantations.** The industrialized North had no use for slave labor, and slavery was against the law there. Northerners considered slavery a great evil, and, in fact, some of them helped Negroes escape from slavery to one of the free states. By the mid-19th century, the nation was divided between slave states and free states. Whenever a new state wanted to enter the Union, the question of whether it would be slave or free was raised. Finally, the South decided to leave the Union and become a separate country—the Confederate States of America. President Lincoln would not allow this. In order to keep the United States united, Lincoln led his nation into a civil war. (For further information about Lincoln and the Civil War, see Chapter 13.) The war ended in 1865 with the North victorious, the country reunited, and slavery abolished.

6. In 1863, two years before the war ended, Lincoln's Emancipation Proclamation freed the slaves in the Confederate states. Shortly after the war ended in 1865, the Thirteenth Amendment to the Constitution freed all slaves. A few years later, the Fourteenth and Fifteenth Amendments gave the former slaves full civil rights, including the right to vote.

FREEDOM AND ITS DIFFICULTIES

7. By 1870, black Americans had been declared citizens with all the rights guaranteed to every citizen. But they were members of a conspicuous minority within a white society. Furthermore, most were uneducated, unskilled, and unprepared to provide for their own basic needs. With freedom, Negroes found many new problems—legal, social, and economic.

8. After the Civil War, Negroes began migrating to the big cities in the North, and this trend continued into the 20th century. In the North, blacks found greater freedom, but conditions were still difficult and opportunities limited. Discrimination in the sale and rental of housing forced blacks into poor, crowded, mostly black communities often referred to as **ghettos.** In general, **facilities** for living and learning were grossly inadequate in these communities.

9. Blacks who remained in the South endured conditions even more difficult and degrading. Southern blacks were forced to obey state laws (called *Jim Crow laws*) which kept them segregated from white people. The races went to different schools, drank from different fountains, used different washrooms, ate in different restaurants, and were buried in different cemeteries. On buses, blacks were required to sit in the back. For Southern blacks, there was no such thing as justice in the courts of law. Once accused of a crime, blacks were almost certain to be found guilty by all-white juries.

10. Southern whites, who wished to keep the power of the vote from the large black population of the South, used the threat of violence to discourage blacks from registering to vote. When a black person did try to register, **devices** such as a poll tax (a tax on the right to vote) or a literacy test (unfairly administered) were used to deny this right.

THE CIVIL RIGHTS MOVEMENT

11. The first break in the South's segregated way of life came in 1954 when the United States Supreme Court declared that no state could separate students by race. Thereafter, many other discriminatory practices were declared illegal.

12. The Supreme Court's school desegregation decision stimulated black hopes for a better life in the United States. During the mid-1950s, blacks throughout the nation began demanding equal rights. Their revolution started as a nonviolent movement consisting of **boycotts,** sit-ins (blacks calmly sitting for hours at lunch counters or in restaurants that refused to serve them), freedom rides (busloads of Northern liberals coming to the South to force integration of public facilities), and **protest** marches.

13. In the 1960s, the struggle sometimes led to violence, committed by both blacks and whites. Many cities experienced riots involving burglary, arson, and street battles between rioters and police.

14. During the 1960s, the greatest black leader was Dr. Martin Luther King, Jr. In 1955, King was a young Baptist minister in Montgomery, Alabama when he formed an organization to boycott his city's buses. Because of regulations requiring blacks to sit in the back of the bus and to give their seats to whites if the bus got crowded, nearly all of Montgomery's 50,000 blacks refused to ride the city's buses for more than a year. Eventually, the U.S. Supreme Court declared that dividing buses into black and white sections was unconstitutional (illegal).

15. The Montgomery bus boycott made Dr. King a famous man and the unofficial leader of the nation's growing Civil Rights Movement. King's philosophy showed the influence of his Christian beliefs and the example of Mohandas Gandhi (the great Indian leader whose nonviolent protests helped to free his people from British control). King urged people to refuse to obey evil laws and regulations, but to protest without fighting and without resisting arrest. For more than a **decade,** King led nonviolent protests and traveled around the country speaking to American audiences in person and on TV. His most famous speech was delivered in 1963 in front of the Lincoln Memorial in Washington, D.C., before a live audience of 200,000 and a TV audience of almost the entire nation. His message included these memorable words: "I have a dream that one day this nation will rise up and live out the true meaning of its creed: 'We hold these truths to be self-evident; that all men are created equal.' "

16. In 1964, at the age of 35, King became the youngest person ever to win the Nobel Peace Prize. During the next few years, his concerns expanded from the problems of segregation in the South to discrimination in the North and, finally, to the suffering of poor people of all races. He was organizing a poor people's march at the time of his **assassination,** on April 4, 1968, when he was only 39 years old. King once said that the assassination of Gandhi only "shot him into the hearts of humanity." Surely the tragic killing of Dr. Martin Luther King, Jr. led to the same result. Today, a great many buildings, streets, and schools are named after him, and his birthday has become a national holiday, celebrated on the third Monday in January. Most important, because of King and other civil rights leaders, black Americans today have a greater sense of **self-esteem.**

17. During the 1960s, Americans of African descent rejected the name *Negro* and began referring to themselves as *black.* (Today, some prefer to be identified as *African-Americans.*) The popular slogan, "Black is beautiful," expressed the new black pride. Blacks also developed a greater sense of identification with their African heritage. As a result, African hairdos and styles of dress became fashionable. Courses in black history became common in college curriculums as blacks became interested in studying about their African past and their role in the development of the United States.

18. The 1970s and 1980s brought a decline in public concern about black needs. The federal government and the general public turned their attention to other problems, and federal funds for many programs that helped poor blacks were decreased. In the 1970s and 1980s, blacks continued to make social, academic, political, and economic progress, but at a slower pace than they had hoped.

BLACK AMERICANS TODAY

19. In 1952, a black writer named Ralph Ellison wrote a book about blacks in the U.S.A. and entitled it *The Invisible Man.* Since the 1960s, blacks have become more visible, especially on TV. Networks and advertisers realize that 12% of Americans are black, and that they, too, are consumers. Now, there are black models in TV commercials, black newscasters, and black actors and actresses in a wide variety of TV shows. Blacks also appear frequently in movies.

20. Black leaders of the 1970s and 1980s have worked hard to increase two kinds of black power—economic and political. Of course, there is a connection between these two, since more political power for blacks can lead to increased federal and state spending for programs to meet their greatest needs—education, financial assistance, job training, and housing.

21. Many urban blacks still live in neighborhoods that are in depressingly poor condition, with deteriorating buildings and empty lots full of weeds and broken glass. In these slum areas, the crime rate is high, drug pushers and addicts are **commonplace,** and the fear of teenage gangs makes residents afraid to go out after dark.

22. Poverty continues to be an overwhelming problem for blacks as they remain far behind white Americans and somewhat behind other minority groups in income and employment levels. The unemployment rate for blacks, about 10%, is more than double that of whites. The median family income for black families is about $18,000, compared to $32,000 for whites. About one-third of all blacks (and about one-half of all black children) are poor. The high rate of poverty is largely because many blacks do not have skills that are needed for better-paying jobs.

23. Realizing that more education will help them get better jobs, blacks are staying in school longer now than in past decades. In 1960, only about 38% of young black adults finished high school. Today, the figure is about 72%. In 1970, about 440,000 blacks were enrolled in college. By 1986, the figure was up to 820,000. However, the percentage of black high school graduates enrolling in college has been dropping in recent years, although most colleges and universities **recruit** blacks actively and offer special services to help them succeed. Many blacks who begin college do not finish, sometimes because of academic difficulties, often because of family financial problems.

24. Blacks are also trying to improve their financial position by operating their own businesses. There are now more than 200,000 black-owned companies in the U.S.A.

25. In politics, black gains have been impressive. Now that more blacks are voting, more are getting elected. In 1987, 6,681 blacks held elected positions in local, state, and federal government, compared to 1,472 in 1970. Among these were 303 black mayors (several of major cities), 311 state legislators, and 23 representatives in Congress. One of the most well-known black politicians is the Reverend Jesse Jackson, who received impressive numbers of votes in his campaigns for the Democratic nomination for President. However, blacks are still underrepresented in government; with 12% of the population, they hold only 1.3% of the elected offices.

CONTRIBUTIONS—PAST AND PRESENT

26. The chief influence of the American Negro culture—nationally and internationally—has been in the field of music. The familiar Negro spirituals, the unusual rhythms and harmonies of jazz, the haunting blues melodies—all these originated with the Negro slaves. It is often said that what is best and most original in American popular music comes from the Negro idiom.

27. Many blacks have become famous entertainers or athletes. Eddie Murphy and Bill Cosby are just two of several famous black comedians. Two superstars—singer Michael Jackson and basketball player Michael Jordan—have become national idols of the young. In intellectual fields as well, blacks have made great contributions. Many are highly respected professional people—teachers, doctors, lawyers, judges, and ministers. One of the most interesting of black American scholars was George Washington Carver, the famous botanist. Carver began his life as a slave. Later, he revolutionized the agriculture of the South. Carver also developed more than 300 products from the peanut (including soap and ink) and 118 products from the sweet potato (including flour, shoe polish, and candy). Among the many outstanding black American authors of the past and present are poets Gwendolyn Brooks and Maya Angelou and novelists James Baldwin, Ralph Ellison, Richard Wright, Toni Morrison, and Alice Walker. Thurgood Marshall has been serving on the Supreme Court since 1967.

28. Given an equal opportunity to learn and to work, black Americans will contribute even more to this country. In order to make full use of its human resources, the United States must make sure that its customs and institutions extend equal privileges to all Americans.

EXERCISES

I. Comprehension Questions. Answer the following questions on paper or in class discussion.

1. Before the Civil War, what was life like for most Negroes in the U.S.A.?
2. What caused the American Civil War?
3. What were some of the main ideas and accomplishments of Dr. Martin Luther King, Jr.?
4. How are black Americans doing today? Are they still second-class citizens in the U.S.A.?

II. Vocabulary Practice. Pronounce the following words after your teacher, and discuss their meanings. Then use some of them to complete the following sentences.

abolished	kidnap
assassination	plantation
boycott	protested
commonplace	recruit
decade	segregation
demand	self-esteem
devices	slaves
discrimination	struggle
facilities	trade
ghettos	underlying

1. ________________ means the killing of a person for political reasons.
2. The immediate cause of the Civil War was the secession of the South, but the ________________ cause was slavery.
3. When you ________________ a product, you refuse to buy it.
4. In the '60s, Northern liberals and Southerners ________________ against segregation by having sit-ins and marches.

5. The Southern ________________ was a large farm on which the owners grew cotton or tobacco. The work was done by ________________ .

6. The 1960s was a ________________ of protest.

7. When slavery ended in the South, ________________ became the way of life. That meant that blacks and whites lived, studied, and played in different places.

8. The slave ________________ was the kidnapping and selling of Africans to white Europeans and Americans. It lasted for about 400 years.

III. Word Study.

A. *Live* spells two different words. One is a verb with a short *i* sound. The other is an adjective with a long *i* sound. There is also an adjective *alive* (pronounced with a long *i* sound). Read the following sentences aloud to practice these words.

1. Martin Luther King, Jr.'s speeches were heard by live audiences and by radio and TV audiences.
2. Black slaves lived in primitive homes.
3. Martin Luther King, Jr. is no longer alive.
4. A live dog is more fun than a toy dog.

B. Pronounce in class the following words from this chapter. Both have a silent *u:*

building
guilty

C. The following words help a reader understand the relationship between ideas. Match each word with its definition by writing the correct numbers on each line. The numbers in brackets give the paragraphs in which the words are used.

1. however [1,23,25]	___ after a long time
2. therefore [2]	___ but
3. furthermore [7]	___ in addition, also, and
4. eventually [14]	___ as a result

IV. Idiom Study. Underline the correct phrase to complete each sentence. The numbers in brackets give the paragraphs in which the idioms are used.

1. *Second-class* [1] means a a) rating of quality not as good as first class b) military rank c) grade in school.
2. Before the Civil War, *free states* [5] were those that a) didn't charge taxes b) gave away land c) didn't allow residents to own slaves.
3. In the 1960s, a *sit-in* [12] was a) a game b) a way of protesting segregation c) blacks sitting in the white section of the buses.

V. Reading Skills.

A. Compare the lives and deaths of Gandhi and King.

1. What kind of protest did both men believe in?______________

2. How did both men die?______________________________

B. Reread the section entitled, "Slavery—from Beginning to End." Then mark the following statements true (T) or false (F).

___1. The slave trade was begun by Americans.

___2. Before the Civil War, most blacks in the U.S.A. lived in the South.

___3. Before the Civil War, some states allowed slavery, and some did not.

___4. The people living in the North didn't care whether or not more states entered the Union as slave states.

___5. The slaves didn't become free until after the Civil War ended.

C. What is the difference between *a civil war* and *the Civil War?* (Both are used in paragraph 5.) ________________________________
____

19

AMERICAN EDUCATION: THE FIRST 12 YEARS

PURPOSE AND SCOPE

1. Americans believe that every citizen has both the right and the obligation to become educated. The citizens of a democracy need to be educated so that they can take part in affairs of government, both local and national. They must also learn **vocational** skills.

2. In order to develop an educated population, all states have **compulsory** school attendance laws. These laws vary somewhat from one state to another, but generally they require that formal schooling begin by age 6 and continue until at least age 16. However, most Americans attend school at least until high school graduation, when they are 17 or 18 years old. About 75% of all American adults and about 85% of younger American adults are high school graduates.

3. The size of the nation's basic educational enterprise is astonishing. From **kindergarten** through high school, about 46 million students are enrolled in school. To educate this vast number of students, Americans employ about 2.7 million teachers, by far the largest professional group in the country.

PUBLIC AND PRIVATE SCHOOLS

4. About 88% of American children receive their **elementary** and high school education in the nation's public schools. These schools have the following important characteristics in common:

a) They are supported by taxes and, therefore, do not charge tuition.

b) In general, they are neighborhood schools, open to all students who live within the district.

c) They are co-educational, which means that boys and girls attend the same schools and have nearly all of their classes together. By providing girls with equal educational opportunity, American public schools have helped to create today's self-sufficient American woman.

d) Public schools are **required** to follow some state guidelines regarding, for example, **curriculum** and teacher qualifications. But, in most matters, schools are locally controlled. Each school district is run by an elected Board of Education and the school administrators that Board hires. This system creates strong ties between the district's schools and its community.

e) Public schools are **nonsectarian** (secular), which means that they are free from the influence of any religion. As a result, children of many different religions feel comfortable attending the public schools, and the public school system has been able to help a diverse population build a common culture.

5. Private schools can be divided into two **categories: parochial** (supported by a particular religious group) and secular (nonreligious). Private schools charge tuition and are not under direct public control, although many states set educational standards for them. In order to attend a private school, a student must apply and be accepted. Parochial schools make up the largest group of private schools, and most of these are operated by the Roman Catholic Church. Private secular schools are mainly high schools and colleges.

COURSE CONTENT AND TEACHING METHODS

6. In educating students for adult work and adult life, American schools try, above all, to be practical. American education has been greatly influenced by the writings of a famous 20th-century philosopher named John Dewey. Dewey believed that the only worthwhile knowledge was knowledge that could be used. He convinced educators that it was pointless to make students memorize useless facts that they would quickly forget. Rather, schools should teach thinking processes and skills that affect how people live and work.

7. Dewey also influenced teaching techniques. Education must be meaningful, and children learn best by doing—these are the basic ideas of progressive education. Thus, science is taught largely through student experimentation; the study of music involves making music; democratic principles are put into practice in the student council; group projects encourage creativity, individual initiative, leadership, and **teamwork.**

8. What do American schools see as their educational responsibility to students? The scope is very broad indeed. Today's schools teach skills and information once left for the parents to teach at home. For example, it is common for the public school curriculum to include a campaign against cigarette smoking and drug abuse, a course in driver's education, cooking and sewing classes, consumer education, and sex education. Most American **grammar** schools have also added computer skills to their curriculum. As human knowledge has expanded and life has become increasingly complex, the schools have had to go far beyond the original three Rs ("reading, writing, and 'rithmetic") that they were created to teach.

9. American high schools have a **dual commitment:** (a) to offer a general college preparatory program for those who are interested in higher education; and (b) to provide opportunities for vocational training for students who plan to enter the work force immediately after high school graduation. For the college-bound, high schools offer advanced classes in math, sciences, social sciences, English, and foreign languages. They also have Advanced Placement (AP) courses, which enable good students to earn college credit while still in high school. But in the same building, other students take vocational courses such as shorthand and mechanical drawing, and some participate in work/study programs which enable them to get high school credit for on-the-job training in various occupations.

10. Today, more than ever before, American schools are committed to helping foreign-born students adjust to life in an American classroom. The Bilingual Education Act of 1968 provided federal funds for bilingual instruction, which allows students to study **academic** subjects totally or partially in their native language while they are learning English. Bilingual education is offered in about 70 languages including Chinese, Spanish, Vietnamese, and several American Indian languages. Of course, this type of instruction is available only where a number of students speak the same foreign language. In addition, immigrant students have benefited from the 1974 Supreme Court ruling requiring public schools to provide special programs for students who speak little or no English. Today, English as a second language instruction is common in American elementary and high schools.

EARLY CHILDHOOD EDUCATION

11. By the age of five, about 87% of American children are attending school, most of them in preacademic classes called *kindergarten*. However, many American youngsters are introduced to their first school setting even before the age of five, through nursery school or day care attendance. In fact, about 29% of three-year-olds and 49% of four-year-olds are enrolled in one or the other.

12. Nursery schools accept children from three to five years of age for half-day sessions ranging from twice a week to five days a week. The typical nursery school is equipped with toys, building blocks, books, puzzles, art supplies, and an outdoor playground. These preschool programs usually charge tuition, although some are **subsidized,** and some offer scholarships. Day care programs are similar facilities that offer all-day care for the children of working parents.

ELEMENTARY SCHOOL AND HIGH SCHOOL

13. In most areas, free public education begins with kindergarten classes for five-year-olds. These are usually half-day classes two or three hours long, although some communities run all-day kindergarten programs. The primary purpose of kindergarten is socialization, but the young students also gain information and skills. For example, they learn to identify colors, count to ten, print their names, work with art supplies, listen to stories, and enjoy books. After kindergarten, American children begin their academic studies. Their schooling is divided into 12 academic levels called ***grades.*** One school year (from late August or early September to mid-June) is required to complete each grade. Academic work—learning to read, write, and do arithmetic—begins when children enter 1st grade, at about age six.

14. The first academic institution that a student attends is called *elementary school* or *grammar school.* In some school systems, elementary school includes kindergarten through 8th grade, and the next four years (taught in a different school building) are called *high school.* In other school systems, there is a third division called *junior high school* (or *middle school*) which usually includes grades 6 through 8, but in some communities includes grades 4 or 5 through 8 and in others includes grades 7 through 9.

15. The typical school day is about seven hours long and ends about 3 P.M. Classes are in session Monday through Friday. Traditional vacation periods include a two-week winter vacation (including the Christmas and New Year's holidays), a one-week spring vacation (often coinciding with Easter), and a two-month summer vacation. In addition, there are several one-day holidays giving students a day off to celebrate.

16. Children going to public elementary schools usually attend a school in their neighborhood. In big cities, many children live close enough to walk to and from school and come home for lunch. However, most elementary schools provide a place where students can eat if it is inconvenient for them to go home at lunchtime. American high schools are larger than elementary schools and serve a larger community. As a result, most high school students take public transportation or a school bus to and from school and eat lunch in the school cafeteria.

17. Grammar schools teach language arts (reading, writing, spelling, and penmanship), social studies (stressing history and geography), mathematics (up to and sometimes including algebra), science, physical education, and health. In addition, elementary school programs often include music, art, and home economics.

18. High school subjects are more specialized. English classes emphasize writing, grammar, and literature. Social studies is split into separate courses such as American history, European history, and psychology. Year-long courses in algebra and geometry are followed by more advanced math work in trigonometry and pre-calculus. There are also specialized science courses in biology, chemistry, and physics. Many high school students study a foreign language, usually Spanish, French, or German. Courses in music, art, home economics, and consumer education are also available, along with various vocational courses. As in elementary school, health and physical education classes are generally required.

19. During the elementary school years, students are grouped into classes, and each group stays together for the entire school day and the entire school year. Generally, the class has the same teacher for most subjects, although art, music, and physical education are usually taught by teachers who **specialize** in these areas. Also, in the upper elementary grades, students in some school systems have different teachers (but the same classmates) for their major academic subjects.

20. In high school, students move from one classroom to another and study each subject with a different teacher and a different group of classmates. Many high schools have what is commonly called a tracking system, which groups students according to academic ability and **motivation.** Thus, more capable and hard-working students take more difficult courses. Depending on the subject, classes may be offered at two, three, or even four different ability levels.

21. High school students have a very busy day. Many take five or six academic subjects as well as physical education. During other periods, students may be doing homework in a study hall, researching in the school library, or participating in activities such as the school orchestra, student government, school newspaper, or math club. Many extracurricular activities also meet after the school day ends. Students involved in time-consuming activities such as athletics, dramatics, or music may be at school from very early in the morning until dinnertime. However, these school activities are well worth the time because they help students find friends with similar interests, develop their talents, gain greater self-confidence, and sometimes even discover their career goals.

PROBLEMS AND SOLUTIONS

22. When an immigrant family moves to the U.S.A., one of the first questions that parents ask is, "Will my children get a good education here?" The answer depends on two major factors: where the children attend school and how hard they are willing to work.

23. In some schools where the community is **stable,** the funding good, and the school environment orderly, a hardworking student can get an excellent education. But in other schools—especially those in poor neighborhoods in the nation's large cities—it is very difficult to become educated. The flight of middle-class families to the suburbs left big city public schools with mostly lower-income students. Many are deprived children from impoverished homes with only one parent. Many come to school ill-prepared and poorly motivated to learn. A large number need help in learning English. Many change residences and schools often, and a changing classroom population is difficult to teach. In some poor neighborhoods, the students do not attend school regularly because they are frightened by violent gangs. In some classrooms, teachers have difficulty keeping the students' attention because disrespectful, uncooperative students disturb the class. Because the quality of education varies so much from one school district to another, parents who are planning to move to a new neighborhood often inquire about the schools—and even visit them—before deciding which community to move to.

24. Researchers are always studying the schools and evaluating the kind of education being provided. Experts ask: "Are today's students learning as much as their older siblings or their parents did? Are they learning as much as students in other countries?" In the 1980s, many studies revealed weaknesses in the American educational system. For example, of the 158 members of the United Nations, the U.S.A. ranked 49th in its level of literacy. It has been claimed that as many as 25 million American adults cannot read the front page of a newspaper. Another study focused on students' knowledge of history and literature. The results were published in a book entitled, *What Do Our 17-Year-Olds Know?*, and the answer is, "not much." For example, 75% of American high school seniors did not know when Abraham Lincoln was President, and 80% could not identify Dickens, Dostoyevsky, and Ibsen as famous authors. In a 1988 study comparing students' knowledge of geography, American young adults came in last of nine countries. In fact, 18% of the American students couldn't even find the U.S.A. on a world map! Still other studies indicate that today's students are weak in mathematical problem-solving and writing skills.

25. What's wrong with American education? To find the answer and to fix the problem, one must look at all of the elements: the students themselves, their parents, their teachers, the school curriculum, the textbooks, and the community. Many students simply do not study enough. (Two-thirds of high school seniors do an hour or less of homework per night.) American teenagers are often distracted by part-time jobs, sports and other school activities, TV, and socializing. Some do not keep up with their schoolwork because of emotional problems, use of illegal drugs, or simply lack of motivation. Clearly, if Americans are to become better educated, students must spend more time studying, and parents must insist that they do so.

26. In the 1980s, criticism of American education stimulated a reform movement. As a result, 45 of the 50 states raised high-school graduation requirements. One government study recommended a longer school year. (Now, the average American student attends school about 180 days a year, compared to 210 for a Japanese student.) Efforts have also been underway to increase parental involvement in schools and to improve teaching. College programs that educate teachers are trying to encourage more academically talented students to choose teaching as a career. Schools of education are also improving their curriculum so that American teachers of the future will be better prepared. School administrators are working on curriculum **revisions.** Publishers are being urged to create textbooks that are more challenging, interesting, and objective. Finally, concerned citizens are urging communities and the federal government to provide more tax dollars for education.

27. What can one say about basic education in the U.S.A. today? It has many strengths, but there's plenty of room for improvement. Since the school reform movement began, test scores have risen somewhat, and Americans are optimistic that reform and improvement will continue. Americans deeply believe in education as the best vehicle for individual and social advancement. Improving the basic school system is one of the nation's top priorities. But meanwhile, it is a consolation to remember that, for most young Americans, formal education does not end with high school graduation.

EXERCISES

I. Comprehension Questions. Answer the following questions on paper or in class discussion.

1. For what two main reasons is education important to Americans?
2. What are the major academic divisions of the American school system?
3. What are some differences between public and private schools?
4. What problems do American elementary and high schools face?

II. Vocabulary Practice. Pronounce the following words after your teacher, and discuss their meanings. Then use some of them to complete the following sentences.

academic	motivation
categories	nonsectarian
commitment	parochial
compulsory	required
curriculum	revision
dual	specialize
elementary	stable
grade	subsidized
grammar	teamwork
kindergarten	vocational

1. The opposite of *optional* is ________________ .

2. The opposite of *parochial* is ________________ .

3. ________________ school and ________________ school are two names for the same type of school, one that provides the first eight years of ________________ work.

4. Five-year-old children begin attending school by going to ________________ .

5. ________________ involves cooperating and working together with other people.

6. ________________ training refers to education that enables a person to develop skills for a specific job, for example repairing cars or cutting and styling hair.

7. Some day care centers are ________________ by the government, which means that the government contributes some of the money needed.

8. What is taught in a particular grade of school is the ________________ for that grade.

III. Word Study.

A. Paragraph 6 has two words with the adjective ending *-less,* (meaning *without*): *pointless* and *useless.* Many adjectives that end with *-ful* (which means *full of*) have opposites that end with *-less.* Write the opposites of the following words, and discuss their meanings.

helpful ________________ careful ________________

harmful ________________ thoughtful ________________

NOTE: Many words ending with *-ful* have no opposite with *-less* and vice versa.

B. 1. What does the word-part *co-* mean? ________________

2. Write the definition of the following words that use this word-part:

coeducational ________________________________

uncooperative ________________________________

C. In schools, what different meanings does the word *grade* have? Write two definitions. (Reread paragraph 13 for help with one of them.)

____

____

D. What does *time-consuming* [21] mean? ____________________

E. What does *ill-* mean in the word *ill-prepared?* [23]

____

IV. Idiom Study. Underline the phrase that best completes each statement. The numbers in brackets give the paragraphs in which the idioms are used.

1. *The three Rs* [8] refers to a) reading, writing, and arithmetic b) religion, reading, and revision c) advanced mathematics courses.
2. *A day off* [15] means a) a month that doesn't have 31 days b) a day in which a person doesn't have to work or go to school c) any holiday.
3. *There's room for improvement* [27] means a) we have enough space to improve things b) things are not as good as they could or should be c) we are building extra space to improve conditions.

V. Reading Skills.

A. Reread the "Purpose and Scope" section of this chapter, and then mark the following statements true (T) or false (F).

___1. American children must go to school until they graduate from high school.

___2. School attendance laws are the same in every state of the U.S.A.

___3. Most Americans have at least 12 years of formal education.

B. Reread paragraphs 6 and 7.

1. What were John Dewey's ideas about *what* students should learn?

____

2. What was his idea about *how* students learn best?

____

20

HIGHER EDUCATION IN THE U.S.A.

WHY COLLEGE?

1. "The more you learn, the more you earn," said the pop singer Cyndi Lauper as she accepted her high school diploma—at the age of 35! Although Cyndi made it without a high school **degree,** most people don't. In the U.S.A. today, about 75% of jobs require some education or technical training beyond high school. The lowest wage earners in the U.S.A. are those without high school degrees; college graduates outearn those without a college education; people with master's degrees outearn those with only a bachelor's; and the highest incomes of all are earned by people with advanced professional or **academic** degrees. These **generalizations** explain why the majority of young Americans go to college. However, despite the averages, more diplomas don't always mean more money. Many skilled blue-collar workers, salespeople, business executives, and entrepreneurs outearn college professors and scientific researchers. And great athletes and entertainers outearn everyone else!

2. But a college education is not only preparation for a career; it is also (or should be) preparation for life. In addition to courses in their major field of study, most students have time to take **elective** courses. They may take classes that help them understand more about human nature, government, the arts, sciences, or whatever else interests them.

3. Going to college, either full-time or part-time, is becoming the automatic next step after high school. Today, more than half of American high school graduates enroll in college. But recent high school graduates no longer dominate the college **campuses**. Today, it is quite common for adults of all ages to come back to college either for career advancement or personal growth. By 1992, about half of all American college students will be older than 25, and 20% of them will be over 35. Serving this great variety of people are about 3,400 institutions of higher learning enrolling more than 12 million students.

4. American faith in the value of education is exemplified by the rising number of Americans who have at least a bachelor's degree. About 20% of Americans are college graduates. However, among younger adults and working people, the percentage is at least 25%, much higher than in most other major nations. In the U.S.A., a college education is not viewed as a privilege reserved for the wealthy or the academically talented. Virtually everyone who wants to attend college can do so.

UNDERGRADUATE EDUCATION

5. American colleges and universities vary a great deal in size. Some colleges have student bodies of just a few hundred, while some state universities serve more than 100,000 students on several different campuses. At smaller schools, students generally get to know their classmates and professors better and are less likely to feel lonely and confused. Larger schools offer a greater selection of courses and more activities to attend and participate in. When selecting a college, the student must consider which type of environment best suits his or her needs.

6. There are two main categories of institutions of higher learning: public and private. All schools get money from **tuition** and from private contributors. However, public schools are supported primarily by the state they're located in. On the other hand, private schools do not receive state funding. As a result, tuition is generally lower at public schools, especially for permanent residents of that state.

7. Schools can also be grouped by the types of programs and degrees they offer. The three major groups are community colleges, four-year colleges, and universities. Community colleges offer only the first two years of **undergraduate** studies (the ***freshman*** and ***sophomore*** years). The number of these schools has grown very rapidly in the past 40 years. In 1950, there were about 600 in the U.S.A. Today, there are about 1,300, and they serve about five million students (about 55% of all college freshmen). Most community colleges are public schools, supported by local and/or state funds. They serve two general types of students: (a) those taking the first two years of college before **transfer**ring to a four-year school for their third and fourth (***junior*** and ***senior***) years; and (b) those enrolled in one- or two-year job training programs. Community colleges offer technical training in many areas of study, such as health services, office skills, computer science, drafting, police work, and automotive repair.

8. Newcomers to the U.S.A. often ask, "Exactly what is the difference between a college and a university?" Some assume that the difference is merely one of size, but it is much more than that. A university is bigger than a college because the scope of its programs is much greater. A university offers a wider range of undergraduate programs and also offers graduate studies. Part of the responsibility of a university is to encourage its **faculty** and its graduate students to do research that will advance human knowledge. Colleges, on the other hand, are primarily undergraduate schools with no commitment to train students for research.

9. Many excellent colleges are *liberal arts* schools, which means that they offer studies in the humanities, languages, mathematics, social sciences, and sciences. Liberal arts colleges generally do not offer degrees in engineering, business, journalism, education, and many other specific vocations that a student can train for at a university. However, students at a liberal arts college (like college students elsewhere) still major in a specific area of knowledge.

10. Some colleges specialize in training students for one particular occupation (as agricultural colleges and teachers' colleges do). Many specialized undergraduate institutions that are not called colleges also provide higher education in one specific occupation—for example, conservatories for music students, seminaries for students of religion, and fine arts schools for artists. For those wishing to prepare for military careers, the United States government maintains four special academies.

11. At the college level, the academic year is about nine months long (usually from September until early June or from late August until May). After completing four academic years with acceptable grades in an approved course of study, the student earns a bachelor's degree. Some students complete college in less than four years by attending summer sessions. At most colleges, the academic year is divided into either two or three terms, excluding the summer session. College grades, from highest to lowest, run *A, B, C, D,* and *F.* An *F* is a failing grade; if a student receives an *F* in a particular course, he or she does not get credit for having taken the course. College students must maintain at least a low *C* average in order to remain in school.

GRADUATE EDUCATION

12. American universities offer three main categories of graduate degrees. In most fields of specialization, a master's degree can be earned by one or two academic years of study beyond the bachelor's degree. A Ph.D. degree (doctor of philosophy) usually takes at least three years beyond the master's. To earn a Ph.D. in almost any field, generally the student must pass oral and written examinations in his or her specialty, produce a long research paper which makes an original contribution to his or her field of study, and pass reading examinations in one or two foreign languages. There are also graduate professional degrees in medicine, dentistry, and law, among other fields.

13. In the 1980s, American institutions of higher learning awarded about 300,000 master's degrees and about 30,000 Ph.D. degrees per year. In recent years, the graduate student population has become much more diversified than ever before. It now includes more women, foreign students, minority group members, older students, and part-time students. Also, the variety of degree programs offered has expanded greatly. Today's graduate students can choose from about 1,000 types of master's degrees and about 60 types of **doctorates**.

LIFE ON AN AMERICAN CAMPUS

14. A college community is an interesting and lively place. Students become involved in many different activities—extracurricular, religious, social, and athletic. Among the extracurricular activities are college newspapers, musical organizations, dramatic clubs, and political groups. Many religious groups have their own meeting places, where services and social activities can be held. Most colleges have a *student union*, where students can get together for lunch, study sessions, club meetings, and socializing.

15. At many schools, campus life revolves around **fraternities** (social and, in some cases, residential clubs for men) and **sororities** (similar clubs for women). These organizations exist on more than 500 campuses. The best known are national groups with *chapters* at schools throughout the country. Their names are Greek letters, such as *Alpha Delta Phi.*

16. Athletics is an important part of life on most campuses. Most coeducational and men's schools belong to an athletic league. The teams within the league play against each other, aiming for the league championship. Football is the college sport which arouses the most national interest. Games, complete with student marching bands and entertainment, are major productions. Other sports—particularly basketball, swimming, and track—are also pursued with enthusiasm. Some schools have competitive tennis, skiing, sailing, wrestling, soccer, baseball, and golf.

17. Is it fun to be a college student in the United States? For most students, the college years are exciting and rewarding, but they are certainly not easy or carefree. Just about all college students face the pressure of making important career decisions and some **anxiety** about examinations and grades. Many students have additional problems—too little money, not enough time for sleep, and a feeling of loneliness because they're living far from home. Still, many Americans look back on their college years as the happiest time of their lives. When students live on campus in college dormitories, they make very close friendships. Sometimes a student is fortunate enough to find a member of the school's faculty that takes a personal interest in his or her academic career. Some students, when returning to their college campus in the fall, feel that they are coming back to their second home. Many graduates feel great loyalty to their former schools and, throughout their lives, they cheer for their school's athletic teams and donate money to help the institution expand and modernize. American graduates refer to the school they attended as their *alma mater* (a Latin expression meaning *fostering mother*). This expression indicates how much the college experience means to students, and how much they feel their school contributed to their lives.

FINANCING A COLLEGE EDUCATION IN THE U.S.A.

18. During the 1980s, the cost of a college education rose about 8% to 10% a year, about twice the rate of inflation. College expenses at many schools are so high that even two-income, middle-class families cannot afford to pay the entire bill, especially if they have more than one child in college at the same time.

19. College costs vary quite a bit, depending upon the type of school attended. For example, at many of the more expensive private schools, annual costs (including tuition, room, board, books, travel to and from home, and other expenses) may exceed $20,000. Of course, public universities are much cheaper. At these schools, tuition is significantly higher for out-of-state students than it is for those whose permanent residence is within that state. Tuition at community colleges averages about half the in-state cost of public, four-year colleges and universities.

20. For those that cannot afford the cost of a college education, financial aid is the answer. Students in the U.S.A. receive about $20 billion per year in financial aid. In recent years, nearly 75% of students in postsecondary programs have been receiving some form of financial aid. There are three main types of financial aid: (a) scholarships (grants), which are gifts that students do not repay; (b) loans to students and/or their parents; and (c) student employment (*work/study*), a part-time job which the school gives the student for the academic year. Most financial aid is need-based; that is, only students who need the money receive it. Financial assistance to outstanding students who do not need the money (commonly called *merit-based* aid) is limited.

21. The funds for all of this aid come from three main sources—the federal government, state governments, and private contributors. Every American college and university has a financial aid office to help students find out what kind of aid they might be **eligible** for and to assist them in completing the complicated application forms. Aliens who are permanent residents in the U.S.A. are eligible for government assistance, but foreign students (I-20 visa students) are not.

22. Difficulties in making ends meet create serious problems for many students. Some—especially those with responsibilities to help support a family—try to work full-time while carrying a full academic course load. They forget to leave themselves time to eat, sleep, and simply live. These students soon discover that they are trying to handle too much, and that an exhausted person performs poorly both on the job and in the classroom. College counselors can help students who need to work out a plan to feed the family and attend college at the same time.

STANDARDIZED TESTS AND THEIR USES

23. Students from other countries who want to attend college in the U.S.A. need to learn about the various standardized tests that can help them demonstrate their knowledge to college admissions personnel. For the adult student who has not finished high school, the GED (Test of General Educational Development) is a logical first step. The GED involves five exams—writing skills, social studies, science, literature and the arts, and mathematics. The tests are available in English, French, and Spanish. Students can study for the GED by taking a review course or by studying a review book.

24. High school seniors wishing to apply to competitive colleges and universities take standardized tests commonly called ACTs and SATs. Each of these tests takes about three hours. The tests enable students to demonstrate general academic ability in mathematics, English, reading, and logic. Most colleges use these scores plus the students' high school grades to evaluate applicants.

25. At the college level, students whose native language is not English will probably be required to take the TOEFL test (Test of English as a Foreign Language) when they apply for admission to a university. Again, courses and textbooks are available to review for this test.

26. When students come to the U.S.A. after completing some college work in another country, they should bring a **transcript** of previous college work and get those credits evaluated by an authorized organization. The transcript will probably need to be translated into English before it can be evaluated. Students who cannot obtain papers to prove that they have already taken certain college courses may want to take some of the CLEP (College Level Examination Program) tests. These tests cover courses commonly taken during the first two years of college, such as English, humanities, math, natural sciences, and history.
27. College graduates wishing to enter graduate programs also find that standardized tests are required. The Counseling Office of a student's present or prospective school is the place to go with all questions about requirements for acceptance to graduate programs.

LIFELONG LEARNING

28. In the U.S.A., the education of adults goes on in many different places for many different reasons. At least 25 million adults (about 13% of the adult population) are enrolled in classes, nearly all as part-time students. Most of these classes are not for college **credit** but for knowledge that the student can use on the job, for job advancement, to pursue a hobby, or for personal growth. Programs commonly called *adult education* or *continuing education* are operated by many high schools and community colleges. In recent years, private learning centers have also opened up, offering inexpensive classes for adults in a wide variety of skills and activities. A typical catalog might offer classes in how to cook a Chinese dinner, invest in the stock market, improve your spelling, make friends, or even give your partner a massage. Many adults enjoy taking classes where they can learn something new and also meet people who share this new interest.
29. Many more classes are taken at the workplace. Hospitals, businesses, and museums, for example, offer courses to help employees improve job-related skills. Some companies, rather than operate their own classes, will offer to pay the tuition if an employee goes back to school to learn a skill that the company needs. In the U.S.A., where technology rapidly makes some skills obsolete and new ones essential, workers at all levels realize that lifelong learning is necessary. Even professional people—doctors, teachers, accountants, dentists, and engineers—continue to study to keep up with new techniques in their fields.
30. Education, whether it occurs on the college campus or elsewhere, is an important element in the life of an American adult. The American

dream of becoming important in one's career and financially successful is most often achieved through education.

EXERCISES

I. Comprehension Questions. Answer the following questions on paper or in class discussion.

1. Why do Americans want a college education?
2. What are some differences between a college and a university?
3. Why are the undergraduate years usually exciting ones? What problems does the undergraduate face?
4. How do Americans pay for their college education?

II. Vocabulary Practice. Pronounce the following words after your teacher, and discuss their meanings. Then use some of them to complete the following sentences.

academic	freshman
anxiety	generalization
campus	junior
credit	senior
degree	sophomore
doctorate	sororities
elective	transcript
eligible	transfer
faculty	tuition
fraternities	undergraduate

1. A school's buildings and the land around them are called the school's ____________.

2. The first four years of college are named (in order) (1st) ________________, (2nd) ________________, (3rd) ________________, and (4th) ________________ years.

3. A student who has not yet earned a bachelor's degree is called an

   ________________.

4. Private colleges and universities generally charge higher

   ________________ than public schools.

5. A student earns ________________ for a course only if he or she

   gets a passing grade in it (*A*, *B*, *C*, or *D*).

6. A student who wants to get a master's ________________ must

   go to school for one or two years after getting a bachelor's degree.

7. The people who teach at a school are called its ________________.

8. Students take courses in their major field of study, and they also

   take ________________ courses.

III. Word Study.

1. Discuss in class and then write in the meanings of the following common abbreviations used at colleges and universities:

   B.S. ________________________________

   B.A. ________________________________

   M.S. ________________________________

   M.A. ________________________________

   Ph.D. ________________________________

   CLEP ________________________________

TOEFL ____

ESL ____

2. Put a check after the things that a person can *earn.*

   money ___

   praise ___

   college credits ___

   time ___

   work___

   a job promotion ___

   an opportunity ___

   a baby ___

   talent ___

3. Reread paragraph 1. What is the meaning of the word *degree* here?

   ____

   Look in the dictionary for two other meanings of this word.

   Write them down. ______________________________

   ____

IV. Idiom Study. Underline the phrase that best completes each sentence. The numbers in brackets give the paragraphs in which the idioms are used.

1. In the chapter title, *higher education* means a) graduate school b) undergraduate and graduate school c) high school.
2. In paragraph 1, *made it* means a) succeeded b) created something c) earned a diploma.
3. Your *alma mater* [17] is a) your mother b) the school that you attended c) your school advisor.
4. *Making ends meet* [22] means a) tying two strings together b) being able to pay for the things you need c) meeting friends at the end of the day.

V. Reading Skills.

A. Finding important details:
Read each paragraph listed in brackets to find the answer to each question.

1. Approximately how many colleges and universities are there in the U.S.A.? [3] ___
2. How many years of college can a student complete at a community college? [7] ___
3. What is the highest (best) grade that a college student can get in a course? [11] ___

B. Using context clues:

1. In paragraph 5, sentence 2, what does *bodies* mean?

____

2. In the last sentence of paragraph 5, what does *suits* mean?

____

C. Finding main ideas:
Reread paragraphs 5 through 8. Then list two ways to divide colleges and universities into categories.

1. ________________ and ________________

2. Community colleges, ________________, and

____

21

VACATIONING IN THE U.S.A.

1. "All work and no play makes Jack a dull boy," says a 17th-century proverb. Most Americans agree and look forward to their vacation. Most American employees receive an **annual** vacation with pay, and it is traditional to use this time off for travel.

2. Traveling within the United States is extremely popular because foreign travel generally takes more time and money. However, Americans who wish to vacation outside the U.S.A. are free to go almost anywhere. Obtaining a passport is a routine matter. Every year about 13 million Americans travel abroad.

3. The most popular vacation periods are during the summer and during the two-week school break **surrounding** the Christmas and New Year's holidays. These periods are also the most crowded and generally the most expensive times to travel, so people who can adjust their schedules sometimes choose to vacation in the fall or spring.

4. American vacationers often travel by automobile. Most families own a car, and those that don't can rent one. The automobile is usually the most economical way to travel, especially for families. It is also fairly fast and convenient. Excellent interstate highways (with motels and restaurants nearby) connect the nation's major cities. They **enable** vacationers to travel at an almost steady speed of 55 or 65 miles an hour. **Tourists** that want to travel faster often fly to their **destination** and then rent a car when they get there.

VISITING THEME PARKS

5. One important American contribution to vacation fun is the theme park. Walt Disney (an American cartoonist and filmmaker) created the first one, Disneyland, in Anaheim, California (near Los Angeles) in 1955. Disneyland offers visitors many incredible experiences, including a journey through a fairyland castle and a boat ride through "jungle" waters. After dark, there's a **spectacular** parade, displaying costumes lit up by thousands of light bulbs.

6. Disneyland's great success inspired the building of other theme parks elsewhere in the U.S.A. and Europe. Many of these parks have rides, restaurants, shops, carnival games, displays, and musical shows. The largest of these is Walt Disney World. In 1988, more than 30 million people visited this huge entertainment complex, making it the most popular vacation spot in the world. Disney World includes three theme parks, all located about 20 miles from Orlando, Florida. The first of these parks, built in 1971, is The Magic Kingdom, home of Disney cartoon and other imaginary characters. It offers exciting train, boat, and railroad rides, as well as the usual **amusement** park rides. Visitors can also explore Liberty Square, with its haunted house and lifelike exhibit of all the American Presidents. As in California's Disneyland, there's an Electric Parade after dark. The second Disney World theme park—Epcot Center—was built in 1982. It contains two main sections: Future World, depicting technologies of the future, and World Showcase, featuring the architecture, crafts, and entertainment of many nations. In 1989, Disney World added its third park, a $500 million facility called Disney-MGM Studios, which has the Hollywood, California movie-making center as its theme. This park has demonstrations of movie stunts and backstage tours to allow visitors to experience movie-making first-hand. Tourists especially love the Great Movie Ride, on which passengers travel past scary gangsters and ugly aliens from outer space; and Catastrophe Canyon, in which visitors experience a fake earthquake. Seeing all three of these parks on one vacation requires at least four days, and many visitors stay longer. A visitor to Disney World needs a pair of comfortable shoes and a lot of traveler's checks.

7. Other theme parks around the country include Great America (near Chicago), which has two themes—regions of the U.S.A. and comic strip characters. Six Flags Over Texas (in Arlington, Texas) has an American history theme. Opryland, USA (in Nashville, Tennessee) has a country music theme. Many theme parks are combinations of amusement parks and zoos. In some, (such as Great Adventure in Jackson, New Jersey and the many safari parks around the country) animals roam free on huge areas of land, and tourists drive or ride trains through the territory. Marine World theme parks, with live dolphin shows and exhibits of saltwater plants and animals, also attract huge crowds. There are also theme parks built around water activities, where swimmers can cool off on water slides and in wave pools. Altogether, the U.S.A. has about 600 amusement parks. In 1987, about 235 million people visited them and spent almost $4 billion.

VISITING THE EAST

8. The nation's major cities are among its most popular tourist attractions. New York City, with a population of seven million, is the largest city in the U.S.A. It is located in the northeastern United States. With a magnificent natural harbor and more than 500 miles of waterfront, it is the largest port in the world. The city has five sections called *boroughs*. The most important borough is Manhattan, the commercial, cultural, and financial center of the city. Manhattan is an island connected to the other boroughs (Brooklyn, the Bronx, Queens, and Richmond) by numerous bridges, tunnels, and ferries.

9. All year, tourists crowd the streets and hotels of Manhattan. They visit the skyscrapers, particularly the impressive World Trade Center (WTC). WTC's twin towers are 110 stories (411 meters or 1,350 feet) high, making them the second tallest skyscrapers in the world. The Center's structural system is an architectural marvel because, despite its great height, it does not bend, even when attacked by strong winds. Another famous New York skyscraper is the Empire State Building (102 stories), the third tallest building in the world. At night, its lighted top brightens the Manhattan skyline. The skyscrapers of Rockefeller Center are also a big tourist attraction.

10. Tourists also come to visit Manhattan's museums and art galleries, shop in its enormous department stores and famous **specialty** shops, and eat in its elegant restaurants. Other attractions are the United Nations Building, the New York Stock Exchange, and the Metropolitan Opera. This world-famous opera company now performs in the Lincoln Center for the Performing Arts, a complex of buildings which also houses theaters, a drama school, a music school, and a library-museum.

11. Live entertainment is **plentiful** in New York City. In addition to its many nightclubs for music and comedy, the city is the nation's most important area for theater. Plays performed "on Broadway" (in the larger midtown Manhattan theatres near the street called Broadway) often involve famous playwrights, producers, and performers. Smaller "off Broadway" theaters feature less well-known talent, but theatergoers sometimes find exciting, experimental productions in these playhouses.

12. New York City is also the home of one of the country's most well-known symbols—the **Statue** of Liberty. This famous figure has been standing in New York Harbor since 1886. It was designed by two Frenchmen—the exterior by Frederic Bartholdi and the interior by Gustave Eiffel (designer of the famous Eiffel Tower in Paris)—and given to the U.S.A. as a gift by the French government. In honor of the statue's **centennial,** Americans contributed nearly $200 million for its renovation. The Statue of Liberty is one of the largest statues in the world. Its height (from its feet to the tip of its torch) is about 151 feet (46 meters), and its weight exceeds 200 tons. This classic figure, holding a torch high in the air, symbolizes American freedom and the opportunity it promises. Years ago, it welcomed nearly all American immigrants as they arrived in the U.S.A. by ship. Today, tourists take a 15-minute ferryboat ride out to Liberty Island in order to go inside this famous statue.

13. Vacationers interested in early American history and American government find the eastern part of the country fascinating. In Washington, D.C., the nation's capital, visitors can watch Congress in action in the **Capitol** building, attend a session of the Supreme Court, and tour the White House, the official home of the President. The Smithsonian Institution, with its six national museums, offers much of historical interest, including the Wright brothers' first airplane and a fine art collection. In Washington, there are also magnificent **monuments** honoring great statesmen, the most spectacular being the memorials to Washington, Lincoln, and Jefferson.

14. One sad but beautiful monument that most tourists visit is the Vietnam Veterans Memorial, a V-shaped black granite wall bearing the names of 58,000 Americans killed or missing in Vietnam. More than 75,000 people a week come to see the wall, designed by a young Chinese-American **architecture** student named Maya Ying Lin and dedicated in 1982.

15. Philadelphia, Pennsylvania is another famous historical city. It proudly displays the Liberty Bell, which rang to announce the signing of the Declaration of Independence in 1776. Visitors can also see the building where the United States Constitution was signed in 1787 and the home of Betsy Ross, who made the first American flag. Only 300 miles northeast of Philadelphia is Boston, Massachusetts, a city with many colonial landmarks and some of our nation's first and finest universities.

VISITING THE MIDWEST

16. Chicago, long known as the second city, became the nation's third city in population in 1982, when Los Angeles surpassed it. With a population of about three million, Chicago remains the largest city in the Midwest and the most interesting one as well. Tourists come to Chicago to visit the theaters, restaurants, fine museums, and wide variety of stores. The elegant shops along Michigan Avenue and the huge department stores on State Street are very popular. Chicago is located on Lake Michigan. The city's Outer Drive expressway along the lake gives visitors a scenic view of the beaches, harbors, parks, and skyscrapers. The city's most famous skyscraper is Sears Tower, the tallest building in the world. Erected between 1970 and 1974, it is 110 stories and reaches a height of 1,454 feet (443 meters). Tourists can go to the top of this building and survey the city from there.

17. Once, Chicago was thought of mostly as a city terrorized by gangsters. (It was the home of the infamous Al Capone.) Today, it is known as a great cultural center with more than 120 theaters and several dozen art galleries. Chicago is also famous for its modern architecture and impressive works of outdoor art, created by internationally known artists. In the city's downtown area, tourists can see Pablo Picasso's 50-foot sculptured head of a woman, Alexander Calder's huge red *Flamingo,* Marc Chagall's 70-foot mosaic of the four seasons, and Claes Oldenburg's pop art piece, a gigantic metal **sculpture** of a baseball bat. Other major attractions are the Museum of Science and Industry, which contains exhibits showing applications of science to industry; Buckingham Fountain, the world's largest lighted fountain; and the Art Institute, one of the world's finest art museums.

18. Two other important cities in the Midwest are Detroit, Michigan and St. Louis, Missouri. Detroit produces more automobiles and trucks than any other city in the world. In nearby Dearborn, location of the Ford Motor Company's main factory, sightseers can visit Greenfield Village and the Henry Ford Museum of American History and Technology, a 254-**acre** indoor-outdoor museum complex. It features an enormous collection of antique cars and other machinery as well as the childhood home of Henry Ford (creator of the first mass-produced car) and the laboratory of Thomas Alva Edison (inventor of the electric light bulb and the phonograph).

19. St. Louis, the largest city in Missouri, is on the west bank of the Mississippi, the nation's longest river. During the 1800s, St. Louis was considered the gateway to the West. Today, tourists visiting the city cannot miss the beautiful Gateway Arch (the nation's tallest monument), designed by Eero Saarinen. Rising 630 feet (192 meters), it dominates the city's skyline. Inside the arch, there are small cars that carry visitors to the top, and every year more than a million passengers take this trip.

VISITING THE SOUTH

20. One of the most popular Southern states for vacationing is Florida. Its tropical climate and beautiful sand beaches along the Atlantic Ocean make it a year-round vacationland. Florida is ideal for water sports and for sightseeing as well. Besides Disney World and several other fascinating theme parks such as Sea World, tourists come to visit the Everglades, one of the world's largest and most interesting swamp areas with many unusual kinds of plants and birds; the John F. Kennedy Space Center in Cape Canaveral; and St. Augustine, the oldest permanent European settlement in the U.S.A.

21. Another great port city with exotic appeal for tourists is New Orleans, Louisiana. Located on the Mississippi River near the Gulf of Mexico, it contains many reminders of Old Europe and the Old South. The famous French Quarter, the Mardi Gras festival, and the Creoles (French-speaking descendants of early European settlers) all give the city a continental flavor. New Orleans is also the birthplace of jazz, and many people visit the city to hear good Dixieland music.

VISITING THE WEST

22. The West lures many tourists with attractions that appeal to vastly different tastes. The Rocky Mountains of Colorado attract skiers and snowmobilers. The game rooms and nightlife of Las Vegas, Nevada attract vacationers who enjoy **gambling** and big-name entertainment. The colorful Grand Canyon and the rushing Colorado River attract nature-lovers to Arizona. California, the nation's third largest state in area and largest in population, offers some of the finest vacation experiences, especially for families.

23. Because there is so much to see along California's Pacific Coast, travelers often fly to the West Coast, then rent a car and drive up or down the picturesque mountain highway **alongside** the ocean, stopping at interesting cities and towns along the way. The major cities tourists want to see are Los Angeles (L.A.), the nation's second largest city, and San Francisco, one of the hilliest and most cosmopolitan of American cities.

24. One section of L.A.—Hollywood—is the home of the American movie industry. Tourists interested in films can spend a day at the Universal Movie Studios and get an idea of how movies are made. Driving around to see the fabulous homes of movie stars is another favorite L.A. pastime. Then, when one tires of searching for celebrities, there's always Disneyland in nearby Anaheim.

25. Visitors to the West Coast often stop to see San Francisco. Situated between the Pacific Ocean and San Francisco Bay, the city is the leading seaport of the Pacific Coast. Ships come and go beneath its beautiful Golden Gate Bridge. Cable cars clang loudly as they climb the city's steep hills. San Francisco is famous for its bridges, cable cars, and breathtaking scenery. But tourists also come to enjoy fine dining—seafood on Fisherman's Wharf and Oriental cuisine in Chinatown.

26. For travelers with the time and money to go far west, the country's newest states—Hawaii and Alaska—offer much of interest. Hawaii, the 50th state, lies in the Pacific Ocean about 2,000 miles west of the mainland. It is made up of 20 islands (8 major ones) that offer vacationers a tropical climate and exotic sights. The most densely populated island is Oahu, where the **capital** city of Honolulu is located. Oahu's Waikiki Beach, lined with hotels and apartment houses, is an international tourist attraction. The scenic island of Hawaii, the largest in area, has tall mountain peaks, active **volcanoes,** forests, and waterfalls. The island of Lanai is almost completely covered with pineapple fields. The Hawaiian Islands are actually mountaintops that were forced up from the ocean floor by volcanic activity. In the past 30 years, they have been getting larger because new acres of land have been created by volcanic eruptions. Every year, about a million tourists come to visit Hawaii and meet its diverse population, including many people of Japanese, Filipino, and Chinese descent.

27. Alaska is a land of contrasts. To start with, it is the largest state in area but the smallest in population. It is more than twice the size of Texas, but its population is only about 500,000. About one-sixth of its residents are of Asian descent (Eskimos and Aleuts). There is a great deal of variety in the climate and geography of this huge territory. Its sights include smoking volcanoes, desert sands, grassy plains, and rain forests. In some areas, the winter temperature can go down as low as -100° F. In the northernmost part of Alaska, for 80 days in the summer the sun does not set, and for 50 days in the winter it does not rise. Understandably, tourists tend to visit Alaska in the summer, when they can enjoy the milder weather and endless daylight. Among its famous sights are the glaciers in southeastern Alaska and Mt. McKinley, the nation's highest mountain (20,320 feet) in south-central Alaska.

ENJOYING THE OUTDOORS

28. Tourists interested in beautiful scenery, natural wonders, and wildlife often visit one of the nation's many national parks. The largest of these—Yellowstone—covers about 3,500 square miles in Wyoming, Montana, and Idaho. Yellowstone contains the world's greatest geyser area, as well as spectacular waterfalls. Other popular national parks in the West are Glacier National Park in Montana, Yosemite in California, and the Grand Canyon in Arizona. In the East, the most famous national park is the Everglades in Florida.

29. Besides national and state parks, many other areas help this nation's largely urban population enjoy a vacation in the country. Some families rent summer cottages near swimming and boating facilities. Some camp out (sleep outdoors) in tents. Some rent a houseboat and cruise down the Mississippi. Dude ranches in the West attract those who love horses. Luxurious resorts cater to vacationers who want comfort, fine restaurant dining, and excellent outdoor recreational facilities.

30. Some people have become involved in a new type of vacation plan called *time sharing*. These people become part owners of an apartment, cottage, or villa in a scenic area, and this investment entitles them to live in the space for a part of the year (perhaps a few weeks). Time-sharing units are also traded or rented.

PLANNING A VACATION

31. Tourists can spend a lifetime of vacations in this country and never run out of variety. Most travelers want to see Disneyland, Yellowstone, and a few thousand other famous American sights as well. How can a tourist find out about them? Libraries and bookstores have a wide selection of guidebooks for travelers. There are also travel magazines and travel sections of newspapers. For information about vacationing in a particular state, tourists can write or call the Tourist Bureau of that state. For those who want help choosing a vacation spot and making reservations, travel agents are eager to assist. Traveling can be expensive, but a knowledgeable travel agent (or a good guidebook) can help tourists find bargains. Word of mouth (advice from others) may provide the best travel tips of all.

32. Americans believe that an occasional change of scene is beneficial, and most foreigners probably agree. One American custom that newcomers have no trouble adjusting to is the annual vacation.

EXERCISES

I. Comprehension Questions. Answer the following questions on paper or in class discussion.

1. What are theme parks? Have you ever visited any?
2. What are the important sights to see in the cities of New York, Chicago, and Washington, D.C.? Why are Florida and California very popular tourist states?
3. Where is Yellowstone Park? What can you see there?
4. Where can tourists get information to help them plan an interesting American vacation?

II. Vocabulary Practice. Pronounce the following words after your teacher, and discuss their meanings. Then use some of them to complete the following sentences. You may need to use the same word twice or three times.

acre	gambling
alongside	monument
amusement	plentiful
annual	sculpture
architecture	specialty
capital	spectacular
Capitol	statue
centennial	surrounding
destination	tourist
enabled	volcanoes

1. The money he inherited from his grandfather ________________ him to leave his job for a year and travel.

2. Most American workers get an ________________ vacation with pay.

3. The ________________ of Liberty is a very large figure of a woman. It is on Liberty Island, so there is water ________________ it. It was dedicated in 1886, so, in 1986, the American people celebrated the statue's ________________.

4. The words ________________ and ________________ are homonyms because they sound alike but have different meanings. Every state in the U.S.A. has its own ________________ city, which is the seat of its government. Washington, D.C. is the

_______________ of the United States. Congress meets there in the _______________ building.

5. The Vietnam Veterans Memorial is a beautiful monument and a fine example of modern _______________.
6. This plane makes a short stop in Philadelphia, but its final _______________ is New York City.
7. There are _______________ in both Alaska and Hawaii.
8. Las Vegas, Nevada, is the place to go if you like _______________ (placing bets with your money).

III. Word Study.

A. Synonyms are words that mean the same. Match the synonyms by writing the correct number on each line.

1. cosmopolitan	___ get
2. exhibit	___ incredible
3. fabulous	___ enormous; gigantic
4. generally	___ usually
5. huge	___ attract
6. lure	___ international; worldly
7. obtain	___ picturesque
8. scenic	___ sightseer
9. tourist	___ display

B. Pronounce the following compound words and discuss their meanings. The numbers in brackets give the paragraphs in which the words are used.

sightsee [20]	skyscraper [9] [16]	mainland [26]
landmark [6]	skyline [9]	waterfall [28]
waterfront [8]	snowmobiler [22]	

IV. Idiom Study. Use the following idioms to complete the sentences. The numbers in brackets give the paragraphs in which the idioms are used.

look forward to [1]	big-name [22]
as well as [18]	word of mouth [31]
change of scene [32]	

1. Everyone enjoys taking a vacation once in a while because it provides a ________________.

2. People go to Las Vegas to gamble and also to enjoy shows with ________________ performers.

3. I always ________________ my summer vacation.

4. My friend told me to visit San Francisco. I got the advice to go there by ________________.

5. In New York City, I saw the Statue of Liberty ________________ the World Trade Center.

V. Reading Skills.

A. Reading a map:
   1. Using a map of the U.S.A., trace a good route for sightseeing in the East, the Midwest, and the West.

2. Locate Hawaii, Alaska, the Mississippi River, and Washington, D.C. on the map.
3. On the map, show your class where you have traveled in the U.S.A.

B. Understanding implications:

At the end of paragraph 6, the text advises you to bring comfortable shoes and traveler's checks to Disney World. What are the implications of these suggestions?

____

____

C. Using reference books:

1. Use an encyclopedia or a guidebook to find out more about one of the tourist spots discussed in this chapter.
2. Prepare a short oral or written report about the place you researched.

22

LEISURE TIME ACTIVITIES

1. To most Americans, work is a necessary chore. According to a recent poll, Americans work longer hours and have 36% less **leisure** time today than they had 15 years ago, so they value the time away from their jobs. The choice of leisure time activities is enormous, and everybody can find something to enjoy.

SPORTS PEOPLE PLAY

2. Among the most popular leisure time activities are sports of every kind. It is said that the American pastime is baseball, but football, basketball, hockey, and, in more recent times, soccer are also very popular activities that Americans enjoy as **spectators** and/or **participants.**

3. Americans spend a lot of time and money on physical activities ranging from bowling to skiing. The object of these activities is not only enjoyment. Doctors have found that vigorous exercise keeps people feeling healthier and looking better. So Americans are working at maintaining or recapturing their youth and vigor.

4. In the spring and summer, neighborhood **teams** organized into leagues **compete** in softball or baseball games, imagining that they are in Yankee **Stadium** playing for 40,000 cheering **fans.** In the cooler weather, basketball is popular, indoors or outdoors. Boys and young men also play football, just for fun, without the formality of yard markers, goal posts, padding, and officials. (American football is not the same game as European football which, in the United States, is called *soccer*.)

5. Golf, one of the most popular participation sports, is played all year except when the ground is covered with snow. Since it is a relatively mild form of **athletics,** it can be played by people of all ages. Doctors highly recommend it for exercise and often practice what they preach. Americans joke about not getting sick on a Wednesday (the doctors' traditional day off) because all the doctors are out on the golf course. Although the only **equipment** needed for golf is a set of clubs, some balls, and tees, the annual expenditure for golf equipment is more than $1 billion!

6. Another popular sport is bowling. It is estimated that 67 million people bowl in the United States. Many bowling leagues (groups of teams that compete against each other) are formed by coworkers or members of organizations such as churches or charitable groups. Bowling is another game that is not too **strenuous** and can be played with a minimum **investment** in equipment.

7. Skiing attracts both **individuals** and families. It is especially popular among young, unmarried people who have the **stamina** and money and who expect to meet other attractive, successful singles on the slopes or in the lounges. Although it requires much more physical **exertion,** is not readily accessible to many Americans, and is more expensive than many other sports, about 15 million Americans participate. Those who do not live in mountainous areas can ski at local "mountains" artificially created and covered with artificial snow. Skiers with more time and money go to resorts with real mountains in places such as Aspen, Colorado. Many skiers go to Europe to the Alps—the ultimate challenge for serious skiers.

8. Tennis has become popular as a participation sport. It is played all year, either indoors or out, does not require much equipment, and provides good vigorous exercise. It is also an individual sport which provides plenty of competition at all levels of ability.

9. Some people get their exercise at health clubs, which have exercise equipment and, in some cases, indoor tennis and racquetball courts. Others join country clubs with golf courses and swimming pools. Those who want privacy equip their homes with exercise bicycles, treadmills, and weights to work out in their bedroom or family room. Walking, running, and jogging are also popular ways of keeping the body fit. Many Americans jog a few miles before going to work in the morning, using jogging trails in parks or simply running around the block several times.

SPECTATOR SPORTS

10. Unfortunately, most Americans participate in sports mainly as *couch potatoes* (sitting in comfortable chairs, munching on potato chips and dip, watching games on TV). Watching athletic events is one of the most popular of all leisure activities. While 23 million Americans played baseball in 1985, 40 million attended major league games, and many millions more watched baseball on television. A typical baseball game takes about two hours to play. On a pleasant weekend afternoon, hundreds of thousands of people crowd the nation's ballparks to enjoy the fresh air, hot dogs, peanuts, beer, and (incidentally) the ball games. Professional baseball's World Series and professional football's Super Bowl (annual competitions between the best teams of each sport) are among the most popular shows broadcast on television. Professional sports teams are native to a particular city, such as the New York Yankees or the Chicago Bears. The association with a city gives the team a ready-made base of fans who live in and around that area. Professional baseball, football, basketball, and hockey are popular TV events and also attract many Americans to the stadiums. College football and basketball are also popular spectator sports. On Mondays, a lot of conversation centers around the results of professional and collegiate games played the preceding weekend. Americans enjoy discussing their favorite teams and players almost as much as they enjoy watching them.

MUSIC, PLAYS, AND MOVIES

11. In 1985, while Americans spent $3 billion to attend sporting events, they spent another $3 billion on theater, opera, and classical musical performances. Rock music concerts also attract millions of people, especially during the summer, when many concerts are held in huge outdoor areas. Mostly younger people, who enjoy the extremely loud music, attend these concerts.

12. Many Americans are not satisfied to be merely spectators and listeners. **Amateur** performances, many of excellent quality, can be found all over the United States on any weekend. Theater groups, orchestras, and bands easily recruit enough volunteers to produce fine music and theater for the local community at very reasonable prices.

13. Another popular source of music is recordings, which are available on phonograph records, tape cassettes, and—the latest technology—compact laser disks. Sales of musical recordings in all forms exceed $5 billion annually, with compact disks quickly becoming the most popular medium.

14. Motion pictures (movies) sell more than one billion tickets a year. Movies are also shown on television and can be rented or purchased as videotape recordings. (About two-thirds of American homes are equipped with video recorders.) Although people once feared that television would ruin the movie industry, movie popularity has soared in recent years. Attending movies is a relatively inexpensive leisure time activity that is very popular.

THE PRINTED WORD

15. Although Americans spend a great deal of time watching TV and seeing movies, books are still very popular in the U.S.A. Hardcover books commonly sell for $12 to $25, so people buy these most frequently as gifts and choose paperback editions (usually under $10) for their personal use. Most people also have a public library in the neighborhood and can get books on loan for two weeks absolutely free. What books do they read? Good works of literature written by Americans are readily available. Since the 19th century, American writers have moved away from the influence of English writers and have developed a voice of their own. Americans are justly proud of their literary giants, but the most popular readings are how-to books (how to fix your car, file for your own divorce, and so forth), escape fiction (including murder mysteries and novels about love and adventure), and biographies, often exposés about famous people. Despite the thousands of books published each year, experts worry that the American people get too much of their knowledge from TV and radio and not enough information from the printed word. Parents, teachers, and librarians are constantly trying to develop in children the habit of reading.

16. Most areas have at least one local daily newspaper which gives news of the surrounding communities and also provides national and international news. However, since 1950, the number of newspapers published in the United States has declined by almost 25%, while the population has increased by almost 70%. Although television has replaced newspapers as the average person's source of news, newspapers and magazines provide more complete news coverage for those who want details and analysis of national and international affairs.

17. Although newspaper sales have been declining, magazines have prospered. They are published weekly, monthly, or quarterly (four times a year) and cover almost every subject imaginable. Some of the most popular are weekly newsmagazines such as *Time, Newsweek,* and *U.S. News and World Report*. There are hundreds of different magazines for special groups—working women, single men, blacks, photographers, computer users, gamblers, and pigeon racers, to name just a few. In addition, there are special publications (called *trade magazines*) of interest to people in particular industries.

THE TUBE

18. By far, the most popular leisure time activity is watching television. There is at least one TV set in 98% of American households, and many have two or three. Two thirds of homes also have a videocassette recorder (VCR), which is capable of recording and playing back sound and picture. Television satisfies many of the other interests that Americans enjoy—sports, news, music, theater, and movies. For those that are at home during the day, there is afternoon fare consisting of game shows and serialized dramas commonly called *soap operas*. (The *opera* part of the name comes from the complicated plots and incredible story lines. *Soap* comes from the fact that, in pretelevision days, the sponsors of serialized radio dramas were sellers of soap and other products purchased by listeners.) For preschool children, TV offers clever programs that educate while entertaining. Saturday mornings are also for the children, who are "treated" to hours of animated cartoons. At dinnertime, the local and national news is broadcast for a half hour or an hour. Evening entertainment consists mostly of situation comedies (sitcoms) which portray some aspect of life (family, singles, elderly, and so forth) in a "humorous" way. Every other line of dialogue is expected to produce a laugh. In case it doesn't, recorded laughter is provided. There are also adventure shows, dramas, and various weekly shows which have the same cast of characters and general theme but a different story each week.

19. The production of television programs is dominated by three national **networks.** They are the American Broadcasting Company (ABC), the Columbia Broadcasting System (CBS), and the National Broadcasting Company (NBC). These are privately owned companies that sell advertising time for a profit. Most television **stations** are affiliated with one of those networks, which provides programming to the member stations. As a result, programs produced by a network are broadcast all over the nation. Another network, the Public Broadcasting System, is a noncommercial company funded by public and private grants. Much of the broadcasting on this network is without advertising. Because it does not depend on advertising for support, it can broadcast programs that do not appeal to mass audiences, such as the plays of George Bernard Shaw or William Shakespeare, concerts, and in-depth discussions of news events.

20. For those that want more TV than the regular stations provide, cable TV is available in many parts of the country. To receive cable TV, one must pay a monthly **subscription** fee. Wires and a special tuner are attached to the TV set to enable the subscriber to receive the cable broadcasts. Cable stations tend to specialize in one type of program. There are stations for sports, movies, music videos, business, health, and the arts. Unlike commercial stations, programs on cable TV are not usually interrupted for commercials.

21. Many people have criticized television programming. They complain that it does not challenge the intellect, shows too much violence, and appeals to the least educated of viewers in order to get the largest audience. To a great extent, these criticisms are correct. But there are also many excellent TV programs available for people who are **selective** in their viewing.

22. Television has become the main source of information and entertainment for the average American. It is estimated that by the time a child reaches 18, he or she has spent almost twice as much time watching TV as in the classroom. Many people are concerned about TV's influence. News is edited and condensed to fit into two or three minutes per event. Unrealistic family and social situations are portrayed, with all problems easily solved within a half hour, giving the young a distorted view of life. How has TV affected the young people who grew up watching it? Unquestionably, children learn a lot from TV shows, but not all of it is appropriate or positive. American concerns about the low level of many popular TV shows has led to TV's insulting nickname, *the boob tube.* Moreover, many educators believe that today's American students read and write less well than students of earlier generations because so much of their knowledge has come to them via TV and film rather than the printed word.

GAMES OF CHANCE

23. In 1988, 54% of Americans made some form of wager, and they spent at least $50 billion on bets both legal and illegal. Where gambling is legal, casino games such as roulette, craps, and various card games attract people from areas where these activities are not legal. Billions of dollars are spent in legal gambling, and probably even more is spent in illegal betting. But by far, the most popular games of chance are the state lotteries, played by at least 42% of the American public.

24. State-run lottery games gained immense popularity in the 1980s. In many states, lottery tickets sell for $1 or $2 each, and some give the purchaser a chance to win millions if his or her set of numbers is selected. There are many different lottery games. Those that pay the most money also give purchasers the worst odds. In some cases, the owner of a single ticket may have less than 1 chance in 10 million to win. Nevertheless, in recent years Americans have spent at least $17 billion per year on lottery tickets. Some people disapprove of lotteries because they are a form of gambling. Others feel that state-run lotteries are okay because they are really a form of voluntary taxation, with the profits going to improve education, roads, or other state facilities. When people don't spend more than they can afford on tickets, playing the lottery can be an exciting and harmless activity, allowing the player the fun of imagining himself or herself an instant millionaire. But no one should seriously expect to win.

OTHER ACTIVITIES

25. Americans, who love hobbies, find a great many different ways to spend their leisure time and extra dollars. Some are stamp collectors, coin collectors, photographers, miniature home builders, boaters, gun collectors, surfers, and enthusiasts of dozens of other hobbies. The most popular hobbies have organizations and publications devoted to the subject. No matter what one's interests, it is easy to find the information, encouragement, and companionship that make a **hobby** fun.

EXERCISES

I. Comprehension Questions. Answer the following questions on paper or in class discussion.

1. Why do Americans spend a lot of time and money on physical activities?
2. Why are golf and bowling popular with people of all ages?
3. What does TV contribute to American life? What harmful influences does it have?
4. Leisure time can be spent passively being entertained or actively as a participant. What are some activities of each type that Americans enjoy?

II. Vocabulary Practice. Pronounce the following words after your teacher, and discuss their meanings. Then use some of them to complete the following sentences.

amateur	networks
athletics	participant
compete	selective
equipment	spectators
exertion	stadium
fans	stamina
hobby	stations
individual	strenuous
investment	subscription
leisure	team

1. ________________ is another word for sports.

2. Swimming and golf are usually ________________ sports. Baseball and football are always ________________ sports.

3. People who go to a ________________ to watch two teams ________________ in a sporting event are ________________. If they cheer for their favorite team, they are ________________ of that team.

4. A person who plays on a team or in a band and doesn't get paid to do it is called an ________________.

5. If you want a magazine delivered to your home regularly, you subscribe to it. You can also get a ________________ to a cable TV channel.

6. Tennis is a ________________ sport requiring a lot of exertion and ________________.

7. If you don't want to waste time watching bad TV shows, you must be ________________ about what you watch.

8. Most TV shows are produced by large companies called ________________ and then are sold to various smaller TV ________________.

III. Word Study. Antonyms are words that have opposite meanings. Match the antonyms by writing the correct number on each line.

1. accessible	___ work
2. amateur	___ unavailable
3. artificial	___ professional
4. endless	___ team
5. individual	___ spectator
6. leisure	___ mental
7. participant	___ natural or real
8. physical	___ limited

IV. Idiom Study. Underline the correct phrase to complete each sentence. The numbers in brackets give the paragraphs in which the idioms are used.

1. If you *practice what you preach* [5], you a) do what you advise others to do b) give a lot of speeches c) pray a lot.
2. The favorite leisure time activity of a *couch potato* [10] is a) eating potatoes b) sitting at home on the couch reading a book c) watching TV.
3. A *soap opera* [18] is a) a kind of an opera b) a radio or TV dramatic story that continues day after day c) a kind of soap for washing clothes.
4. *In case* [18] means a) if b) although c) because.
5. TV is sometimes called the *boob tube.* [22] That name is a) complimentary b) insulting c) neither complimentary nor insulting.

V. Reading Skills.

A. Checking comprehension:
   1. If you play tennis with your friend and try to win the game, you are a) complaining b) completing c) competing [4].
   2. "I want a book *and/or* [2] a magazine" means a) only one of these b) one or both c) both.

3. "*Escape fiction*" [15] helps the reader escape from a) prison b) ordinary life c) an exciting world of fantasy.
4. Paragraph 5 ends with an exclamation point because

   ____.

5. In paragraph 18, what is implied by the quotation marks

   around the word *humorous?* ______________________

6. What is the meaning of the heading "Games of Chance"

   (above paragraph 23)? __________________________

B. Using reference books: In an encyclopedia, read the rules of one of the sports mentioned in this chapter (baseball, football, basketball, bowling, soccer, tennis, and so on). Then prepare a short oral or written report explaining how the game is played.

23

We the People
of the United S
Article 1

THE CONSTITUTION AND THE FEDERAL SYSTEM

THE CONSTITUTION

1. Daniel Webster, the 19th-century American statesman, once said: "We may be tossed upon an ocean where we can see no land—nor perhaps the sun or stars. But there is a chart and a compass for us to study, to consult, and to obey. That chart is the Constitution."

2. June 21, 1988 was the 200th anniversary of the adoption of the United States **Constitution.** It is the oldest written constitution still in use. Yet, since the addition of the Bill of Rights in 1791, the Constitution has been changed (amended) only 16 times, and one of those **amendments** simply canceled another.

3. What is this Constitution? It is the basic law from which the United States government gets all its power. It is the law that protects those who live in the United States from unreasonable actions by the national government or any state.

4. The Constitution defines three branches of government. They are the **legislative** branch, which enacts (makes) laws; the executive branch, which enforces them; and the **judicial** branch, which **interpret**s them (decides what they mean).

5. The legislative branch is called **Congress.** It is made up of two groups of legislators—the Senate and the House of **Representatives.** The Senate is often referred to as the *Upper House.* It has two **senators** from each state. Senators are elected for six-year terms. Every two years, one-third of them face reelection.

6. The *Lower House* is the House of Representatives, which has 435 members, all elected every two years. The representation of each state is determined by the state's population. While the smallest states have only one representative each, California's representation in the 100th Congress (1987 to 1988) was 45.

7. For the purpose of electing representatives, each state is divided into Congressional districts. The districts within a state are about equal in population. One representative is elected from each district. One of his or her major duties is to protect the interests of the people in that district.

8. The job of Congress is to pass laws. Before a proposed law (**bill**) becomes a law, it must be approved by both houses of Congress and by the president. If the president disapproves of (**veto**es) a bill, it can still become law if at least two-thirds of the members of each house of Congress vote for it.

9. The president, the nation's chief executive, must see that all national laws are carried out. Of course, a very large staff of advisers and other employees assist the president. In fact, the executive branch employs about three million people located all over the world. The most important group of advisers is called the **Cabinet**. The Cabinet consists of the heads of the 14 departments of the executive branch, such as the Secretaries of Education, Defense, and Agriculture. Cabinet members are chosen by the president with the approval of the Senate. The president also appoints ambassadors and other consular heads, as well as judges of the federal courts.

10. The vice-president is the only other elected person in the executive branch. The chief constitutional **duty** of the person holding this office is to serve as president of the Senate. The vice-president's most important function is to become president upon the death, resignation, or disability of the president. Out of 35 presidents elected, eight have died in office, and one **resigned.** In each case, the vice-president became president.

11. The judicial branch consists of the federal courts. One of the unusual features of the American judicial system is the power of the courts to declare legislation **unconstitutional** and, therefore, **void.** Federal laws are unconstitutional if they are not authorized by the Constitution or if they violate a person's rights that are protected by the Constitution. For example, if Congress passed a law that members of the House of Representatives be elected for four-year terms, that would be unconstitutional because the Constitution says that representatives are to be elected for two-year terms.

12. United States laws are in some way controlled or affected by all three branches of government—Congress makes them; the president approves and enforces them; and the courts determine their meaning and validity. This is one example of the government's system of checks and balances, by which each branch of government prevents improper actions by the other branches.

13. The checks and balances were put to an important test in 1974 when it was discovered that President Nixon had been involved in obstruction of justice (hiding crimes) in connection with the *Watergate* scandal. Both Congress and the prosecutor demanded that the president give them certain papers and tape recordings which he had. The president refused because he said that neither the judicial nor the legislative branch could tell the president, the head of the **executive** branch, what to do. He was relying on a doctrine known as the *separation of powers*. This means that one branch of the government cannot interfere with the others.

14. During this conflict, two important questions were raised: (a) Could the president withhold information about possible crimes from Congress and the courts? and (b) Did the doctrine of separation of powers mean that the courts could not order the president to give evidence to the prosecutor?

15. After considering these questions, the Supreme Court ordered the president to give the evidence to the prosecutor, and he obeyed. After examining the evidence, Congress began the constitutional procedure to remove the president from office (**impeach**ment), but before the process was completed, President Nixon resigned from office. The checks and balances prevented a major governmental **crisis,** and the presidency passed peacefully and smoothly to the vice-president. The "chart" had kept the country on course, even when the captain tried to stray.

16. Probably the most significant portion of the Constitution is the Bill of Rights, the first 10 amendments to the Constitution. The first of these assures freedom of religion, speech, and the press and the right to complain to and about the government. Speech is protected no matter how unpopular or repulsive, so long as it does not create an immediate and serious danger to life or property. Free speech means that the government cannot prevent people from saying or writing whatever they want, nor can it punish people for expressing ideas that criticize the government. Free speech is at the very heart of democracy. Former Supreme Court Justice Louis Brandeis once stated that, for a democracy to work, people must be allowed to express new, unusual, and unpopular ideas so that they can be debated and examined and then adopted or rejected. After all, democracy itself was a **radical** idea in the 18th century, and it still is in many parts of the world.

17. Freedom of religion means that each person can belong (or not belong) to any church. An individual can follow any church's teachings as long as these do not seriously interfere with the rights of others. Religious freedom also means that neither the **federal** government nor any state government can encourage or prevent the practice of religion. This concept has been referred to as the *wall of separation* between church and state.

18. The Fourth, Fifth, Sixth, and Eighth Amendments protect people suspected or accused of crimes. But they also protect the ordinary person. Government officials and police cannot arrest people or search them, their property, or their homes without some reason to believe that they have committed a crime.

19. Certainly, the most important of the remaining amendments is the Fourteenth. It grew out of the Civil War and was passed to protect former slaves from oppressive and discriminatory state laws. But its effect has been much broader than that. First, it gives state citizenship to all United States citizens living in a state. Then, it prohibits states from violating the rights of American citizens. But the most significant provision is that no state may "deprive any person of life, liberty or property, without due process of law; nor deny to any person within its jurisdiction the equal protection of the laws." These last provisions apply not only to United States citizens, but to all persons in the state. The original Bill of Rights did not protect people from state action, but only from federal action; the Fourteenth Amendment has been interpreted by the Supreme Court to apply almost all of the provisions in the Bill of Rights to the states. Thus, the Fourteenth Amendment is one of the most valuable protections that people living in the United States have.

THE FEDERAL SYSTEM

20. The United States is organized as a federal system. This means that the power to govern is divided between the national (federal) government, located in Washington, D.C., and the state governments. Whatever laws are passed by Congress (federal laws) must be authorized somewhere in the United States Constitution. That is what is meant by the statement that the United States government gets all of its powers from the Constitution.

21. The original purpose of a national central government was to perform those tasks that could not be performed efficiently by each state individually. Such things as dealing with foreign nations, establishing a monetary system, and regulating commerce between the states could be done better by a single national authority. Other governmental responsibilities, such as public school systems, local roads, and police and fire protection, were left to the states and their subdivisions.

22. While the federal government's power is limited by the Constitution, the individual states are given the power to pass any law that is not prohibited by the Constitution. In those areas where both the states and the federal government have the power to pass laws, state laws cannot conflict with those passed by the federal government.

23. Most of the state governments are quite similar to the national government. Each is headed by an elected executive called a *governor*. The legislative branch may be called a state legislature, general assembly, or have some other name, but it generally functions much as Congress does. Most of the state legislatures also have two houses. The state court systems generally follow the three-level federal court plan, which provides for a trial court, an appellate court, and a supreme court.

24. States are divided into smaller governmental units, such as cities, towns, villages, and counties. These units have some legislative authority, which they receive from the state, and they are responsible for control within their boundaries.

25. The United States and its Constitution have withstood many crises and criticisms. Since the Constitution was written, this nation has changed from a rural to a highly industrialized society. And the population has grown from less than 4 million to almost 250 million. Still, the "chart" that Daniel Webster mentioned continues to keep the nation securely on course. The American experiment in democracy has proved conclusively that government "of the people, by the people, for the people" can function effectively for the betterment of its citizens.

EXERCISES

I. Comprehension Questions. Answer the following questions on paper or in class discussion.

1. What are the three branches of the federal government, and what job does each do?
2. What is the Cabinet?
3. What is the Bill of Rights? Name some of the freedoms it provides and protects.
4. What is the federal system of government?

II. Vocabulary Practice. Pronounce the following words after your teacher, and discuss their meanings. Then use some of them to complete the following sentences.

amendments
bill
Cabinet
Congress
Constitution
crisis
duty
executive
federal
impeached
interpret
judicial
legislative
radical
representatives
resigned
senators
unconstitutional
veto
void

1. The first 10 ________________ to the U.S. Constitution are called the Bill of Rights.
2. One of the jobs of the Supreme Court is to ________________ the Constitution.
3. In a ________________ system of government, the governing powers are divided between the state governments and the national government.
4. A proposed law that is being considered by a legislative body is called a ________________.
5. If Congress votes in favor of making a bill a law, the President can still stop that bill from becoming law by using his ________________ power.
6. President Nixon ________________ from office before he could be ________________.
7. Every state elects two ________________ to the Senate, but in the House of Representatives, the number of ________________ from each state varies, depending on the state's population.
8. A ________________ idea is one that suggests very great changes.

III. Word Study. In English, many verbs can be made into nouns by adding the suffix *-tion* or *-ment*. All of the following verbs, except one, have a noun form that ends with one of these suffixes. Write these *-ment* and *-tion* nouns. Be careful. Sometimes additional spelling changes are needed before adding the suffix. Use a dictionary for help. Which of the nouns is the same as the verb form of the word?

1. amend________________	8. prohibit________________
2. apply________________	9. protect________________
3. appoint________________	10. regulate________________
4. conflict________________	11. resign________________
5. elect________________	12. separate________________
6. govern________________	13. state (say)________________
7. interpret________________	14. violate________________

IV. Idiom Study. Underline the correct phrase to complete each sentence. The numbers in brackets give the paragraphs in which the idioms are used.

1. The *Upper House* [5] of Congress a) meets in a room above the Lower House b) is called the Senate c) has more members than the Lower House.
2. Each member of the *Lower House* [6] a) is elected by one district of a state b) is called a senator c) is appointed by the president.
3. The expression *checks and balances* [12] refers to a) the federal government's bank account b) the relationship between the two houses of Congress c) the relationship between the three branches of the federal government.
4. *Obstruction of justice* [13] means a) committing crimes b) withholding evidence about a crime c) helping the police catch a criminal.
5. *Free speech* [16] means a) it doesn't cost anything b) people have the right to express all kinds of ideas c) there is no charge to hear speeches made by senators.

V. Reading Skills.

A. Checking comprehension:

1. Reread paragraphs 13, 14, and 15. Why was President Nixon's argument with the Supreme Court important? What did the outcome show? ____________________

2. What is the meaning of *House* as it is used in this chapter?

____

B. Understanding sentences with *nor:*

1. Reread paragraph 16, sentence 4. Can the American government punish a person who says something bad about the country? ____________

2. Reread paragraph 17, sentence 3. Can the federal government encourage the practice of a particular religion?

____

C. Identifying figures of speech:
Figures of speech compare things that are not really alike. The comparison is figurative (imaginary) not literal (real).

1. Write down the first two words of the sentence in paragraph 15 that uses a figure of speech. ____________

What is the Constitution compared to in that sentence?

____

What is President Nixon compared to? ____________

2. Find the figure of speech in paragraph 17. What is the U.S. doctrine of separation of church and state compared to? ________________

24

CHOOSING THE NATION'S PRESIDENT

1. Every four years, Americans participate in a **unique** and exciting **ritual**—the selection of the nation's president. Beginning early every presidential election year, those who would like to be president of the United States compete with others to win **delegates** to the political **conventions** held in the summer. Delegates are chosen from each state. Some of them are selected at state **caucuses** (similar to town meetings) and others by party leaders from each state. But most are chosen by **primary** elections. Primaries give voters an opportunity to indicate who they want to be their party's presidential **candidate.** In a primary election, each voter can vote only for a presidential candidate in one party.

THE CONVENTIONS

2. The summer before the election, each of the two **major** political **parties** holds a national convention to select the people that will be its candidates for president and vice-president. The number of delegates from each state is determined by its population and its support for that party in previous elections. The total number of delegates at a convention ranges from about 2,000 to about 3,500.

3. After routine formalities, convention business usually begins with the creation and acceptance of a party **platform.** A platform is a very general statement of the party's philosophy, positions, and goals on **issues** of national and international concern. A majority of the convention delegates must vote for the various planks of the platform in order for them to be accepted. (A plank is a statement on one subject.)

4. The next business of the convention is the nomination of prospective presidential candidates. For each nominee, a long, complimentary nominating speech is made in which the nominee's strengths and accomplishments are recited. This is followed by a long, noisy **demonstration** with delegates waving flags, bands playing, and thousands of people singing, yelling, clapping, and waving signs. When the convention quiets down, one or more seconding speeches are given for the nominee. These are followed by similar displays of support.

5. After the demonstrations, the delegates get down to the serious work of choosing their party's presidential candidate. The most important qualification is the ability to get elected, but the delegates also consider a nominee's integrity, philosophy, and talent for leadership. Votes are taken alphabetically by state. Several roll calls may be necessary before one nominee wins the majority of votes needed to become the party's candidate. In the early votes, some delegates may **withhold** their support from serious contenders by voting for an important politician from their own state, called a *favorite son*. This is done so that the state delegations can bargain with the major nominees by agreeing to switch their votes in exchange for some political favor or governmental position. For example, an agreement might be made with a nominee that, in exchange for a state's votes, the nominee will name a certain person as his or her choice to be the vice-presidential candidate. Eventually, enough deals are made so that one person receives a majority of the delegates' votes and becomes the party's nominee for president.

6. After the presidential candidate is selected, the vice-presidential candidate must be chosen. Traditionally, the delegates give their presidential candidate the *running mate* of his or her choice. It is also traditional (and good politics) for a party's presidential and vice-presidential candidates to come from different sections of the country and have somewhat different political views. Thus, the party achieves what is called a *balanced ticket*, a pair of candidates (running mates) that appeal to many different blocs of voters. Even though nomination of the vice-presidential candidate is usually prearranged, the rites of nominating and seconding speeches, accompanied by demonstrations, are performed, followed by a vote of the delegates. After the candidates give their acceptance speeches, the convention is adjourned until it is time to nominate presidential and vice-presidential candidates again in four years.

7. Of course, it sometimes happens that one candidate wins enough delegates during the preconvention period to be **nominated** for president without a contest at the convention. If that happens, the process is shortened, and all of the speeches and demonstrations are focused on that candidate and the vice-presidential candidate.

THE CAMPAIGN

8. Serious campaigning for the election traditionally begins on Labor Day in early September. From that time until Election Day in early November, voters are bombarded from all sides—by radio, television, newspapers, mail, and personal communications—with political material. Sometimes long-standing friendships break up as arguments over issues and candidates rage. Ordinarily soft-spoken people become outspoken advocates for their candidate. Neighborhood political workers and precinct captains from each party knock on every door and remind voters of all that the party has done for them and for the country since the last election.

9. Each candidate tries to convince a majority of the American voters that he or she is best qualified to lead the country for the next four years. Since the candidate has only two months in which to do this, a very concentrated **campaign** is necessary. All of the resources of modern communication are used to acquaint the voters with the candidates' views and personalities. Television has become a powerful influence, and the candidate who does not have personal appeal on TV is at a great disadvantage. In 1960, a series of televised debates between Richard Nixon and John Kennedy probably influenced enough voters to change the course of the election. It has been said that, if Abraham Lincoln were running for president today, he probably couldn't win because he wasn't physically attractive.

10. Although modern communications have better acquainted voters with candidates and issues, the resulting costs of election campaigns have created a serious problem. The various candidates who participated in the 1984 presidential campaign spent a combined total of almost $250 million. About $180 million of this total was contributed by the federal government on a matching funds basis. That is, the candidates raised from private **donations** an amount equal to what they got from the government. Private donations such as these may mean that the person elected has many "friends" who expect political favors in return for their financial help.

11. Because campaigning is extremely expensive and because a candidate must receive a majority of the electoral votes to be elected, presidential politics has, to a large extent, been limited to two major parties—the Democrats and Republicans. Although no third-party candidate has ever won a presidential election, third parties have often played an important role by focusing attention on particular issues and influencing the policies of the two major parties.

12. No candidate can hope to win by appealing to one or two groups of voters, such as farmers or businesspeople. Because of the need for broad appeal, the philosophies of both parties usually take a middle course so as not to alienate any large blocs of voters.

13. "Does it matter who wins?" Newcomers to the U.S.A. often ask, "Are there any real differences between the two political parties?" During an election campaign, one hears a lot of political labels. Ranging from those who are very resistant to new ideas to those who favor great change, the labels go like this: reactionary, **conservative,** moderate (middle-of-the-road), **liberal,** and radical. Most Democrats are moderates or liberals. Most Republicans are moderates or conservatives. People sometimes refer to liberals as being *to the left* and conservatives as being *to the right.* In terms of specific programs, Democrats (or liberals) tend to favor more spending for social programs (to help poorer people) and less spending for military programs. Republicans' (or conservatives') priorities are just the reverse. Traditionally, Democrats have also favored a stronger federal government while Republicans have emphasized states' rights. The government does change somewhat depending on the party in power, but not as much as political campaign speeches might lead one to believe.

14. Each party has a familiar symbol: For the Democrats, it is a donkey, and for the Republicans, an elephant. These symbols were created by Thomas Nast, a famous 19th-century political cartoonist. The Republican Party is also called the GOP (Grand Old Party).

15. To preserve free democratic elections, the rights of all candidates are carefully guarded. They may speak their minds openly, even to the extent of severely criticizing other candidates and their viewpoints, without fear of punishment. This is true even when an **opponent** is an *incumbent* (currently holding office).

THE ELECTION

16. On the Tuesday following the first Monday in November, voters cast their ballots for president and vice-president. Some members of Congress and many state and local officials are also elected at this time. Thanks to voting machines and computers, Americans usually know most of the winners by late evening. In fact, the television networks often predict the results of an election as soon as the voting stops. They do this by conducting exit polls—asking voters in scientifically selected precincts how they voted.

17. The president and vice-president are not actually chosen by how many people vote for them (the popular vote); instead, they are chosen by *electoral votes*. When citizens cast votes for presidential and vice-presidential candidates, they are selecting their state's electors (people chosen under state laws and procedures to cast each state's votes for president and vice-president). Each elector is expected (although not legally obliged) to vote for the candidate who wins the majority of popular votes in his or her state. These electors as a group are called the *Electoral College*.

18. The number of electors for each state is equal to the total number of representatives and senators who represent that state in Congress. Thus, states with larger populations have more electoral votes. Because the candidate who receives a majority of the votes in a particular state receives *all* of that state's electoral votes, it is possible for a presidential candidate to win a majority of the popular votes but not a majority of the electoral votes, and thereby lose the election. This can happen if an opponent wins by small margins in large states and loses by large margins in states with few electoral votes. (See Popular and Electoral Votes chart in this chapter.) At least two presidential elections have been decided this way, most recently in 1888, when Benjamin Harrison defeated the incumbent candidate, Grover Cleveland. On the other hand, in the 1988 presidential election, George Bush received only a small majority (54%) of the popular vote but an impressive 79% of the electoral vote. It is also possible that an elector expected to vote for one candidate will exercise his constitutional right to vote for someone else. However, since electors are important members of their parties, this rarely happens.

Popular and Electoral Votes in the 1976 Election

State	Democrat (Carter)	Republican (Ford)	Electoral
Nebraska	234,000	360,000	5R
Idaho	127,000	240,000	4R
Ohio	2,012,000	2,001,000	25D
Pennsylvania	2,329,000	2,206,000	27D
Totals	4,702,000	4,807,000	52D, 9R

19. To be elected, candidates for president and vice-president must receive a majority of the votes in the Electoral College. If no candidate receives a majority, the House of Representatives chooses the president from the top three candidates, and the Senate chooses the vice-president from the two candidates having the highest number of electoral votes.

20. This Electoral College method of choosing the president has been criticized as old-fashioned and undemocratic. However, states with small populations do not want to change it because they have a greater proportional vote in the Electoral College than they would have if the president were chosen by popular vote.

THE INAUGURATION

21. The newly elected president and vice-president are inaugurated in January during a solemn, nationally televised ceremony. The president then moves into the White House and appoints members of the Cabinet (the president's closest advisors, who are also the heads of the various departments of the Executive branch). Sometimes the new president and the majority of the members of Congress belong to different parties. When this happens, it is more difficult for the president to fulfill promises made during the campaign.

22. Since the two major parties are not extremely different, there is seldom a sudden shift in national policy as a result of a change in the political party in control. Change can be detected only with the passage of time, as the new administration becomes accustomed to its powers and responsibilities.

EXERCISES

I. Comprehension Questions. Answer the following questions on paper or in class discussion.

1. What is the purpose of a primary election?
2. Each political convention has three major jobs to do. What are they?
3. How is the vice-presidential candidate selected during the convention? How is a vice-president elected?
4. What is the difference between popular votes and electoral votes? Which are more important?

II. Vocabulary Practice. Pronounce the following words after your teacher, and discuss their meanings. Then use some of them to complete the following sentences.

campaign	liberal
candidate	major
caucus	nominated
conservative	opponents
convention	parties
delegates	platform
demonstration	primary
donation	ritual
inauguration	unique
issues	withhold

1. Every four years, the two ________________ political parties have a national ________________.
2. At each convention, various people are ________________ to be the party's candidate for president of the United States.
3. The people who vote at these national conventions are called ________________.
4. The Democratic Party appeals to the more ________________ voters, and the Republican Party appeals to the more ________________ voters.
5. The planks of each political party's ________________ tell that party's viewpoint on important political ________________.
6. The presidential candidates from each party ________________ for a few months before the election.
7. The president is elected in November but does not take office until the following January, after the ________________.

8. Americans have a ________________ system for choosing presidents. (No other country has exactly the same system.)

III. Word Study.

A. Compound words:

Discuss the meanings of the following compound words used in this chapter:

long-standing [8]
soft-spoken [8]
outspoken [8]
old-fashioned [20]

B. Words with the letters *ex:*

The letters *ex* are sometimes pronounced [eks] and sometimes [egz]. Look up these words in an English dictionary, check the pronunciation symbols, and write [eks] or [egz] on the line next to each word. Then say the words aloud.

example___
expensive___
expect___
exit___
exchange___
extremely___

C. Words with the letters *qu:*

The letters *qu* are usually pronounced [kw], but in words that end in *-que,* the sound is usually [k]. Check the pronunciation symbols in your dictionary, and then write [kw] or [k] on the line next to each word. Then say the words aloud.

unique___
acquaint___
qualified___
equal___

IV. Idiom Study. Complete each sentence with one of the idioms from the list. The numbers in brackets give the paragraphs in which the idioms are used.

favorite son [5]	matching funds [10]
running mates [6]	exit polls [16]
balanced ticket [6]	Electoral College [17]

1. If both the presidential and the vice-presidential candidates are liberal Democrats from New England, the party does not have a ________________ .

2. Political candidates *run* for office. George Bush and Dan Quayle were ________________ in the 1988 presidential elections.

3. A ________________ is a candidate favored by the people from his or her own state.

4. The ________________ elects the president of the United States.

5. ________________ are surveys conducted on Election Day to find out how people voted.

V. Reading Skills. Using the information from this chapter, make a list of some things that are good and things that are bad about the American system of choosing its president.

GOOD	BAD
1. ________________	1. ________________
2. ________________	2. ________________
3. ________________	3. ________________

25

CITIZENSHIP: ITS OBLIGATIONS AND PRIVILEGES

1. Every person living in the United States, citizen or not, is **entitled** to most of the nation's basic freedoms and protections. Still, there are many **advantages** for people who intend to live in the U.S.A. permanently to become citizens. Of these, the most important are the right to remain in the United States and the right to participate in its government. Once a person becomes a naturalized citizen, his or her rights are the same as any native-born citizen, except that he or she cannot become president or vice-president of the United States.

HOW TO BECOME A CITIZEN

2. With few exceptions, everyone born in the United States is automatically a citizen. An alien who wishes to become a citizen must fulfill certain legal requirements. In general, a person wanting to become a **naturalized** citizen must first obtain permanent resident status. After five continuous years in that status, one can apply for citizenship. The applicant must prove that he or she has actually lived in the United States for at least half of these five years. The applicant must also have lived at least six months in the state in which application is made. Next, it is necessary to demonstrate an understanding of the English language and of the history, principles, and form of government of the United States. The applicant must also show that he or she is a person of good moral character who believes in the principles of the United States Constitution. Once a person is approved for citizenship, he or she goes before a judge and promises loyalty to the United States of America.

RESPONSIBILITIES OF CITIZENSHIP

3. No individual, no matter how important or wealthy, can act in a way prohibited by law. Of course, not all laws are perfect. Some are unwise, others are too harsh, many are foolish. But they cannot, for any

of these reasons, be ignored. The citizen who disapproves of a particular law can legally and peacefully work to get it changed through participation in government.

4. One way that citizens participate in government is by voting. Unfortunately, in every election, a large percentage of those entitled to vote never come to the polls. In 1988, for example, only about 50% of those eligible voted for a presidential candidate. When a large number of citizens do not vote, those who do have a greater **voice** in determining the outcome of the election. If only 50% of the people vote, 26% of the total population can elect the president and the members of Congress. The idea of majority rule is, thus, lost.

5. Another way that citizens can participate in government is by communicating with their representatives. In order for elected officials to represent their constituents properly, they must know what the voters think about current laws and **pending** legislation. Do voters feel that certain laws are **outmoded** and should be discarded? Are they for or against a particular **bill?** Is there something their government should be doing but isn't (or shouldn't be doing but is)? A representative who wants to stay in office (be reelected) is strongly motivated to vote as his or her constituents desire. But very few voters take the time to write their federal or state representatives and express their views. This creates an opportunity for a small, active minority (such as those opposed to restricting gun use and ownership) to influence legislation out of proportion to their numbers, and it leads to a distortion of the representative form of government.

6. Letters are not the only way in which citizens can influence their representatives. Among the basic constitutional guarantees are the rights to assemble peaceably, to petition the government, and to freely express opinions about the government's policies. Peaceful protests outside government office buildings (and many foreign embassies and consulates) are very common. Groups (such as those opposed to the government's Central American policies or to apartheid in South Africa) march with signs, singing and chanting, to let their government know what they favor or oppose. However, in expressing dissatisfaction, people must respect the rights of others to express opposing views or be **neutral.**

7. One of the most **controversial** duties of a citizen is service in the military forces. Although the United States does not now have compulsory military service, from time to time in its history a draft has been in effect. Of course, during World War II, citizens were required to serve in the armed forces, and most did so willingly. But in more recent times, the government has met with a great deal of resistance to its draft laws. During the Korean War and, especially, during the Vietnam War, many people refused military service, demanded non**combat** assignments as conscientious objectors (people who had strong personal or religious objections to killing), or left the country. Much of that **resistance** was due to the **lack** of support for the United States' fighting against countries that were not threatening its safety directly. Opposition to the war in Vietnam was so strong that the United States was finally forced to abandon its military efforts there. The effects of the antiwar protests have made a **lasting** impression on political leaders. It is **unlikely** that the United States will engage in combat when there is no genuine threat to the country.

8. One of the more unpopular obligations is the payment of taxes. For most people, the largest of these is the federal income tax. Since 1913, the United States government has been collecting income taxes. As the cost of running the government has increased, so have tax rates. When the federal income tax was first enacted, people had to pay 1% on annual incomes of less than $20,000. Income in excess of $500,000 was taxed at 7%. Today's income tax rates are between 15% and 33%. Currently, income taxes provide more than half of the money collected by the federal government each year. In 1987, the federal government received about $412 billion in income taxes. These taxes are necessary to support a federal budget which, in 1988, was about $1 **trillion**. The money is used for many things. In addition to the cost of operating the government itself, there are expenses for defense, education, foreign aid, research, aid to the poor, and countless other services provided by governmental agencies.

9. Federal income tax rates are graduated, which means that people with larger incomes are taxed at a higher rate than those earning less. An unmarried person earning $15,000 a year pays about 10% of that in taxes, while someone earning $50,000 pays about 15%.

10. Income tax is paid by nearly everyone who earns money in the United States—citizens, alien residents, and visitors. Employers are required to **withhold** a percentage of their employees' salaries and pay it to the government to be applied toward the employees' tax. Self-employed people and those earning a substantial amount in addition to their salaries must make quarterly payments toward their annual taxes. By April 15 of every year, each person whose income in the previous year exceeded a certain minimum must file a tax return—a statement (on forms supplied by the government) listing income, expenses, number of dependents, and other information. After making calculations on the return, taxpayers can determine how much they owe. Those who have paid more than their share get a **refund.** Those who have paid less must pay the balance. Every year around April 15, Americans complain that Uncle Sam is taking all of their money. Uncle Sam (a thin, bearded man whose suit is decorated with the stars and stripes of the American flag) is a symbol of U.S. government.

11. Although the federal government has a lot of information about each taxpayer and penalizes those who file false returns, the income tax law could not be enforced without the honesty and cooperation of the vast majority of taxpayers.

12. For most people, the federal tax is not the only tax on their income. Most states and many cities collect income taxes. Many other taxes are levied by federal, state, and local governments. Funds from these taxes are needed to provide services and facilities such as courts, schools, roads, and parks. Besides income taxes, the most common taxes are those imposed on property and purchases. The owner of a car, for example, pays several taxes: a sales tax when buying the car, an annual vehicle registration tax, and a personal property tax. If the person dies while owning the car, the **heirs** may have to pay an **inherit**ance tax on the car's value.

13. Despite the grumbling one hears about high taxes, Americans know that the taxes they pay make possible the valuable services they receive. Also, when all American taxes are added together, they total less than 20% of the nation's gross national product. This is one of the lowest percentages of all industrial nations.

14. Another duty of the citizen is to serve on a **jury**, if selected. A jury is a group of people (usually 12) who are chosen to listen to evidence presented in court. Members of the jury must decide which of the battling parties is right or, in criminal cases, whether the accused person has committed a crime. The jury is basic to the American system of justice. The right to a jury trial is guaranteed by the Constitution in Article Three and in the Sixth and Seventh Amendments. This right is also guaranteed by most state constitutions.

15. Jury panels are usually selected from voter lists. From these panels, which may include several hundred people where courts are busiest, 12 jurors are selected to hear each trial. Many people find jury service an interesting and rewarding experience and look forward to being called again.

RESPONSIBILITIES OF THE GOVERNMENT

16. Of course, the government also has obligations to those who live in the United States. Some of these are basic to government, such as providing defense from foreign invaders, police services for preventing and detecting crimes, courts, a legislative body (Congress), postal services, and the like. What additional services the federal government should provide has always been the subject of debate. Generally, conservatives have felt that the federal government should not provide services much beyond the basics, while liberals want the government to provide assistance wherever it is needed. Money for medical care for the poor and elderly, assistance for those who cannot afford decent housing, and aid to education at all levels are areas of controversy. During the 20th century, the amount of direct assistance given to individuals has generally increased. After considerable debate, Social Security was established in the 1930s to provide a modest pension for people who are retired. Most workers are required to contribute to the Social Security system by paying taxes into the fund. The amount of monthly pension payments a person receives depends upon his or her wages and the age at which the person retires. Medicare, which is also funded through Social Security taxes, provides payment of some of the medical expenses of those 65 years or older.

17. Many people think that the government should provide funds for college education for those in need, day care for pre-school children of working parents, help for nursing home expenses, a national health care program, and other benefits. But these are very expensive programs and, with a national debt of two trillion dollars, Congress is not likely to provide these services in the immediate future. However, attitudes change, and the government must reflect the views of the majority of its citizens.

18. The unique character of the American government is not what it does or does not do. It is the way in which governmental decisions are made—by people elected by the citizens. Americans have the power to change their representatives (at the end of their term in office) if they are dissatisfied with the decisions being made. Representative government is slow and inefficient compared to a monarchy or dictatorship. But having the ordinary citizen involved in the decision-making process has produced a government that Americans have no reason to fear and many reasons to admire. Most Americans believe that, in spite of its shortcomings, their system of government is the finest in the world.

19. In 1782, Americans chose as their national bird the bald eagle, one of the largest and most powerful birds. This high-flying bird has long been a symbol of freedom and courage. Americans hope and believe that they will always have the courage and strength of purpose to protect the cherished freedoms that their government provides. Protecting these freedoms is the ultimate responsibility of the American government and its citizens.

EXERCISES

I. Comprehension Questions. Answer the following questions on paper or in class discussion.

1. What requirements must a permanent resident of the United States fulfill in order to become an American citizen?
2. What are some of the responsibilities of an American citizen? Name at least five.
3. What different kinds of taxes do people living in the U.S.A. pay? What do they get for their money?
4. Do you think that the American government provides enough services and benefits to its citizens and residents? If not, what else is needed? Can taxpayers afford more?

II. Vocabulary Practice. Pronounce the following words after your teacher, and discuss their meanings. Then use some of them to complete the following sentences.

advantages	naturalized
bill	neutral
combat	outmoded
controversial	pending
entitled	refund
heir	resistance
inherited	trillion
jury	unlikely
lack	voice
lasting	withhold

1. John's father died and left John all of his money and property. John was his only ________________. John ________________ everything that his father had.

2. Employers ________________ some money from each paycheck that an employee receives, and these deductions are applied toward that worker's annual income tax.

3. Mr. Brown's income tax return showed that he was ________________ to a ________________ (some money returned to him).
4. Should we increase taxes? That is a ________________ issue.
5. Some people are for higher taxes, and some are against the idea. I have no opinion on the matter. I'm ________________ .
6. To ________________ an opinion is the same as to express an opinion.
7. There are two types of American citizens: native-born and ________________ .
8. A ________________ dollars means a thousand billion. It looks like this: $1,000,000,000,000. It is ________________ that I could ever earn that much money even if I lived to be a million years old.

III. Word Study.

A. The prefix *anti-* means *against*. It is used in this chapter in the compound word *antiwar*. Can you think of any other words beginning with *anti-*? If not, use a dictionary for help, and write down two of them. ________________ ________________

B. The words *heir* and *air* are homonyms. Underline the correct word to complete each sentence.
   1. The (air; ear; heir) in this room smells of smoke.
   2. The lawyer read the will to us, and we found out that we were all (hairs; heirs; ears) to a large fortune.

3. A woman who inherits a lot of money is sometimes called an (earring; heiress; error).

IV. Idiom Study. Underline the correct phrase to complete each sentence. The numbers in brackets give the paragraphs in which the idioms are used.

1. *To stay in office* [5] means a) to refuse to leave one's place of work b) to live in an office c) to keep a political position by getting reelected.
2. A *conscientious objector* [7] refuses to a) pay taxes b) engage in military combat c) serve his country.
3. *Uncle Sam* [10] means a) the American people b) the American government c) a relative.
4. *And the like* [16] means a) and similar services b) and other services that people enjoy c) and more.

V. Reading Skills.

A. Using context clues:
   1. In paragraph 7, the word *draft* means a) a kind of beer b) joining the army c) being required to serve in the nation's armed forces.
   2. In paragraph 7, a *lasting impression* means a) a final impression b) an impression that will not be forgotten c) an important impression.

B. Studying American money:
   Look closely at various American coins and bills. Read the words and study the pictures on them. Try to identify the people, buildings, symbols, and sayings. What symbol that was discussed in this chapter is on the back of both the quarter and the $1 bill? ________________